THE MESSENGERS

To Martin

Hope you enjoy the
book, and the words
are in the right order!!

All the best

Malcolm.

 MALCOLM ANDERSON

First Published 2011

Library and Archives Canada Cataloguing in Publication
 Anderson, Malcolm, 1961-
    The messengers / Malcolm Anderson.
 ISBN 978-0-9683158-4-2
    1. Marathon running. 2. Runners (Sports)--Biography. I. Title.
 GV1061.14.A54 2011   796.42'520922   C2010-906950-1

Published by The Experience Publishers
www.experiencebooks.ca
1-877-755-5155
info@experiencebooks.ca

Cover design by Jacqueline Venditti.
The back cover images of Sean Meissner, Jose Nebrida, Lenore Dolphin and Bob Dolphin are courtesy of Adrenaline Event Photography.

THE MESSENGERS

For Callum and Jack

MAY YOUR MIND SET YOU FREE
MAY YOUR HEART LEAD YOU ON
MAY YOUR MIND LET YOU BE
MAY YOUR HEART BE STRONG

James, From the Song 'Waltzing Along'

PASSION
A strong enthusiasm

ENDURE
To undergo a hardship

TRANSFORM
To make a thorough or dramatic change

INSPIRE
To instill or create a feeling in a person

"The marathon is widely known as the ultimate test
of athletic endurance, 26.2 miles of running,
a grueling and punishing event that tests the limits of one's
resolve to overcome fear with sheer guts and determination."
Steve Edwards

"Travelling and running marathons have been the most
satisfying thing I have ever done both physically and spiritually.
I feel honored to be able to participate in such an adventure."
Cheryl Murdock

This book is about people who have each completed one hundred marathons (26.2 miles/ 42.2 kilometres) or ultras (long distance races more than the marathon distance). They are remarkable, passionate inspiring people. These are their stories.

In November 2006, I was standing on a train platform in what to me felt like the middle of nowhere in Athens, Greece. It was early evening and growing dark. A bitterly cold wind sliced through anyone who was unfortunate enough to be exposed to it.

I was standing beside another runner who, like me, was contemplating hypothermia, and a dozen others who no doubt were thinking the same. We had assembled on the platform having just registered for the Athens marathon – 'the' Marathon – in an old airport hangar several miles out of downtown Athens. Dave was busy trying to stay warm by rubbing his hands and moving quietly on the spot. We got talking, about running of course. What he told me turned my understanding of marathons upside down.

In his early forties, head shaved, and standing about 6 feet tall, Dave had a huge smile. He told me in a very understated matter-of-fact way that it was "a special run because it would be his 200th marathon."

200th marathon?

Here I was about to run my first of what would be three marathons in a two-month period thinking that I might be pushing it. Dave stunned me again when he casually mentioned that the Athens marathon would be his 40th of the year. He and his wife Linda lived north of London and either traveled in the United Kingdom or somewhere in Europe to run a marathon (or two) every weekend. He'd done that the previous year as well.

Our train eventually arrived. We quickly threw ourselves in and reacquainted our bodies with warmth. Dave and I continued talking for the next forty minutes – well, to be more accurate, I kept asking him about his running – where he'd run, why, his favorite runs ... how did he manage to run so many *all the time*. My knowledge of marathon running grew exponentially.

Dave introduced me to Linda and his friends – other members of the United Kingdom 100 Marathon Club. Linda had recently run her 100th marathon in Frankfurt, Germany. She showed me the necklace and pendant club members had given her when she completed her 100th marathon. We grimaced at the cold wind when we got off the train, and parted ways, wishing each other all the best for the race. I walked away realizing I knew very little about the world of marathon running.

It occurred to me that I may be able to understand and memorize a training schedule but I don't know the context in which I run marathons – the richness within which runners – normal people – embrace the marathon experience. Dave was running his 200th marathon. Years of distance running experiences. Not just the runs themselves, but getting there, the places, the people, the socialization – the total marathon experience.

Consider this:

- Running a marathon or an ultra is a significant, potentially life-changing achievement; training programs note it can take several months to adequately prepare for a marathon. But imagine running 10 marathons in just one year. Even then, it would still take you 10 years to run 100 marathons, assuming life doesn't get in the way and you're injury free. That also means you have to find, plan for, and travel to, 10 marathons, every year, for 10 years. That may not be difficult if you live in New York, or Seattle, or London, but what if you live in Perth, Australia, thousands of miles from anywhere? And what if you don't even drive? What if you're blind? What if you're deaf? Or in a wheelchair?

- By the end of the 2008 climbing season on Mount Everest, *Wikipedia* notes that there had been 4,102 ascents to the summit by about 2,700 individuals. More people have climbed Mount Everest than have run 100 marathons.

I wanted to find out why runners who have run 100 or more marathons and ultras keep doing it? What can we learn from them?

I refer to these runners as *Messengers*. They have many messages to share.

The messengers are passionate about long distance running and what it means to their lives. Their stories are inspirational. And they all seem so damn happy.

2

"Give the distance the respect it deserves and train properly, and then nothing is impossible."

John Sturley

The current world record for the fastest marathon is 2 hours, 3 minutes and 59 seconds (2:03:59). That's an average pace of less than 2:57 minutes per kilometre (or 4:44 per mile). It was set at the Berlin marathon in September 2008 by Ethiopian Haile Gebrselassie. The current world record for women – 2:15:25 – was set by Paula Radcliffe of Great Britain at the London Marathon in April 2003.

But, as incredible as these times are, they are only a very small part of the marathon world. We tend to celebrate the fastest times to reach a given distance when running, but there are many other achievements by others in these events, equally remarkable, that go unnoticed. These achievements have nothing to do with speed but everything to do with what is possible from each of our own contexts.

Long distance runners all take a similar journey. They try to achieve the goals they set given their own beliefs, attitudes, abilities, courage and commitment. While we may like to think a personal best (PB) is always within our reach, most runners don't keep coming back to run marathons over and over again just to beat their PB. There are many other reasons why they keep coming back to run the long distances. That's what we'll see in pages that follow.

Indeed, as Jim Fixx wrote in his 1977 best seller The Complete Book of Running – a book that transformed thousands of people's lives – "the qualities and capacities that are important in running – such factors as will power, the ability to apply effort during extreme fatigue, and the acceptance of pain – have a radiating power that subtly influences one's life … To learn the meaning of not winning in running is to learn the meaning of not winning elsewhere in our lives. For what we learn through running radiates into the remotest corners of everything we do, making everyday failures seem less poisonous."

I interviewed more than 120 messengers – those people who have completed one hundred or more marathons or ultras – from around the world. Some of the messengers have completed well over 200 marathons and ultras; some have completed several hundred. A smaller group of runners has each completed more than a thousand. Some of the numbers become, simply, numbing. If you were to start running marathons, for example, at the rate of 25 a year – about every two weeks – it would take you forty years to reach the 1,000 mark. If we want insights into the total experience of long distance running and what it means for our spirit – for the human soul – who better to ask than these messengers?

They come from the United Kingdom, Ireland, Canada, the United States, Australia, New Zealand, Sweden, Denmark, Germany, South Africa, Japan, Netherlands and Belgium. All ages and both genders are represented. The number of races upon which the collective experiences are based easily reaches somewhere between 20,000 to 25,000 marathons and ultras. That's a great deal of official race distance, and it doesn't take into account any training runs.

The interviews are supplemented with additional material from running magazines, websites, emails from runners, and numerous newspaper clippings and race reports. The messengers have openly shared their stories with me; not unlike what happens when you run part of a marathon with a complete stranger. In fact, some of my interviews occurred while I was running.

I met Robbie, for example, who you'll meet later, during the Windermere marathon in the Lake District of England. As we were running through the spectacular landscape, not far from Wordsworth's home and just, literally, down the road from where Beatrix Potter once lived, Robbie was telling me stories about himself, his running and his travelling that would have anyone on the edge of their seat. A great night out. Or a great time spent running. I wish I'd had a pen and paper at the time, but it was a wonderful way to run around some spectacular countryside. Living in the moment. Sharing the experience.

In any case, Robbie wrote out, longhand, some of his story and mailed it to me. I was able to read some newspaper clippings as well. I ran for a while with Carla that day too, who a year or so later, went on to run her 100th marathon.

The messengers have a love of life; a strong desire for, and commitment to, health. They have a passion for people and places. They set goals. Running long distances has saved their lives and transformed their lives. They have transformed other peoples lives as well.

George Sheehan, the iconic runner, doctor, philosopher and author, wrote in his book *Running and Being* that "running is not a religion, it is a place." He likened it to a monastery. The monastery is a place for the body, and a place for the mind and for the soul. "The monastery is a place for ordinary people, for sinners as well as saints … a retreat, a place to commune with God and yourself, a place for psychological and spiritual renewal." Sy Mah, who once had the world record for the most marathons ever run, said that "life was a matter of self-discovery; that truth resides in one's own heart and honest effort."

Although the runners in this book don't use these words, the message is the same. It's as if they have each arrived at Apathia, or if not, are well on the way to it. Apathia was that state of mind espoused during the Hellenic period of Greek civilization as representing a state of tranquility and peace of mind. One achieved this 'state' by being indifferent to pleasure or pain, and simply 'going with the flow'.

Brenton Floyd ran his first marathon at age 10 and went on to run his 100th at age 15. John 'Maddog' Wallace has run a marathon in more than 100 different countries, and Holly Koester completed her 100th wheelchair marathon in 2008. Most of Jeff Hagen's 100 marathons are actually ultras – more than the 26.2 mile marathon distance; he will run his 100th ultra at the end of 2010. The total distance run for his first 100 is the equivalent of over 300 marathons. Rory Coleman sends himself a birthday card each year to celebrate his 'cold turkey' transition from a downward spiraling drinking, smoking, party-goer to a tea-totaling endurance athlete and race organizer. The husband and wife team of Yen Nguyen and Peter Bennett travel the world running marathons. They're one of several couples whose stories are told in the pages ahead. Pam Reed twice won outright the Death Valley Badwater Ultra (135 miles from the lowest part of the North American continent to one of the highest – Mt Witney) in temperatures that rose above 130 degrees Fahrenheit (54.4 Celsius). Australian lawyer Ray James successfully battled alcoholism in large part through his passion for running, moving one addiction aside for another. After a heart attack in his fifties, John Dawson realized he needed to get fit. Two hundred and fifty marathons later, he was training Simon Beresford, the first person with Down's Syndrome to complete a marathon, and invited to 10 Downing Street, the British Prime Minister's residence, for doing so. Larry Macon, aged 65, ran 104 marathons in 2008. At 28 years of age Leslie Miller became the youngest female in the world to complete 100 marathons: "It's who you are", she said, "it's exciting to challenge yourself." When Linda Major completed her 100th marathon in Frankfurt, the members of the United Kingdom 100 Marathon Club formed a Conga line as they danced together over the finish line to celebrate. Another member of that club, Steve Edwards, will, before he turns 50 in 2010, have completed 500 marathons with an average time of 3:17. Todd Byers has run 80 of his last marathons barefoot.

Paul Watts has not let the fact that he is blind prevent him from running more than 200 marathons. Dave McGillivray (in 1978 and 2004), Marshall Ulrich (2008) and Jerry Dunn (1991) have raised hundreds of thousands of dollars with transcontinental runs that have taken them across the United States.

Inspiring, passionate and committed. Proud. Transforming lives. Overcoming adversity. Making distance running a lifestyle. The messengers have a love for everything that running marathons and ultras provide to their own existence. They are messengers to us all.

3

"Run, Pheidippides, one race more! The meed is thy due!
'Athens is saved, thank Pan,' go shout!'
He flung down his shield,
Ran like fire once more: and the space twixt the Fennel-field
And Athens was stubble again,
a field which a fire runs through,
Till in he broke: 'Rejoice, we conquer!'
Like wine through clay,
Joy in his blood bursting his heart, he died – the bliss!"

From the poem Pheidippides, Robert Browning (1879)

In all our acts and all our communication we constantly convey messages; messages for and about ourselves, and messages for others. Some are implicit messages, others explicit. We learn. We transfer knowledge. We keep growing and develop a better understanding of who we are, what we do and how we do it. We heighten our awareness, understanding and interpretation of the world in which we live, the different places and the different people. We share our thoughts and experiences. We are all messengers in some way.

The great messenger of the gods in Greek mythology, the divine messenger, is Hermes. Hermes is the patron of boundaries and travelers, helping travelers have a safe and easy journey. Many ancient Greeks would make a sacrifice to Hermes before they traveled. Hermes is also the patron of athletics, looking out for runners and other athletes with injuries who need help. Hermes delivers messages from Olympus to the mortal world. His shoes have wings on them (that would be nice), so he can move easily between the mortal and immortal worlds. He is a god in other respects too, as there were not enough gods to cover all functions in those days. The word 'hermeneutics', which essentially means the real and hidden understanding and interpretation of *meaning*, is derived from Hermes.

Hermes shares his messenger role with another god, Iris. Iris is often mentioned in Homer's *Iliad*. She is represented as either a rainbow or as a young girl with wings on her shoulders. If Zeus had a command to be communicated to the mortal world it would be Iris who would descend to the earth as the messenger, appearing either in some borrowed mortal form or in divine form.

Less divine in the real world of the ancient Greeks were the *hemerodromoi*. The ancient Greeks used hemerodromoi (all day messengers) to deliver important messages across the countryside. The Greek philosopher Socrates said he wished he could keep up with the hemerodromoi. But it is Pheidippides that is the best known of these messengers, although there were many others. Like Euchidas who ran from Plataea to Delphi in 479 after the battle of Plataea to deliver sacred fire. He drank some water (to purify him), crowned himself with laurel and then ran back to Plataea, all before the end of the day. Upon his return he too collapsed and apparently died. We don't know for certain if he died as such embellishments were common at the time, but there is an epitaph to him that records his run – a distance of 1,000 stades (approximately 113 miles).

In a 1974 research paper in the journal *Classical World*, Victor Matthews notes that it's "a strange paradox that the modern Olympic event which sports enthusiasts are most likely to identify with the ancient Greeks [the marathon] is one that had no place in the ancient Olympic games." The longest ancient Olympic event was the *dolichos*, which was just under three miles. What we do identify with are the ancient distance runners – the Hemerodromoi.

The hemerodromoi were professionals – they never competed in running events but they served as essential communication links; they were more effective than horses over difficult terrain and would be present when the message was delivered, which provided opportunities for interpretations and discussion if required. Upon their return they could comment on how the message was received. For example, the extent of emotions, who read the message, their facial expressions and so on. In many respects there were considerable advantages over email.

The runners in this book are our modern day hemerodromoi. They too are messengers. They have messages for all of us.

4

"Throw away the watch and run as you feel."

Jim Barnes

In October 2009 I was at an 80th birthday party for Bob Dolphin. His wife Lenore, their daughter and friends had organized the Saturday afternoon party in a hotel room in downtown Portland, Oregon. There was cake, chocolate, birthday celebration stuff and countless people coming in and out of the hotel room congratulating Bob. There were tiny packets of M&M's with small text on them saying it was Bob's birthday. Nothing terribly unusual about all this.

Except for a few things. The next morning Bob was running in the Portland marathon. Impressive at 80 years old. More impressive, however, is that this would be his 452nd marathon since he took up running at age 48.

Even more astounding was that Bob successfully ran the Victoria Marathon in British Columbia the following weekend, slicing 50 minutes off his Portland time in doing so. He has every intention of completing 500 marathons. I was there in Yakima, Washington when Bob ran his 400th marathon in 2007. At his current rate of 20-25 marathons a year, he'll complete his 500th sometime in 2012. Bob is just one example of a growing number of people who are running marathons, and half marathons, on a regular basis these days.

He and his wife Lenore are known throughout the marathon community as 'Team Dolphin' and they are the also directors of the North American 100 Marathon Club. Lenore has volunteered in well over 300 marathons, and together they are the directors of the annual Yakima River Canyon Marathon in the heart of Washington state's apple growing region. It's a low key, down to earth marathon with a point-to-point course that winds through a quiet river canyon. And it's plain fun and friendly, with a great pasta party before the marathon and a banquet afterwards in the Selah Community Hall. It's also been the race venue for the Marathon Maniacs Club and 100 Marathon Club reunions. Runners come from around the world to run this race; not because it's a wonderful run, although it is, but moreso because of the camaraderie and friendships built over the years and the opportunity to continue and renew these friendships over a weekend.

It is a place that, like other marathons, is free of barriers and hierarchies. In marathons, the elite runners run the same race as those who are running their first. Friendships are built upon the common bond of distance running. Runners with sub 3:00 hour times mix and socialize with runners who finish in over 5:00 hours. Finishing times don't matter. Times are seldom the topic of conversation. The experiences of races and places are shared and arrangements made to meet again at other events. It's addictive. One could even think that the running of a marathon is a sidebar activity for what's really going on.

But wait a minute. We're talking about 'a marathon'. 26.2 miles. The distance made famous and popularized in the 1908 Olympics when Dorango Pietri came stumbling into the Crystal Palace Stadium in London, collapsed several times and was finally assisted over the line in first place by worried officials thinking he was near death. The American team lodged a complaint, saying he was assisted. The complaint was upheld and the second place runner, American Johnny Hayes, was awarded the gold medal. Pietri was given a special one-off trophy by the Queen the day after the race to recognize his courage.

The distance was seen as 'too far' – only runners in peak physical condition could complete the distance; even then, they risked mental and physical suffering, pain and death. These runners were outliers. No way could the average athlete perform such amazing feats of endurance. The mystique of the marathon was born, and for years it stayed that way; the word 'marathon' becoming synonymous with achievement, endurance, durability, commitment and resilience.

Things have changed. The distance is not as foreboding as once thought. Mere mortals, as marathoner and author John Bingham would put it, can run marathons, and not risk death and danger, but actually enjoy it. And they can run a lot of them.

Running 100 marathons is a canvas for painting the many positive traits of the human character. The simple act of putting one foot in front of the other for 26.2 miles changes people's lives. Run 100 marathons or more, and you must think anything is possible. And why wouldn't you? The 100 marathon individuals 'live rich'. Their stories reflect personal successes in many forms. We can learn a lot from their experiences whether we ourselves run or not.

To have run 100 marathons is truly remarkable. Just like completing one marathon, it's a tangible achievement that no-one can ever take away from you. The world record holder for completing the most marathons is a wonderfully unassuming man, still running strong in his late seventies. As of August 2009, Horst Preisler had completed more than 1,650 marathons, more than 360 of which are ultras. One person. He started running in his late thirties when his wife Christa told him he was putting on a bit too much weight around his waist. Little did she know. He listened and he acted. Horst is an ordinary person like you and me. An extraordinary, ordinary person perhaps.

When I started doing the research for this book I was asked several times by some weary 100 Marathon club runners if I was going to write that these were people who were, quite simply, 'mad', 'nutters', 'crazy people' ...for running so many marathons. My response then, as now, is that far from being mad, they are amazing, and we can all learn something from them.

Fortunately, they believed me. I've been graciously welcomed into their world of mega-marathon long distance running. What started off as a project examining 'the impossible' turned into a project that shows what is possible and very doable.

Especially if we believe in ourselves.

5

"Marathon running is such a good metaphor for life in general
when times are tough and you want to give up
but you don't, you persevere."

Chris Warren

The 2,500th anniversary of Pheidippide's legendary run from
Marathon to Athens is commemorated with a special medal in
2010. Two organizations, SEGAS (the Hellenic Athletics Federation and Organizer of the Athens Classic Marathon event)
and AIMS (Association of International Marathons and Distance
Races) jointly decided to have a medal produced that is offered
for sale by marathon races around the world in 2010 (at a cost of
10 Euros).

The medal was produced by *1000KM Productions*, a South African company founded in 1992 by messenger Paul Selby. Paul
has an engineering background and in 1971, having arrived in
South Africa from England, formed what turned into a successful
manufacturing, sales and marketing company. During that time he
ran a 3 K leg of a relay race, and, as he told me over the telephone
from his home in South Africa, "found out about running."

Two months later he ran his first marathon. Six months later he ran
the first of 25 Comrades ultra races; probably the most famous ultra race in the world, with approximately 56 miles (87 kilometres)

of undulating South African landscape to cover between Durban and Pietermaritzburg in the province of Natal. Paul has now run more than 500 marathons and ultras, and more than 100,000 kilometres of training and competing in over 1,000 road races. Of Comrades he says "It's a life changing experience. It is so tough. You hurt, you struggle and suffer. Then you see the next runner in the same plight. Comrades is a life adventure in one day."

Since 1996 Paul's company has produced medals for the London Marathon, and since 1997, also for the Berlin Marathon. It supplies a number of leading event organizers in Europe, the United States, the United Kingdom, and around the world. By 2003, Paul said they were exporting over one million medals annually.

In 1990, he and his wife Jenny introduced the 1000 K challenge in South Africa in memory of Jenny's late husband, Johnny Kambouris, who was the Chair of Paul's running club (Jenny has also run in ten Comrades). Runners try and run 1,000 K in the year between Comrades races. Between 2009 and 2010, 700 runners had entered the challenge. Eleven runners, including Paul, have completed *all* 19 years.

Paul speculated briefly that his passion is an obsession. "If there's a marathon on somewhere I'll do it. Last year I broke an ankle, it was a challenge to get through that." He has also been raising funds for charities, especially cancer, for years. "It's become a large part of my life" he says. "The running community has been great; I've made so many friends, met so many great people, and the life that goes with it … People need to get out on the road and enjoy the sport."

Dave Major chose the Athens marathon for his 200th marathon because "it was Athens and I have always been interested and fascinated with the history of this event. It felt right to run history rather than just observe it and on my 200th I couldn't ask for a more significant event to celebrate. It felt that Pheidippides himself was with you every step of the course." He added, "The word marathon is something that means so much to me. It arguably saved my life, it has formed my social scene, shown me parts of the world I would never dream of visiting, and therefore to run from the place which named the event I live by was for me emotional."

Australian Lester Smith ran his first marathon at age 35. He has kept a log book of his running for 25 years: "It's an extension of what I do at work; I like numbers." He is an environmental scientist with Australia's Commonwealth Scientific and Industrial Research Organisation (CSIRO), examining the effects of environmental contaminants. Lester said he watched a "20-minute video about a marathon event about 18 months before I ran my first marathon – I loved the camaraderie among the competitors that I saw on the video. I got out of bed on January 1st 1985 and said I'm going to run a marathon this year."

He started running very slowly – using a walk-run approach – and built up from there, "nurturing the body for the first 5-6 years", then at pace – with a 3:30 time, and then a 3:10 time, which is where he is right now – "I've never tried to push it any harder", he said. "People are quite astonished that I can find tranquility at the 35 K point of a marathon." When we talked, Lester had completed 112 marathons.

"Compared to what I do now, I hardly did any training. I said 'well that was interesting, a bit painful, so I'll train a second one.' For me, I have to set new directions and new goals. I will have a try at three hours – it's something I need to try – and I'll see where that takes me."

Now, running is intricately woven into his life. "I love the fact that I can get up in the morning, get out and run around the hills – at 5:30 it's very pleasant with the cows, the sheep, the vineyards ... I use it to relax – a form of Zenism. Until you do it you won't fully understand what we get out of it, and we get much more out of it than just running; its life changing." Running is *his time*, he said, and his family likes it that way too.

In a more philosophical tone, Lester was adamant that there is more to distance running than simply running the distance hard.

"You'll be disillusioned if all it is is the drive to run your best race. I firmly believe that there are marathon runners that have gone a couple of extra steps further and found something."

Lester's main goal though is to "enjoy the passion and love of running." He also likes to help other runners through training, mentoring and coaching. "I love to be out there, talking to every-one – support on the bad days, pats on the back on the good days … we're a happy bunch."

What do the messengers, the modern day hemerodromoi, say about themselves?

American Andrew Kotulski put it like this: "we like our own im-age – we like the people who are like us … we're all a little weird." Runners who complete hundreds of events are not 'in it' just for the physical exercise. Jeff Hagen from Washington state said that "ultrarunners and marathoners make great running companions, both on training runs and in races. They tend to be less intense than short-distance runners, and the farther they run the more mellow they seem to be. A bit like mountaineering where there is difficulty, adversity; a bond is struck."

Indeed, the notion that the messengers are adventurous was con-sistently referred to: "Marathoners like to see and do different things" Todd Byers commented. Dave Bell said "we're not afraid to try; rather than sitting on the sidewalks, we do." Wally Herman, from the vantage point of more than seven hundred marathons and ultra races, felt that "marathoners are great, but ultra-marathoners are greater. They suffer more, the rougher edges are rubbed off … I like endurance activity and it's more of an experience. The flip-side, you might find, is that ultra-marathoners are more of the loner type than marathoners."

Marathoners, said 300+ marathoner Lois Berkowitz, have "a very yielding quality, and a very unyielding quality … marathon run-ners are focused on what they can do; they're not afraid to try, unlike a lot of the general public … You meet all ages – marathon running does something to eliminate all aging."

Leslie Miller, echoing the sentiments of many of those interviewed, felt that long distance runners are "very good people, very honest, very giving people... and also a bit odd ... we have to be a bit odd to do what we do." Jack Brooks said that the people – the other runners – are one of the compelling reasons he's attracted to the sport – "marathon runners are nice, hospitable, friendly, social folks." What's more, as Susan Daley, with more than 400 marathons to reflect on said, "marathon runners are encouraging of one another, and one another's goals. They're very supportive of one another."

Yen Nguyen felt that messengers reflect a combination of traits, including obsessiveness, addiction, and discipline. "They're highly motivated and determined." Many others, like Jim Scheer, stressed the high level of determination, being goal-oriented and 'persistency' as key traits. 'Perseverance' was frequently mentioned by the messengers as a predominant trait, as was mental toughness, especially with the 100-mile, 24-hour and 48-hour events. One runner commented that it is "patience, perseverance, and the personal satisfaction that you do something you didn't do before – that sense of achievement", that were the key traits of the messengers.

"Perseverance" said Pam Penfield, "would rate up at the top of the list of traits, and, of course, being very goal oriented." Indeed, "the fantastic thing" said Osy Waye, "is that there such a huge difference in people, but there's always that perseverance – something in you." Long distance runners, said John Zeleznikow, "have the ability to keep going on and on and not let the little things worry you." Jack Brooks added that there is the ability "to continue running fast on tired legs." Both Norm Franks and Jeffrey Horowitz singled out 'stubbornness' as a key trait – determination, persistence and the desire to not give in.

Another messenger said they were "quiet, interested in health and fitness, and dedicated to do their best." Leslie Miller added that "it's this bond of struggling through ... that 'I couldn't have done this without you' belief ... and just the support you get – especially the ultras. You get support from the front and the back of the pack." As Jack Brooks put it "even at the top level most marathon runners are not stuck up or pretending they're important … they're pleased you're enthusiastic about the sport."

Above all else, however, it is the desire and need for the social aspects of long distance running – the friendships made and nurtured – that is seen as the most dominant characteristic. What typically begins as a desire to improve one's health and fitness evolves over the number of races completed into a passion for the total experience, a central component of which are the friendships that emerge. And it is a shared experience in which bonds among runners are developed and strengthened through the common challenge that faces the messengers at every start line. The social rewards become equal to, if not more important than, the physical rewards of successfully completing the challenge of the long distance.

The time it takes to complete each event, each challenge, is less important than the satisfaction of completion and the ability to share the experience with those who have a similar passion. To complete the challenges in different places builds new knowledge, exposes the mind and soul to new ways of looking at things and increases the understanding of the surrounding world, all of which only serves to enhance the total experience further, and increase the desire to take on even more new challenges.

John 'Maddog' Wallace,
Machu Picchu, Peru.

Lois Berkowitz receiving
her award for the third time
around the 50 states.
The runner handing it to
Lois is her friend, and fellow
messenger, Paula Boone.

Australian messenger,
Lester Smith.

Steve Edwards, creating a world record for the fastest 10 marathons in 10 days, 2008.

Holly Koester, Yakima River Canyon Marathon, 2007.

Leslie Miller, youngest women to run 100 marathons.

Some members of the UK 100 Marathon Club in Munich, Germany for Linda Major's 100th marathon (Linda is wearing bib number 1282).

Jim Boyd completing his 300th marathon in 2009, after having completed his 299th marathon the day before.

6

"Levels of physical inactivity are rising in many
countries with major implications for the general health
of people worldwide and for the prevalence of
non-communicable diseases such as cardiovascular disease,
diabetes and cancer and their risk factors such as
raised blood pressure, raised blood sugar and overweight.
Physical inactivity is estimated as being the
principal cause for approximately 21–25% of breast and
colon cancer burden, 27% of diabetes and approximately
30% of ischemic heart disease burden."

World Health Organization, 2010

"Don't waste a minute of your life.
I enjoy all my training and running marathons.
I try and have a great laugh and not take it too serious."

Robbie Wilson

More people are looking to run marathons than ever before. Ironically it's at a time when obesity and being overweight is at an
all-time high. The data are staggering and alarming.

The World Health Organization (WHO) estimates that globally
there are over one billion overweight adults, of which more than
300 million are considered obese. In 1997 the WHO formally stated that obesity was a global epidemic. A new word, *globesity*, has
emerged to reflect this phenomenon of obesity and over- weight-
ness. Being overweight is a major risk factor for chronic diseases
such as Type 2 diabetes, cardiovascular disease, hypertension and
stroke, and some forms of cancer.

The WHO identifies physical inactivity (6%) as the fourth leading
risk factor for global mortality (behind high blood pressure (13%),
tobacco use (9%) and high blood glucose (6%)). Being overweight
or obese accounts for another 5% of mortality. Equally important is the fact that physical inactivity levels are rising in many
countries. There are significant implications for the health of the

population worldwide with the rise in preventable illnesses and diseases and the accompanying pressures on the national health care systems. The WHO also points out that physical inactivity is a growing problem not just for the developed world but also for the low- and middle-income countries.

According to the World Health Organization over 90% of type 2 diabetes and 80% of coronary heart disease can be avoided or postponed if individuals have good nutrition and regular physical activity, and eliminate smoking and respond to stress more effectively.

Psycho-social issues are also much more prevalent in individuals who are overweight. Earlier deaths and reduced quality of life are the outcomes of the overweight epidemic and that's without going into the multitude of issues surrounding the effects on health systems as they attempt to respond and manage the epidemic. WHO identifies the key causes of all this being the increased consumption of energy-dense foods that have high levels of saturated fats and sugars, and reduced physical activity.

In some parts of the world, rising incomes levels and increased urbanization have contributed to diets with a higher proportion of fats, saturated fats and sugars, replacing diets that were high in complex carbohydrates. In the developed world there has been the continual trend towards a sedentary lifestyle, made possible through automation and technological advances. In 2009, the WHO estimated that at least 60% of the global population gets insufficient exercise.

In the United States, the Center for Disease Control and Prevention (CDC) states that American society has become *'obesogenic,'* with increased food intake, non-healthful foods, and physical inactivity. In 2009 the CDC noted that since 1980, American obesity rates for adults have doubled and rates for children have tripled. More than one third of all American adults (more than 72 million people), and 16% of American children are obese. In 2000, it was estimated that health costs associated with obesity were $117 billion.

In England, it's estimated that about 46% of men and 32% of women are overweight, with another 17% of men and 21% of women being obese. In New Zealand, more than one third of adults are overweight (36.3%) and more than one quarter is obese (26.5%).

And yet, at the same time, there's been a huge surge in the number of people running marathons.

The 2009 Running USA Road Running Information Center annual marathon report estimated that in the United States in 1976 there were 25,000 marathon finishers. This rose to 224,000 in 1990 and to 353,000 in 2000. By 2009 the figure had risen again to 468,000. Women comprised just 10.5% of the finishers in 1980, but by 2009 they represented almost 41% of all finishers. *Masters* runners – those aged 40 and over – represented 26% of all finishers in 1980, but this figure rose to 45% by 2008.

Median finishing times meanwhile have also increased. For men the median finishing time has increased to 4:16 in 2008, up from 3:32 in 1980, while the women's median time has increased to 4:43, up from 4:03 in 1980. In 2009 alone, 40 new marathons started up in the United States.

The trends are similar in other parts of the world. Lottery systems are now in place for several of the large marathons, such as New York and London. In 2009, the Tokyo Marathon received 310,000 applications for the 32,000 available slots.

7

"I run for a tapestry of reasons.
Woven in the fabric of my being is a need to control
some facet of my life. To subjugate a truculent body to my will,
to prove myself every day against a latent temptation/desire to
sleep in, over-eat; succumb to the rigors of aging."

Elaine Doll-Dunn

"We all have different starting points
for the marathon experience."

Big Dave Carter

Although Bob Dolphin's first ever race was as a 15 year-old running a 3.5 mile race in Worcester, Massachusetts, in 1944, he was not, he said, "a runner." It wasn't until 1979 at age 48, that he made a decision which has shaped his life ever since.

Each day he would drive a couple of miles from his home to work. One day his car wouldn't start so he decided to walk. He enjoyed it so much that the next day he decided to walk again. His supervisor, a runner, loaned Bob his copy of Jim Fixx's *Complete Book of Running*. The book, published in 1977, was an inspirational best seller with over a million copies sold. Fixx, a member of the high IQ club Mensa, had been significantly overweight and smoked two packs of cigarettes a day just ten years earlier. And so after some days of enjoyable walking, Bob figured he could try running the distance and things took off from there.

His first race as a "middle aged runner" was the *Human Race*, a 10 K in Columbia, MO, in 1980. In September 1981, at age 51, he ran his first marathon – the *Heart of America Marathon*. He ran it in a time of 3:53, but said it "wasn't a fun day", with six major hills and hamstring cramps in the last 10 K. But there was a sense of accomplishment at the finish line.

Messengers start running marathons for many different reasons. Something in each of them generated a spark that led to a substantial change in their life. For some, it was a personal challenge. For others, it was about health and fitness, and for others it was a sense of looking into the future and where they could end up if they didn't take care of themselves. Some messengers started running marathons through the inspiration, encouragement, support and needs of friends and family members. And some started simply because of a bet.

Australian Jim Barnes realized later in life that he was putting on weight and had to do something about it. "I'd started putting a lot of weight on and needed to exercise, and running had always appealed to me when I was younger." Like many, fellow Australian Stan Miskin was athletic at a younger age, playing football and tennis. As he got older the weight started to accumulate. Stan knew he had to do something, so he started jogging. Soon after, it was clear he was hooked. Stan's first marathon was in Melbourne in 1978, at 53 years of age. Twelve years later he returned to run it again as his 100th marathon, in a time of 4:00.01. In between he also ran 26 ultras.

Charlie Lyn tells the story of Stan's training. Stan set up a card table at one point along his training route and had his car at another. Both locations were stocked with drinks, oranges, towels and dry clothing. Stan would run past one of these sites every 20-25 minutes. One day his card table and supplies were stolen. He arrived at the scene disoriented, thinking he must have set it up further along the road. As Charlie writes "He was eventually found by his wife and daughter in a dehydrated state." On his long run days he ran from one shopping centre to another. Along the route he would drop in on friends for a few minutes, have a chat and some water, and continue on running again.

Fifty-two year old Julia Thorn is the first Australian female to have completed 100 marathons, but was 30 years old before she ever ran a step. She had, however, biked long distances, like across Australia for example, and is used to cycling over 100 kilometres in one day. She ran for a few years then took a break while she raised a family between 1990 and 1997.

Julia ran her first marathon in Rotorua, New Zealand in 1997, finishing in a time of 3:51. She said prior to the race that "when I've done this I'll never do it again." But she had a great experience and within a week she was set to do another. "Although I'm not a confident person" she said to me, "the marathon running has helped by setting goals and has increased my confidence." When she had run her 20th marathon she started thinking of the 100; her thinking was further reinforced by the fact that she could become the first Australian woman to run 100 marathons. "I don't really suffer that much in marathons – a bit of discomfort but it's not huge – it's a physical tiredness but you get over that. You need to run within yourself – it's a skill to run it so you're not a basket case at the end."

Like many of the messengers, she underwent a transition mentally as at a certain point she had to let go thoughts of running a PB. Her 3:28 in Christchurch New Zealand in June 2004 was her fastest time and she hovered around that for a while. "Now I'm slower – it's probably fatigue in my legs – maybe a self-preservation thing." That said, she still recovers from a race quickly. "My family thinks it's easier than it is because I just carry on as usual after I've run one and when I'm training." Now, with 100 marathons and ultras recently completed, her new goals are longer distances, including 100 milers and 24-hour races.

German long distance runner Peter Wieneke was a banker until he retired in January 2009. He began running marathons in the early 1990s. When we talked at the end of 2009, he had amassed 752 marathons and ultras. This currently ranks Peter at about number 15 world-wide for the most marathons completed.

Peter has been active all his life, playing soccer and competing in judo, boxing, swimming, and table tennis among other things. His marathon running started when his Thai friend, Bu, who ran the

Hamburg marathon, convinced Peter to try the sport. Like many of the messengers, it started slowly. Peter ran two marathons in 1994, three in 1995 and six in 1996. But since 2000, he has run between 60 and 83 marathons and ultras each year. He has raced in a range of long distance events including several 100 K races, 6-hour, 12- hour and 24-hour races, and several multi-day stage races. Peter moved into the longer distances when he realised that after marathons he wasn't tired and felt he could run more.

In 2005, at the age of 59, Peter completed the gruelling 246 K Spartathlon from Athens to Sparta in 34 hours 51 minutes; 36 hours is the maximum allowed. The Spartathlon course is based on the route established by a team led by John Foden in 1982. They sought to recreate the route from Athens to Sparta based on Herodotus' description of Pheidippides, the Athenian messenger, who arrived in Sparta on behalf of the Athenian military leader Miltiades to seek support against the invading Persians. Foden was a British Royal Air Force Wing Commander who was passionate about Greece and ancient Greek history, but curious as to how someone could possibly cover the 250 kilometres (1140 'stadia') in 36 hours as Herodotus' account of the messenger's route indicated. Since Foden was a long-distance runner, he decided to try the route to see if it was possible. It is mountainous, including the Parthenio mountain (1200 meters), where Pheidippides reportedly met the God Pan. Peter said that Spartathlon "was the greatest fight I've had in my life." In addition to the mountainous terrain, strict cut-off points and the time limit, the temperature would go up to 35 degrees Celsius during the day and down to 5 degrees Celsius at night.

Peter is happy to say that "his family fully accepts and respects his hobby." According to his Swedish wife, Anna, "it's more like an adventure – more like a family – you reacquaint with friends each time at a race; it's exciting." His goal is to have run 1,000 marathons and ultras in two years time, and to run his 1,000th with his friend Bu in Thailand. He's never had an injury so it's looking good at this point.

One of the reasons that Peter can run so many marathons in a year is because of fellow German distance runner Christian Hottas. Christian has created an official marathon route in a park near his home in Hamburg, Germany. Approximately 16.3 laps of the course equals the 26.2 mile (42.2 K) marathon distance. He arranges regular marathons that may be held anywhere from once to four times a week. In accordance with by-laws set by the German 100 Marathon Club, and similar to those in other countries, the race must be advertised, the official distance measured, and a minimum of three runners must participate. He invites people to run these marathons with him. As in other countries, a minimum of three runners is required to make it a legitimate event. Times are recorded and a certificate provided to those who complete the race. He has organized over 400 marathons on this course in this way over the past few years. The runs may coincide with the celebration of the birthday of a movie star or famous person in history for example, and will be named after these individuals. When I was in Hamburg, Christian showed me the certificates of completion for such events and we drove by the park where the runs are held.

Back in 1986, Christian came to the realization during a vacation in Norway that his body weight had increased from the 65 kg he weighed in 1975 to 98 kg. "Being 171 cm tall, I decided to do something to reduce my weight …running seemed to be the easiest and most natural sport for my intention." So he changed his diet and started to run.

Another runner who has participated in Christian's events is Mogens Pedersen from Denmark. Mogens is a 45-year old steel construction worker who ran his first marathon in 1992. With three young children, Mogens found that running was a great flexible way to get exercise as he could do it any time he wanted, or was able to, given the commitments to the children. He's completed more than 220 marathons and runs them now for fun and relaxation, and as an opportunity to meet up with friends. In fact, there is a growing interest among runners to participate in the smaller marathons that are not only cheaper than the large city marathons (e.g., 100 kronas versus 600 kronas), but more sociable. Friends can arrange to race the same event and meet up afterwards without having to search for one another among thousands of competitors. For some messengers such as Mogens, the smaller events bring us back to the very basics – the 'why' in our running – as Mogen said "in the early morning at 5am, no wind, silence, … you can only hear yourself running."

German messenger Sigrid Eichner holds the world record for the most marathons completed by a woman. Her plan, at the time of writing, was to complete her 1,500th marathon in May 2010. Also in her plans for 2010 was a 1,150 K race across France in 18 days. Sigrid is a retired school teacher in her late 60s. When I met her in Germany a couple of years ago, just after she had raced across France, she was looking forward to retiring. Then, she said with a huge smile, she would be able to run more marathons. Her running career began with the shorter distances: "I just liked running", she said, "the fun of it, and to enjoy the feeling afterwards." What Sigrid likes most about running marathons and ultras is "the contact with other people, the pleasure of being alive, the fun of sharing the same experience with others, the joy of having overcoming myself and having conquered a difficult course, and the satisfaction after the run. I like difficult races where you never know how it will end."

To the runners who are interested in running the longer distances Sigrid's advice is to "be brave enough to tackle a challenge you want to tackle, don't give in to others who say don't do it, and just do what you are dreaming of. The main thing is to be prepared in your mind to endure pain and the difficult phases throughout a run. The attitude towards a race is in your mind, just be prepared!"

Meanwhile, back in the United States, at age 33 Gunhild Swanson started running because she was concerned that she was putting on some middle age spread. This was in 1977 when she was raising four children. Gunhild signed up for an exercise class at the local YWCA. At the end of the class they ran 10 minutes around the gym one way, and then 10 minutes the other. She heard of a local 12 K race being organized by Olympic marathoner Don Kardong and friends: The Bloomsday Race. Gunhild got hooked. She ran Bloomsday in 1978 and in 1980 turned to marathons.

Michael Dutton of Everett, Washington, played football at Western Washington University but his career was finished when he got tendinitis in both shoulders. He said his self-esteem and confidence hit "an all-time low." At 265 pounds, the potential for adverse health effects were very real if he didn't take a course of action. His brother suggested running would help. Michael started running and changed his diet. He lost 80 pounds in a year. Over time his distance increased and he decided to run a marathon. "I was only going to run one marathon, but I finished first in my age group, and won a trophy, and I was hooked." Three weeks later, he ran another marathon and has continued to do so. He ran the Crater Lake marathon in Klamath Falls, Oregon and was "overwhelmed by the course's beauty. I almost felt like I was in heaven. That's where I want my wife to throw my ashes."

Chris Warren from Washington State was a non-runner who didn't enjoy running. His long time girlfriend had signed up to run a marathon with a charity group and Chris was waiting for her at the finish line. "It was very inspirational listening and watching everyone running in at the finish line. I said if all those shapes and sizes can do it, so could I." Six months later, in 2000, he ran the Seattle marathon.

Chris hasn't stopped running, and has now completed more than 170 marathons and 13 ultras. After he reached his 100th he was "driven", he said, to achieve a higher level in his own club, the Marathon Maniacs, of which he is one of the three co-founders, so he ran 53 marathons in 52 weeks, running doubles on several weekends. He would like to run 15-20 marathons a year. He "absolutely loves the fact that at a marathon it's such a positive environment to be around – everyone wants to be there."

Jim 'Manic' Mundy, who works with the London Ambulance Service in England, started running after watching the London Marathon on television in 1989, at age 38. "It inspired me to enter a half-marathon in top hat and tails, shocked to find the rest of the entrants in shorts and vests. I had found the world of road running, ran a few more halves and joined a running club before running the London Marathon in 1991. Like most club runners, I ran one or two a year until 'retirement' in 2002, having completed 15 marathons and five ultras." He started seriously running marathons after Jack Brooks dragged him out of his pre-mature retirement to run his 100th with him in Calvia, Italy. Jack introduced Jim to "the notorious 100 club!!" Jim has since gone on to run the Brathay 10 marathons in 10 days challenge in two consecutive years, and plans to run a trans-continental race in 2010.

Sixty-three year old Noriko Sakota from Japan began her distance running career after walking for exercise at a gymnasium. She then participated in a 10 K running race during a sightseeing trip. Six months later she ran her first marathon. That was the Kogake-Kakegawa marathon in Japan in April 1992. She finished in a time of 4:35. Just four years later, she completed her 100th at the Enoshima Joy Marathon. Noriko is now second behind Sigrid Eichner of Germany with the most marathons ever run by a woman, with 850 marathons and 14 ultras.

Fellow Japanese 100 Marathon club member Masami Nakamura from Tokyo began running marathons to experience the "hardness of the distance." He ran his first marathon in Honolulu in 1989 at the age of 54. When asked why he still runs marathons he said it's too difficult a question to answer. In December 2009, he completed his 700th marathon. Now at age 74 he is retired, but continues running long distances while pursuing his other passions of karate and bowling.

Masami lives near the Imperial Palace in Tokyo. He organizes a private marathon that runs along the roads around the palace twice a month. He arrives early in the morning to Takebashi, the spot where the marathon starts and finishes, to run this now very popular race. Although many club members run this marathon, it is open to anyone. If more than three runners want to run another marathon and Masami agrees to arrange it, an extra one will be held (often on Sunday).

When he was in his forties, Hisashi Yoshifuji was troubled with back aches. His doctor advised him to start a regular program of walking. His walking transformed into running and at age 46 he ran his first marathon – the Sasayama ABC marathon in March 1986. Since then, he has completed 678 marathons and 109 ultras. He says he runs for his health and the immense sense of satisfaction and achievement he feels each time he completes a race. His mottos are not to run excessively, not to compete with others and to run for fun.

American Dave Bell began running in 1993 and ran his first marathon in 1995. He was inspired to do so after hearing the story of his friend who was talked into running the 56-mile Comrades ultra in the 1980s. Dave wanted to run Comrades but knew that he first needed to run a marathon.

Texan Steve Boone has worked on computer systems for about 40 years. One day, a customer bet him he couldn't run a marathon. He said he could. In college Steve had no problem running 5 miles in 25 minutes. At the time of the bet Steve was pretty active playing soccer. He won the bet but got "beaten up" doing it. That was in 1988. Then he ran the New York marathon and loved that. The next year he ran four more, and ran seven others in the following year. The number kept increasing. Now he typically runs about 40 marathons a year. "Initially", Steve said, "it was and still is to a certain extent, a personal challenge. Then I started making friends out there. Then I met my wife, Paula at the Boston Marathon 12 years ago (that was her 4th marathon)." Now they run and travel across the country together throughout the year.

John Bozung from Utah ran track and cross-country in high school but stopped running when he felt that the distance – about 2 miles at a time – wasn't far enough. He also taught skiing in high school and college and so was relatively active.

Several years later, in 1985, his brother-in-law challenged him to a 10 K race – the Will Rogers Pallisades 10 K. He beat his brother-in-law and kept running throughout 1986 and 1987. In 1987 he completed the Los Angeles Marathon in 4:30 and swore he'd never run one again. He completed the Minneapolis marathon in 4:00 and didn't hit the wall. "It felt good", he said. In 1993, he set his sights on completing the four 'big ones' – Los Angeles, New

York, Boston and Chicago, and also St. George, Utah. In December, he added a 50 K race. By then it was clear he was hooked. He wasn't hurting anymore and seemed to recover quickly. Thinking there must have been "some method in my madness", he began his streak; currently over 170 consecutive months of running a marathon each month.

Englishman Jack Brooks ran his first marathon at age 41 "because when I first mentioned the idea a number of people told me that I wouldn't be able to manage it."

American Todd Byers, who has run over 80 marathons barefoot, and more than 250 in total, was a runner in high school, but didn't run the longer distances. After completing an aerospace engineering degree in the mid-1980s he moved to Seattle. Not knowing anyone, he took up running. Todd saw the movie *Marathon* starring Bob Newhart, and figured if Bob could run a marathon so could he. He trained and successfully completed the Emerald City Marathon in April 1986. "I never intended to do a second marathon", he said. Later on, he lost a bet with a friend and ended up doing an Ironman. "Now, it's about seeing people and seeing some of the country. People tell me if I didn't stop and talk to everyone I'd probably run a marathon in a couple of hours."

A friend bet John Wallace of London England, five pounds that he couldn't run the London marathon. He bet another five pounds that John wouldn't dress up. Now 50 years old, the school caretaker has run over 250 marathons dressed as Superman, and registers for events as Clark Kent. There are other runners dressed as Superman, but John is the original. He's had a fascination for Superman since he was a child, and picked up his original costume at a fancy dress shop. He has now used seven different costumes. Superman started running marathons because he wanted to get fit. He's raised over $100,000 for charities doing so. He aims to run at least 300 marathons but with four children, he says, "it's harder to run than it was in the past."

Dennis Cunniffe's "love of running" came later in life when he watched Cliff Young, at the age 61, run from Sydney to Melbourne, Australia. This was in 1984 when Dennis, a bricklayer by trade, was 45 years old. Dennis said in the Australian magazine *funRunner* "The first thing I thought about watching this was his age. And then I realized that it did not matter how old you are – it's never too late to start – so I started to train. Now I love running because it makes me feel fit and strong. I feel I am getting two things out of this sport – I'm travelling and running – the two things I love to do." As far as anyone knows, Dennis is the only deaf person in the world to have run 100 marathons. He ran his first, Sydney, in April 1984 and his last (115th) in October 2000. His 100th was in Canberra in April 1998. All 115 were run under 5 hours, with a PB of 3:17. His wife, Yvonne, told me that Dennis always felt he had an addiction to running; "he felt very guilty if he did not run." He still covers about 5-10 K when out for a run.

From an early age when American Paula Boone first saw the marathon event in the Olympics, she felt she could do it. She said she used to run track at high school, but then didn't run for about 10 years. Running was a great escape from what she says was a miserable marriage (to her now ex-husband). One day she met up with a bunch of runners who were going to run the Boston marathon. They took her through the training ropes. Her first marathon was the Antelope Island Marathon in Utah in 1996. Paula's friends told her they could get her to the finish in under 4 hours. She finished in 3:58:14, and was the 2nd woman overall. She qualified for Boston in her third ever marathon. She met Steve Boone at Boston and "the rest as they say is history." Paula would like to run Boston again, where she and Steve met (it was his 107th), but as she puts it "I don't see much chance of losing enough weight and getting back to those fast times – I'm too happily married now!" As of the end of 2009 Paula had run close to 300 hundred marathons.

Across the Atlantic, UK 100 Marathon Club member Linda Major is also closing in on three hundred marathons. Linda told me that it was the challenge of the marathon event that appealed to her when she began. "I suppose it's the challenge of seeing how much I can push my body. I never really had a goal in life but always tried to keep myself fit. I was born with a hole in my heart and I have always had that nagging in the back if my mind."

Linda ran her first marathon in 2001 and, claiming she'd never run another, "dabbled in 5 K and 10 K races", which, she says, are a different group of runners. She started running marathons again in 2003, and figured that one a month was "reasonable." She never thought of reaching 100, but after while, she said, "they add up; maybe you can get there ... then you're hooked." For Linda "it's a great way to see the world and meet lots of people, who you keep in touch with and become firm friends."

Linda's fellow club member Fu-Lok Chueng said his first marathon was "something to tick off the 'done it' list." He said "marathons do not require sporting prowess or talent, though it would help, unfortunately I have neither ... Left foot, right foot, left foot, right foot, breathe in, breathe out (repeat for 26.2 miles). It would be very hard to get this wrong!" Glyn Morris, also from the UK 100 Marathon club, said simply that he "decided to give marathon running a shot", at the Bungay Black Dog Marathon, after running shorter races for a year in 1994. "I gave it everything on the day to finish with a mixture of euphoria and extreme exhaustion, vowing never to run another marathon ever again." Glyn ran his 100th marathon in 2007.

Another UK club member, former Chair of the club Peter Graham was 24 when he started. He'd planned to run just ten marathons but said after his fifth – New York – he "was hooked." He ran his first 100 marathons in nine years. Now in his mid-forties he has run over 250 marathons, and has stopped keeping records of how many he has run. He runs now, he says, "for the sheer enjoyment." At the time of writing, he has just nine states to complete and he will have finished a marathon in all 50 US States. His favorite countryside marathon is the Yakima River Canyon Marathon in Washington state, which he has run five times. He's run more than 100 different marathons and rates the 40 plus events in the United States among his favorites.

Rinus Groen, a Dutch insurance fund manager now in his fifties, has been running for 34 years. In 1976, he bought a booklet called "trimboekje." In this, the mileage from every run completed during a half year was added and when the runner had run over 100, 150 or 200 K they received a small bronze, silver or gold statue. When Rinus looked at the distance a marathon would provide he realized this would significantly increase his tally so he entered marathon events. Reaching 100 "just happened" by running two to four marathons every year.

Canadian Wally Herman has now run over 700 marathons. His first was the Kitchener-Waterloo Octoberfest marathon in 1975. This first one, he said, would "be it"; he'd get it out of his system … "but then you're hooked." Wally describes his latent interest in endurance; he did not start to run until age 50, although he had hiked and cross-country skied. He got interested in marathon running in the 1970s; like many others, spurred on in part he said, by Frank Shorter who won the Olympic marathon gold in 1972. Wally was able to run more and more marathons when he took early retirement from his civil service job with the Canadian federal Department of Industry, Trade and Commerce in his early fifties. "I just take marathons as they come. Every day is a great day. Every marathon is a great marathon", he says.

When David Hamilton from New Zealand finished his first marathon at Rotorua in 1979, he lay down under a tree, gazed up through the leaves and thought: "Oh God! Who invented marathons?" Then, he said, the challenge was to try new courses and conquer them all, and to run a sub-three hour race. "That took me four serious attempts and didn't happen until marathon number fourteen." By then, he had discovered that if he ran marathons often enough he didn't need to do so much training, because each marathon was training for the next. "A few years ago, I realized that if I got stuck in I could run 100 marathons before the end of the century, so that became the goal."

When I asked David what it takes to run 100 marathons, he replied "a love of a challenge, a lot of travel, a lot of organization and a lot of patience. It also helps if you are slightly mad and have a selective memory to blot out the bad parts." He doesn't consider himself to be particularly gifted in an athletic sense. At school, he said he "once tried to get out of running a mile track race because I thought the distance was too great for me. After I finished school I didn't play any sport for nearly 20 years until the running boom came along. I guess as this whole marathon thing evolved I came to realize it was something I could achieve, because success was measured by finishing and time was secondary."

Someone who has run many of the same races as David is another David from New Zealand, Dave Penfold. Dave said he started running marathons for the challenge of it all although his very first marathon occurred "by accident." He thought he could run a half marathon but when he arrived at the event he discovered they didn't have a half marathon, so he ran the full instead. "It was quite the shock – quite the adventure really, as I'd only ever run a 17 K run before." It was a 5-lap course and each time he went by his car he thought about stopping, especially with bad chaffing and bleeding nipples, but he continued through the pain and finished in 4:41. A friend then sent him New Zealand legend Arthur Lydiard's book on running *Run, the Lydiard Way*, and he started running more and more longer runs. Six weeks later, he went to Wellington and ran his second marathon, knocking an hour off his time. "That got me going", he said. The following year he kept running, and met up with others who were running marathons more frequently. He started to do the same. He looked to do one a month, which set the pattern ever since, with his 50th completed around his 50th birthday. After he reached his 50th he started looking at 100.

Twenty years later, 65 years old, and with a hobby farm with 40-50 head of cattle and a passion for racing cars (he's building a formula two-seater), Dave has clocked over 210 marathons. He loves the longer runs and the "congruence" as he puts it, between the head and the physicalness of the distance run.

He enjoys running early in the morning and watching the first light. One morning he saw a plume in the distance – it was Mt Ruapehu erupting 80 K away. When he got peritonitis, a bacterial infection that causes an inflammation of the membrane which covers the abdominal organs and walls three years ago, he thought "it was all over"; he realized then, he said, that "you need to make the most of your life while you're above the ground."

In a similar vein, American Jeffrey Horowitz runs marathons to "experience the challenge, to feel vibrant and alive, to define myself as the kind of person who doesn't stop when things are merely difficult." After running marathons for almost 20 years, reaching a tally of 100 "just happened; it wasn't a goal by itself for a long time", he said.

Jeff Galloway has written more than 15 books on running, several specifically on marathoning. He has also mentored and coached hundreds of thousands of individuals over several decades, and receives more than one hundred email messages each day from runners. He was on the American 1972 Munich Olympics team, running in the 10,000 metres and as an alternate for the marathon. As Bill Rogers, 4-time winner of the Boston marathon put it, "Jeff Galloway is perhaps the one individual in the American running community who can combine a superior knowledge of our sport with the highest level of achievement - making the Olympic team."

And he's also run over 120 marathons. Jeff's first marathon "was an accident." When he was home for Christmas after his first year at college he registered for the first annual Atlanta Marathon "because of the size of the trophy." He said he made "a lot of mistakes" and hit the wall at Mile 19, but went on to win the event. He was a runner at college, inspired by an 8th grade track conditioning program that he says planted the seeds of his addiction. "Two months of running forest trails produced a young runner addicted to the positive well being that comes after a run, the camaraderie, fun, and mutual respect which I've since learned that distance runners share everywhere, at any age."

After his successful first marathon, Jeff didn't run another marathon for two years. These days he runs three to four marathons a year, with about 50-60 miles of slow training each week.

In one of Jeff's books he writes about Cathy Troisi, who came to one of his running schools and became noticeably enthusiastic when Jeff described his run-walk approach to training and running marathons. Cathy had never run before, and, in her fifties, thought it was too late to begin training for something like a marathon. She had, however, wanted to run the Boston marathon for a charity. Jeff's run-walk approach gave her hope. We'll return to Cathy later.

Another marathon coach, and an author of 35 books who has influenced thousands of runners, is Indiana-based Hal Higdon. Hal has competed in the Olympic Trials eight times and has won four world masters championships (i.e., over the age of 35); including the 3000 meter steeplechase in 1975, which still stands as the American Master's record (9:18). He was one of the founders of the Road Runners Club of America and also a finalist in NASA's Journalist-in-Space program to ride the space shuttle. In 2003 the American Society of Journalists and Author's gave Hal its Career Achievement Award, the highest honor given to writer members. He has been running, and writing, he says, for over half a century. In fact, it seems he has always been running. "Marathon running was something I got into because I was good at it", he told me. He said he's run over 100 marathons "because I'm really old (he's seventy-eight) and they've just accumulated over time … Now I've slowed down to the point where I'd be out on the course too long."

Hal said that when he was running at the elite level he was training every day, had a full-time job and with his wife Rose raised three children. He recalled at age 34 he was leading the Boston marathon at the 15-18 mile marks, but faded, and finished fifth. At that point he said, he realized he was never going to have that moment again. But now, he's moved into the simple enjoyment of it all. In Honolulu, for example, he started in the last row alongside a couple who were kissing at the start line. Hal decided to aim for running each mile faster than the previous one, which he did.

In 2009 Hal's novel 'Marathon' was published. It details the 72-hour countdown of a major city marathon, complete with suspense and intrigue, and the insider's eye of what goes on behind the scenes of a major marathon. Hal's book "captures the essence of the marathon", said Amby Burfoot, Editor at Large of the Running World magazine.

Yen Nguyen is an accountant who lives in Houston, Texas. Originally from Vietnam, Yen came to the United States at the age of 13, sponsored by the Lutheran Church. Her family lived in Minnesota for a few years before her father decided they had to live somewhere warmer – so they moved to Texas. She has completed over 330 marathons and ultras since she first started running marathons in 1996.

Although Yen had never run a marathon she had been running for a while at the downtown YMCA in Houston. One Saturday morning, she was talking to another woman in the changing rooms. The heavier-set woman was on her way to the Houston Marathon Expo saying she'd run several marathons. Yen couldn't believe it as the woman didn't look like your stereotypical marathon runner. The woman suggested that since Yen ran fairly regularly at the YMCA that she too could enter the marathon. And so on that Expo day in January 1996, the day before the marathon, Yen signed up, not telling her family what she was intending to do. Despite her quads "screaming" at Mile 24, Yen completed the marathon in a time of 5:36. "It hurt", she said.

This was a long way from Yen growing up, "as a chubby kid." One of her boyfriends even dumped her in high school, she said, for being "too chubby." These days, as she has done every day for many years, she runs about nine miles a day, on the rooftop track of the downtown YMCA, mainly before work. Yen will sometimes supplement this with some walking after work. "I feel sick when I'm not running each day", she said.

In England, Selina 'Shades' da Silva ran her first marathon in 1995, and her 100th in 2003. Selina said she got started running marathons after watching the first ever London marathon on TV. "I couldn't believe ordinary people could do that sort of thing." She resolved to have a go herself as a personal challenge. She said "I only intended to run one marathon." In her 17th marathon Selina met two other runners who had run more than 100 marathons each and at that point she set her sights on her own 100 goal. Selina has now run more than 220 marathons, is a regular online coach for UK Runners World, and completed the Brathay 10 marathons in 10 days challenge in 2008. Running, she says, is her first priority.

Fellow UK club member Osy Waye was drawn to marathon running just like Selina. He watched the London marathon and it looked like a lot of fun with plenty of costumes and dressing up. Although he had never done any running at school, he'd always done a lot of walking. So at age 38 he put his lottery entry into London. "The atmosphere, that's what it's all about" he said when we met in London's Hyde Park. "I love the big city marathons ... I never look at my times."

For some runners the move into marathon running is the result of an awakening, a growing awareness that they need to address their health. They're motivated from within and often inspired by others.

Retired firefighter Mike Brooks from Maine, New England began his own journey into distance running in 1992 after hearing of another firefighter's wife who had been diagnosed with multiple sclerosis. He biked 150 miles to raise money. Back then he smoked two packs of cigarettes a day. But he stopped smoking and took up running. Mike told a reporter in 2003 "I found the further the distance I ran, the better I liked it ... I'm lucky I've got an understanding wife." In September that same year, he ran his 100th marathon at the U.S. Air Force Marathon in Ohio, just eight years after running his first marathon.

Ron Fowler of Seattle, Washington started running marathons to see if he could "do the challenge." But he also found that running greatly reduced his stress levels from working in the insurance business, which he did for 30 years. In the summer of 1969 a neighbor gave him Ken Cooper's 1968 book *Aerobics*. Cooper, a doctor and former US Air Force Colonel, founded the Cooper Aerobics Center and The Cooper Institute, and has published a number of books. The basis of his Aerobics book is a point system for improving the cardiovascular system. Cooper's book inspired Ron. "I never feel totally rested from running", he told me, "but I still get all the benefits from running …perhaps more mental than physical benefits." He's been running almost continuously now since the 1970s, having run his first marathon in 1978. He's now run more than 180 marathons.

Down under in Australia meanwhile Brian Gawne joined the Shepparton Runners Club in part he says because his father had died of a heart attack at age 56. Brian himself played Australian football until he retired at age 31. Conscious of his father's early death, he eventually built up his training to run his first marathon, the Big M Frankston to Melbourne marathon. He ran it in a time of 3:42 and said he'd never run another. At age 61 he ran his 100th marathon (and he's run another 20 ultras). He's a member of the Spartans runners group, as he has finished 30 Melbourne marathons. His wife Lyn also started running marathons in 1981. In a 2009 article in *Run For Your Life*, Brian talked about his involvement in a children's running club, which has about 30 members. He encourages them but does not push them, wanting them to enjoy the experience and hoping he can offer advice when needed. "I run because I love it. I like being fit. It helps me keep my weight down and allows me to eat and drink what I like."

Dave Major of England has now run more than 400 marathons. He's been suffering from asthma since he was two years old. He's taken a range of different drug medications over the years to control his daily infliction. In his teen years Dave's asthma became easier to live with and he started drinking and smoking heavily "like all good teenagers with money in their pockets." His health deteriorated in his twenties and at 29 he was told by his doctor that he would be confined to a wheelchair by 35 if he did not radically change his lifestyle. On the 1st September 1994 he started to run/walk just a mile a day "but late at night because I was 210 pounds and very embarrassed." Dave says that due to his embarrassment he "felt running was a sport I could follow without having to join a gym or sports club and face the general public."

American Jim Scheer had played one year of semi-professional football but "after a year of tackling the big guys" he said, "he figured it wasn't a way for lifelong fitness." He too was inspired by reading Ken Cooper's book *Aerobics*. His workmates used to ask him why he ran, and he always replied "because I don't want to look like you." Looking back, he says, many of his co-workers have died from ill-health. His brother also died because of his lifestyle. Now retired, Jim has run more than 300 marathons, motivated by his recognition many years ago that good health was essential.

A combination of factors, each in itself heavily influential, led Englishman John Sturley to start running marathons. Following a painful and protracted divorce, and the subsequent death of his father, John, in early 1984, "took up 'jogging' to counter the effects of depression, anger, frustration and an ever-expanding waistline." After running his "still-favourite distances of 10 miles and the half marathon", he stepped up to marathons. The numbers kept on growing. "I wanted to belong to a select band of runners who seem to enjoy the marathon distance", so he joined the UK 100 Marathon Club. "The feeling of satisfaction of still being able to push myself to the limit and to survive to race another day is especially important to me, as I have had a heart triple-bypass operation." In answer to the perennial question of "why", John always replies "Because I can. There are many who cannot."

Chicago Lawyer Susan Daley began running marathons in 1991 because her friend was "doing it and it seemed like something to do." Susan now runs a marathon, on average, twice a month. "I pretty much go where I want" she told me. As Chicago is a flying hub, it's very easy to fly almost anywhere. She looks for easy access, and marathons with no cut-off times that will prevent slower runners from completing the race. Susan's not running marathons to beat world records. "Sometimes I'm last", she says, "I've got pictures of the ambulance driving behind me. When I started in 1991 I would think, yes, I could run faster, improve my times, qualify for Boston. But over time it's more that I just want to finish the marathon and have a good time." She's now finished a marathon 400 times.

Sometimes a simple suggestion or request can lead someone into a life changing activity. If you're into the marathon running circles in Australia you will have likely met or at least heard of Bob Fickel. Bob ran his first marathon in 1981. Before that he ran the 1980 City to Surf 14 K in Sydney, his first "big race." He had started training for it with his first wife's cousin. She pulled out but Bob completed the event. He has now done 30 consecutive City to Surf races, and in 2009 finished in 70 minutes. His real passion, however, is the long distance. He will have run his 200th marathon in 2010, which, given the fewer races in Australia and the distances required to race them, is a significant achievement.

In England, a friend of Bill Inskip had to go to the Falklands war in 1982, just before the South Coast marathon for which he had registered. He asked Bill to run for him. The bug was caught. Many marathons later, Bill joined the UK 100 Marathon Club to meet others who had run 100 plus marathons, and, he said, "for the t-shirt." Bill nearly stopped running but after an accident where he broke both legs he wanted to see if he could still do it. "I guess if it is in the blood and you love it then keep running for as long as you can for the buzz".

In 2008 at 85 years of age, American Paul Gionfriddo ran his 100th marathon at the Lakefront Marathon, Milwaukee. He finished in a time of 6:21. At that time he was still running 25-30 miles a week. He's run several more since then. More remarkable but equally inspirational is that he started running when he was 60 years old. It began when General Electric Medical Systems, where he worked, now known as GE Healthcare, arranged a 3-mile run. He told a reporter in 2008 that "each of the groups had to have one member to be at least 55 years or older. I happened to be the oldest one in my group, and they tapped me and said 'you gotta run' and I said 'oh, no I don't'!" He ran it, and really enjoyed it.

In England, Pam Storey had never played a lot of sports until she began playing badminton later in life. She then started as a founding member of a jogging club, but would do intervals of running and walking. When she joined an athletics club a coach put her on a training program for completing a sub 3-hour marathon. At the same time, she married a marathon runner. With just one month left of the training she sprained her ankle, but still entered the marathon. After 17 miles, however, she ended up in an ambulance.

Not long after, she did complete her first marathon, in a time of 4:20. Pam remarried – to Gil – another prolific distance runner, and has gone on, in her late fifties, to complete more than 120 marathons. She ran her 100th in Dublin with John Wallace (aka Superman), dressed as Supergirl. As she doesn't drive, she is extremely grateful that her partner Gil, has taken her to so many events. Like many other distance runners, Pam raises money for charity. Her primary charity is Advance International Ministries, which supports Kiyindi, a village in Uganda. So far the charity has built a job training centre, medical centre and a bible school. Electricity and water have also been brought to the village.

Fewer than thirty runners in New Zealand have completed 100 marathons, and one of them is Robert Treneman. When he left school Robert's boss pushed him to run, so he did. He got fit, was attracted to the long distance, and completed his first marathon in a time of 4:18, then a second in 3:07. At the age of 19 he ran a 2:54 marathon. When he had run about 40 marathons he met runners who had run 100 and thought "I could do that." With marathons he said, "the fitter you are, the easier they are." In 1996 he ran his 100th marathon in Boston.

Fifty-year old Steve Yee is a wastewater process analyst in Washington state, and a co-founder of the Marathon Maniacs. He's completed more than 250 marathons and ultras. His first ever race was The Bar-S Stampede 10 K, which he describes as "one of the most miserable race experiences I've ever had." He was an intern at the Cudahy Bar-S Meat Company at that time. The company sponsored the race so Steve and a few of the employees signed up. "I went all out in that first mile and quickly bonked thereafter. Runner after runner passed me and I think I ended up five places from being the last finisher. At least the hot dogs at the end of the race helped soothe my bruised ego."

Six months after he had started running, he ran his first marathon, The Tacoma Marathon. He started running marathons because it was a greater challenge than just running 5 and 10 Ks. It felt like the normal progression, taking it up to the next level. He enjoys the challenge. "In a shorter race, even if you screw up you're not in much pain afterwards. In a marathon, it's all about pacing, the training regimen you have to do and the satisfaction of completing a marathon. Those are feelings that just don't happen when competing at shorter races."

Although he didn't know if he'd be able to complete his first marathon, he finished it in a time of 3:03. Steve says his friends and family think he's "truly nuts." He writes on the Internet that his Mom says "go get married and start a family", so he wouldn't be lonely and run so many races.

Shinichi Nose of Japan started running when his doctor advised him to lose weight. He completed his first marathon at the age of 60 in Honolulu, 2004. He and his wife ran the marathon to celebrate their 30th wedding anniversary. She had run marathons herself prior to this race. When he joined the Japanese 100 Marathon Club – known as the Full Hyaku club – in 2006, he had run ten marathons. In the following two and half years he ran 90 more to reach his 100. As of early 2010, he had run over 130 marathons. When I asked him why he runs marathons he said it is to keep in good health, to socialize with his running friends and because he always feels good when he completes a marathon. His goal is to complete 200 marathons before he turns 68.

The world of long distance running is a small one. Tom Adair, President of the 50 States Club, contacted Shinichi on my behalf about this book and he graciously offered to do translation for me. I sent a copy of my previous book *A Marathon Odyssey* to Shinichi as a way of saying thank-you.

There is an image of Athens on the cover of that book. Shinichi emailed that it brought back memories of when he ran the Athens marathon, which happened to be the same year I ran it.

I remembered at that point, that I had taken a photo of Japanese runners wearing bright pink (I didn't know it at the time, but that is the Full Hyaku club's colors). I emailed Shinichi the photo, asking if he knew the runners. He emailed back saying "what a great surprise!!" It turned out the photo I took is of Shinichi, the tour guide Ms. Kamata, and Noriko Sakota, whom we meet in this book, who was running her 700th marathon in Athens. That photo is in this book too, along with the group photo of the Full Hyaku members who travelled to Greece for the Athens marathon.

Australian ultra-runner Kelvin Marshall lived on the Melbourne marathon route. One year, he was standing at the 8-10 K mark watching the runners go past. He told himself he'd do it the following year.

Kelvin played Australian football (Rules) in his earlier years when he was at school in Melbourne. Each team member had to run 20 K every week. Kelvin figured he'd do it all at once on the weekend. Growing up without a car, each Sunday he and his dad walked everywhere, often with their dog, sometimes they were out for five hours at a time. And at high school everyone had to go into the cadets course, which included an option to do Bushwalking. He bushwalked in places where he has since done a lot of running. "I enjoy the endurance – with trail races you don't even notice how hard it is sometimes because you're enjoying the scenery – the physical challenge – it's you against nature."

American Dave McGillivray wanted to be an athlete in high school, but he was continually picked last in gym class and at recess and was cut from both the basketball and baseball teams. He still believes this was due to his "small stature and people's incorrect perceptions" about height. In his 2006 book *The Last Pick*, written when he was 51, Dave writes that he has had a "lifetime of journeys" through the course of what he calculates to have been 130,000 miles of running "thus far."

Among many other accomplishments, Dave has been the race director of the Boston Marathon since 2001. Joan Samuelson, the first female Olympic gold medalist in marathon running (1984) writes of Dave "With the heart the size of Boston, I can't think of anyone who does more things for people, without expecting anything in return … his work ethic, his energy, his athletic feats, and his generosity are legendary."

But Dave *did* make the soccer team in high school. And during his soccer training runs he noticed he always seemed to be ahead of his teammates, a point also noticed by the cross-country coach who was watching. Coach Joe Orpin asked Dave if he'd consider running cross-country, to which Dave first replied "no" because he didn't see running as a legitimate sport. But the coach kept talking, and eventually convinced Dave to try the new "sport."

After reading the issue of the *Boston Globe* that described the Boston Marathon to be held that day, Patriots Day, Dave set about running the event. He borrowed a friend's generic race number, 942, got his brother to be his support crew and called his grandfather to tell him what he was doing. His grandfather, who had always been supportive of anything Dave did, would wait for him to finish. Dave was seventeen at the time and, he said, "invincible", as all 17 year olds feel. He'd not run the distance before but didn't see that as a major issue.

It was a major issue. At mile 18 he pulled out due to "body parts not working", muscles spasms and blisters. He was taken to hospital in a police cruiser, and picked up later by his parents. When he finally got home he called his grandfather to tell him what had happened. His grandfather had waited until the very last runner had crossed the line and he had watched the clean-up crew.

Dave apologized and told him that he'd failed. His grandfather said he hadn't failed; but rather, he'd learned, and that he needed to do his homework and train for the next one, and he'd be there watching him the next year. Dave agreed to run the following year.

Two months later his grandfather died suddenly of a heart attack while riding a train in Boston. Dave resolved to train hard for the upcoming 1973 marathon, running between 100-120 miles a week in preparation. And, at age18, he entered the race, this time officially.

The day before his next Boston marathon he caught a virus and was very sick. His parent's said he couldn't run, to which he replied, "please give me a chance"? They agreed.

The race was challenging and difficult, with Dave doing everything he could just to "keep going" amidst the aches and fever. He was throwing up in the first few miles. He saw his Mom, who was crying, and his Dad at mile 13, which helped him along, but by the time of the hills he was doing the "survivor shuffle." He was throwing up every few miles and had no option but to run, walk, run, walk. At 21.2 miles, he sat down with his head between his knees crying and apologizing. He looked over and saw the cemetery where his grandfather was buried. He picked himself up and continued running, finishing in a time of 4:35.

Dave has now run over 120 marathons. He's run 38 consecutive Boston marathons, 21 of which have been at night (He can't actually run it while directing the race, so instead runs it after the last runner has crossed the line), which is so in keeping with Dave's overall spirit and drive. Also, since he was 12 he's run the equivalent distance each year on his birthday. When we talked he was contemplating running the requisite 55 miles on his upcoming 55th birthday. "Every year I look forward to it", he said, "and get more nervous about it too."

8

"It is hard to describe what a relief it is to fulfill an achievement like this. At first, a goal only 'absurd', later 'maybe ... in a far and distant future', later again 'perhaps within some years'... and suddenly 'quite close'. Well, fact is that it took me less than four and a half years to run the first 100 marathons ... What is important is all the adventures, travels and most importantly many, many good friends that the marathons have given me."

Tor Rønnow on completing his 100 marathons.

A common characteristic of our messengers is their focus on setting and achieving goals. How specific goals emerge may be different from one runner to another, but in each case they systematically work towards achieving those goals. The goals may enter their consciousness after a simple conversation with another runner; "I'm going to run a marathon in all fifty states", for example, or "I'm going to run fifty marathons before I turn fifty." Or "I'm going to run over fifty marathons in one year." Or "I'm going to be this country's most prolific marathon runner ever." Typically the goal setting is a very personal thing, although "completing 100 marathons" is still very much a magical, common goal.

What any of these goals requires is patience, faith and confidence in one's physical, mental, spiritual and emotional capacity to achieve it. Having the financial resources and time also helps! Regardless of how committed or dedicated you are, it takes time to run 100 marathons. Although it is possible to run 100 in one year, almost everyone will need several years to reach 100. And that will require a significant amount of traveling also. Even if you can run one a month, it will still take close to nine years to reach 100.

Bob Dolphin reached his goal of 400 marathons at his own, and favorite, Yakima River Canyon marathon in Washington state in 2008. I asked him after he finished that what his next goal was. "Five hundred marathons" he replied almost immediately. All going to plan, he will reach 500 late in 2010. The specific date will depend on where exactly Bob would like to reach this milestone. But he also wants to run some more 50 K's to reach 50 ultras, and he wants to run all 50 States, the Canadian Provinces, and all the continents, as well as race walk another marathon. "I want to run marathons for the rest of my life."

Optimism abounds as well. Several messengers identified running a marathon at 100 years of age as a goal: "In the future", one runner said, "I would love to be the first person to run the London marathon when I am 100." Welshman Gilbert (Gil) John, nicknamed the 'ultragoat', stunned people one time when he was asked what his ambition was. Gil replied it was to run a world record marathon at age 100. Gil is very goal oriented: "You've got to have a new target don't you", he said to me the day before the Windermere marathon. His latest goals are to complete 100 ultras and to complete 100 different marathons. When fellow Welshman Steve Jones, a former world record holder met Gil in a pub after the London marathon one year, Gil was introduced as the Welsh record holder for marathons at the time. It must have been quite a shock given that Steve was a former world record holder for the fastest time. But Gil at the time had completed 212 marathons. Currently Gil has completed over 370 distance events, including 86 ultras.

It's an interesting example though of how we view world records. In the athletic world the typical focus is on the fastest completion time for specific events, but why is it that we are so focused on speed, especially when endurance events are more about going the distance? Why is it that other achievements such as the longest runs or the most events completed are not more important? Or are the numbers of races completed important at all? Australian John Zeleznikow said to me that "Just to do it [to run a marathon] makes you stand out and you don't have to be a world champion."

American Todd Byers commented that he wants to "continue going around the world, seeing parts of the world I haven't seen … I'm slower now, which means I get to see the new places in much more detail." When Todd completed his 100th marathon in Seattle his friends had got together and made a big 'Congrats Todd' banner. His name was called out as he crossed the finish line, and everyone signed his banner. It was displayed over the back wall at the awards ceremony. "I've still got it", he said.

There is the friendly competitiveness as well, as many messengers will be looking at who has more marathons and who they can catch up with. Steve Boone has run more than 400 marathons and his wife Paula has run over 270, but Steve say's they "are babies", when compared to the likes of Norm Franks, Wally Herman and others, each of whom has run hundreds more than Steve or Paula. "When you run marathons" Steve said, "you're not looking behind, you're looking ahead. It's the same when you compare yourself with other marathon runners."

Like several other messengers, Texan Rick Worley set himself a continuing goal of consecutive marathons completed – in his case over weekends. Between January 1997 and January 2001, 159 consecutive weekends, he completed one or more marathons for a total of 200. Englishman Roger Biggs, at the beginning of 2010, has a streak of 60 marathons in 60 weeks. Other messengers, meanwhile, set goals for consecutive months of completing marathons. American John Bozung has a current streak of 174 months (fourteen and a half years) in which he's completed a marathon, and Dave Major has completed at least 50 marathons in each year for the past four years.

John Maddog Wallace kept adding more and more countries to the list of those in which he'd completed a marathon. For many years Wally Herman, a good friend of John's had a tally of 99 countries and very few people were anywhere close to him. But over time, John made it his goal to reach 100 and eventually, he achieved his goal. John said to a reporter "I thought, I'm never going to catch Wally in the number of marathons he's run ... And trying to be the first to do anything in running is very, very difficult. So I'm going to try to run the most number of countries in the world. I finally caught Wally last year."

John is similar to many runners in that he needs goals to give himself direction. Osy Waye, an English messenger, is another example; "Why 100?" he said, "It's in my personality – I like achieving targets. Where I've lacked in speed I'm very good with endurance."

One of the top endurance athletes in the world, Pam Reed, said over the telephone to me that "You can't just have one goal because if you do you're setting yourself up – and if you don't achieve your goals, then what ... I had to learn that with my experience at Leadville one year – for months I'd focused on winning the event – I had hoped to win, but dropped back during the run and finished third." "It's better", Pam said, "to have other tangible goals but also to keep in mind the intangible non-event specific goals", like hers for example, "To be able to run and not feel like I'm running", and, echoing many runners, to make "more time to do stretching – I don't like doing it."

The messengers are no fools, however. They know that training for and completing distance running events is good for their health. And setting long term goals like running a marathon at age 100, or, to be the oldest person ever to run a marathon as Robbie 'Red Hat' Wilson wants to, gives the goal a sharper focus. Maddog, for example, says his overall goals are to stay healthy and injury free. Japanese Hisashi Yoshifuji says he hopes to run marathons "forever." American Rick Haase says his long term goal is to "run as many interesting races as I can before I have to use a walker", although his shorter term goal is simply "to stay healthy." Wally Herman, in his late seventies now, says his next goal is simply the next marathon, "but it's a short term and long term goal." Todd Byers meanwhile, says "when it stops being fun I'll stop doing it." British runner, 75-year old John Dawson, says "it's foolish to set too high a goal or goals for yourself. I'll go on for as long as I can."

Englishman Keith Scrivener says "everybody needs goals in life and me more so after my series of what should have been fatal illnesses. In my case because of my marathon target and the support of my wife Meryl and my three children, my running club and Sir Roger Bannister I still have a fantastic quality of life."

Paul Alsop is another goal-setter. He said that "When I was about 55 my wife and I decided that we wanted to go trekking in the Himalayas for my 60th birthday. In order to get fit for the trek, I started running marathons again. It was then that I thought I would like to run 100 before I was 70. I completed my 100th in May 2007, my next goal is to complete 200 by 80; I am currently ahead of my schedule."

In April 2009, Mike Brooks took on his "longest race ever." His goal was to run 500 miles to raise $10,000 for Camp Sunshine on Sebago Lake in Maine. Camp Sunshine is a retreat for very sick children, some terminal, and their families. He has raised money for the camp on other occasions, including at the 135-mile Badwater in Death Valley, California, and at a 6-day race. Mike also entered the Sri Chinmoy 10-Day race on a one-mile paved loop in Flushing Meadows Park, Queens, New York, where only three of the 44 runners were from the United States. When interviewed by *Marathon and Beyond*, Mike noted that "the first 6 days went pretty much as planned except for four days with temperatures over 90 degrees."

His goal was to run about 75 miles on Day 1 and then about 55 miles per day after that for as long as he could, for a total of 500 miles. By Day 6, with 334 miles on his feet, he was experiencing back problems, and fatigue was setting in. Although he'd had regular sleeping breaks, by Day 7 he said he was leaning to the left; the more hours that passed, the greater the lean and the pain. By Day 9, with blistered feet and pain on the balls of his feet he had completed 469 miles. He only needed thirty-one miles over the last 24-hours to complete his goal. But by now both the lean and pain were "extreme." He said "I could only go a few hundred feet and would have to lean on something or bend over to control the pain in my back." Despite help from the on-site chiropractor, massage therapist, and doctor, nothing helped. So after completing 491 miles he had to stop just nine miles short of his 500 mile goal.

Australian Bob Fickel ran in the Sutherland Relay for Life 24-hour run in Sydney for several years. In 2003 he ran as his sister Lorraine, who had breast cancer, watched from the sideline. His sister died in 2004, but Bob ran the entire event that year by himself, raising $12,000 in her honour. To keep him awake he runs on coffee and good music, and at a slower pace than he typically would, around 8km per hour.

British messenger Michaela Sanders is a goal setter, from identifying running distances during a race, from lamp post to lamp-post to broader running goals and life in general. But her overall outlook is one best captured by her comment, "Don't spend the rest of your life making more regrets." For her 50th marathon in Amsterdam, a dozen friends came with her to run and celebrate. Michaela had severe flu, felt sick and couldn't eat, but with so many friends having spent money to come and share the weekend with her, she felt compelled to run. Her husband Mark, who has since also become a member of the 100 Marathon Club, ran in front of Michaela, passing her jelly babies along the way. She was running for everyone else. As she noted, "resilience, tenacity and stupidity."

One of the most significant goals of course is reaching 100 marathons. There isn't an instant desire to reach the magical 100 as soon as someone runs a marathon. Rather, the desire typically enters the consciousness after many marathons; often after either seeing others wearing 100 Marathon Club shirts (as frequently mentioned by British messengers) or talking to 100 Marathon Club members. In 1997, for example, Dave Major stood on the start line of a marathon in the south of England and looked at the club vest in front of him. It said in big silver letters "100 Marathon

Club." "That was it", he said, "I wanted one. The only problem was how would I find and run the other 96 I needed!!" On his 50th marathon in Spain, Dave was celebrating with other British runners in a bar. He didn't realize at the time that most of them were members of the UK 100 Marathon Club. Sitting next to the chairman of the club by accident Dave was asked how many marathons he had run. When Dave said 50 the chairman replied "that's good you can be a WANNABEE." "That was it", said Dave, "I now really wanted that Vest!"

Fellow British messenger Selina da Silva notes that completing her 100th marathon "felt fantastic" although there was a great deal of stress over the last ten of the countdown, in part, because everyone wants to know when you'll do it. You become hypersensitive to every potential injury. As Selina mentioned "you're so keen to avoid injury that you get nervous just crossing the road". In a similar vein British messenger Peter Graham said he could have easily run another marathon in between his 99th and 100th but decided to wait two months before doing his 100th. He added though that "the grief in going through the whole of September without doing a Marathon was a bit depressing."

In 2005, British messenger Glyn Morris "discovered the 100 Marathon club." He made up his mind to join. "In order to get there as quickly as possible, and because I had more time on my hands than was healthy, I decided to run a marathon every week ... Because there weren't enough local marathons to fit in with my agenda, I'd need to travel abroad, and also step up to ultras, which at the time was a pretty daunting prospect." In 2005 he managed to complete 51 marathons. Included in his 2005 year was a 175-mile seven day race – the Marathon of Britain, from Malvern to Nottingham, which as Glyn notes he "finished on the Friday, which gave me plenty of time to recover for the Nottingham marathon on the Sunday." In 2006 he slowed his pursuit but still took in the Marathon des Sables in March as well as starting to run 12 and 24 hour races. Glyn completed his 100th at the London Marathon in April 2007, "so I was able to enjoy my 100th on a very sunny day with my club mates and the fantastic London crowds, and I can now hang up my running shoes. Maybe not, but I can finally relax and concentrate on my now preferred distance of ultra running."

Four time Lake Tahoe Triple Marathon winner and Oregon-based Sean Meissner set himself the goal of running 100 ultras before his 35th birthday on July 31st, 2008. It didn't happen. He had already run his 100th marathon in Washington state in 2007 (Chuckanut), his second race run in a skirt. He did, however, reach 100 ultras in March 2009 in Maui, Hawaii. Sean briefly described the 34-mile race" "CRAZY rain and wind (120 mph!!). Course shortened by 2 miles. Severe hypothermia at the finish...happy to finish, lucky to win. Ultra #100!"

Dave Major wrote about getting to 100 marathons based on his own and other people's comments. "As early as 50 marathons some people start planning their big celebration. This is normally based on certain criteria as "Where do I want it (for example, local, special, unique), Is it a private achievement, do I want to party, do I want to have as many of my 100 clubbers around as possible, can I obtain the number 100 from the race organizers? Then the required communication would kick-in accordingly, with the line being drawn in the sand'.

In the run-up, future messengers are in the countdown mode. Depending on how far ahead they have made their commitment, which could be races, weeks, months or even years away, their thoughts start to turn to ensuring all their races have been planned accurately and according to where and when the 100th will be run. Some doubts start to creep into their thinking. What happens if the race is cancelled? How do they make up the extra event? What if I am ill? Or injured? Is there any time available for recovery time?

Dave talks about what some club members refer to as the 'nervous nineties' "the time when the pressure you have applied to your achievement takes hold. You will be thinking every day about the 100, worrying that you will not finish, retire, be ill, be incapable of running another mile etc. As each one passes the nervousness grows along with the excitement of your peers. You are now the main focus of the running club and cannot wait for the weeks / months to roll by. The feeling that you just want it to be over grows immensely."

By the time number 99 occurs, the runner realizes that it will be the last one before becoming a member of the 100 Club "forever"!! "You will at all costs complete", says Dave. And then the 100th is the big day. "You will feel you can run forever, you won't want the day to be over and when you do complete the race, depending on your arrangements, it is like a huge weight is being lifted from your shoulders."

To many runners, the 101st is both the easiest and hardest. Now they can wear the club colors but they no longer have that sharp "100" focus. "All those years of apprenticeship have been completed and now that's it", says Dave. The next series of races – the 102-120 – is where members may stall. They may lose all their focus and reason to carry on. Fair enough. What else could there be to achieve? This is when other goals and targets are established. These may include 100 road races, 100 trail races, different countries, certain number of races before various birthday dates, and so on. Statistically, it's noted that a number of club members semi-retire for a while right after completing their 100th.

Dave's wife, Linda Major, talked about the angst of reaching 100. Ever since her first runs, when she injured her ankle, she's found she always has weak ankles. The first time she thought she could run on it, but she ended up on crutches for six weeks. The second time she hurt her ankle was with just six marathons to go for her 100. Linda ran four of them with her ankle strapped up, the first two of which she could barely walk the next day. But "When you get that number 100 in your head", she said, "there is nothing that will get in the way." And so it was that Linda reached her 100th in Munich, Germany, with the help of a contingent of 100 Marathon Club members. All of whom did the conga dance with Linda as they went over the finish line.

Another Dave, Boston Marathon Race Director Dave McGillivray, told me that in the 1970s and 1980s it was all about competition, and he himself was running 2:30 times (his PB is 2:29). But now, running marathons is about participation, self-esteem and self-confidence. Dave now considers running marathons to be a 'reality check'. Known for his logistical expertise, Dave was pivotal in managing the road events of the 1996 Atlanta Olympics. In the same year, as Boston's race director, he oversaw a 75 person organizing committee to hold the 100th running of the Boston Marathon. Over 38,000 runners from around the world competed.

One of those thousands was New Zealand messenger Robert Scott. Robert cites that 100th Boston marathon as his best ever marathon experience. He's run well over 150 marathons, 88 of which are sub 3-hour marathons (with a PB of 2:41 in 1995).

When John Maddog Wallace ran his 100th marathon at Boston's 100th anniversary, he put away his typical competitive focus and drive and instead "ran it for fun." He jumped the barricades at Wellesley to get the hugs and support of the nurses there, and on his t-shirt he had "John's 100th Marathon." "'I got a lot of applause", he said, "I had a really great time."

Also at that 100th Boston anniversary race for his 100th marathon was Takatoshi Yashino from the Japanese Full Hyaku club. He had run his first marathon, the Honolulu marathon, in 1991. This, he said, was part of his desire to lose weight and maintain his health. He's now run over 300 marathons as well as several ultras.

Takatoshi is the current Secretary General of the Japanese club and handles almost everything to do with its management. He plans two reunion marathons and festival ceremonies every year. The annual general meeting is usually held in the autumn at a different venue every year. He also arranges an overseas marathon tour every year (about 30 members competed in the 2010 Barcelona Marathon, Spain) and he organizes a monthly private marathon in Hiratsuka City where he lives. This marathon usually involves about 20-30 club members and others. He also edits monthly club newsletters. Shinicihi Nose, a fellow club member, said "Our club may be called 'Yoshino's Club'."

I asked Jeff Galloway, the prolific author and trainer, about his 100th marathon. He ran his 100th at that same Boston run as Robert, Maddog and Takatoshi. It was one of Jeff's most memorable experiences as he ran it with his father, who was 75 years old at the time. Jeff's whole mission in that race, he said, was to run with his dad the entire way.

It was an amazing experience for Jeff and one that was symbolic in many ways. Jeff had always looked up to his dad growing up. Somewhat surprisingly Jeff was "a fat kid" growing up. His dad tried Jeff in football but that wasn't his passion. He also put Jeff into cross-country, and the rest is history. As Jeff got leaner and fitter over the years and became a world class Olympian, his dad became more and more sedentary. When his dad was 52, he attended a high school reunion. He found that of the 25 boys who had been on the class of 37' football team, 13 had already died from degenerative diseases. Over the next seven years Jeff's father lost 55 pounds as he got back in shape and started running, including a number of marathons. After a doctor raised concerns about his health and irregular heart rhythms, something he'd had for years, Jeff's dad decided to run his last marathon at Boston's 100th (and Jeff's 100th).

And so they ran the Boston 100th together, with a goal of beating 6 hours. His dad, who had run about 40 previous marathons, didn't want to take the walk breaks Jeff was encouraging. He struggled a bit at Wellesley and on the Newton Hills, and struggled some more as they ran into downtown Boston. But when his dad saw the finish line he took off, with Jeff running right behind him. Jeff was able to catch up and they crossed the finish together – in a time of 5:59:48. Jeff's dad quipped that he would've run faster but Jeff slowed him down.

"Accomplishing an unconventional or seemingly unattainable goal is a challenge, one we can all meet if we choose. If you undertake a project, physical or otherwise, you must first make the decision to reach the goal, then put all your energy into it and not doubt yourself in the process."

Dave McGillivray, Boston Marathon Race Director
Author of The Last Pick.

9

"Marathons set you on a mission, bringing together mind,
body and spirit, which is unique."

Jeff Galloway

"You make time in your life for things
that are important to you."

Sean Meissner

In his 2000 bestseller book *'The Tipping Point'* Malcolm Gladwell introduces the concept of the 'law of the few' to help explain how social networks work and how messages are quickly passed on by people. Messengers, he notes, make something spread. Gladwell identifies three types of individuals; connectors, mavens and salespeople.

Gladwell coined the phrase 'connectors'. These people, he says, link us up with the world; "people with a special gift for bringing the world together …a handful of people with a truly extraordinary knack [... for] making friends and acquaintances." *Connectors* know many people and are typically the most central nodes in a social network. *Mavens* are those who have a vast knowledge about a given content area. They are information gatherers for a social network and may evaluate the various strands of information and other messages that come through the network; they may pass their evaluations on to others, along with the messages. The *sales people* meanwhile are those individuals who are artful in the way of persuasion – they help convince others to try new things – it could be a new race, a new destination, a different form of traveling or running related product, for example.

If you want to contact someone in the messengers' world it won't take long get connected. Certain individuals are 'connectors' that, not surprisingly, connect others. Many of the messengers in this book are also connectors.

One is Tom Adair the President of the 50 States Club in the United States. Like fellow messengers Don McNelly and Susan Daley, he is a member of the *Full Hyaku Club*, the Japanese 100 Marathon Club.

Tom has run more than 300 hundred marathons, which is quite a few for someone who only ever wanted to run one marathon. Tom had been an avid tennis player for 18 years, but, he said, "the shining wore off the apple." At his wife's hospital cocktail party one evening he was talking with strangers and mentioned that he'd recently run a half-marathon. Someone who did not know much about marathons replied that he was sorry that Tom was only able to run half of the marathon. Tom replied "well I better go and run the other half."

"It wasn't pleasant", Tom said, "but I did it." Now, retired and 68 old, he's done much more than that. In his third marathon he met Norm Frank, who told Tom about a 50 States Club. It spurred Tom on to his fourth marathon, and beyond. Then his goal was to run 60 marathons, and the 50 States. By his fifteenth race, however, Tom had reset his sights on completing 100 marathons.

Tom said he had real sense of accomplishment with his first marathon but today, 300 marathons later, he sees marathon running as "a fraternity of friends – and to renew friendships one race to the next." In other words, it is a social movement made up of connections with runners from around the world. And it's also about that road to Apathia – that sense of the unperturbed. Tom explains, for example, "When I'm training by myself it's a time for prayer … to be there with my own thoughts. I can't do that anywhere else."

Friendship is paramount. "If someone runs a 3:30 or a 5:30, it doesn't affect friendships, we never discuss times." Sometimes, Tom says, "there are bad days running and the runners with many marathons have plenty of these experiences – they don't always talk about them but the experiences they have are always there and they can appreciate the challenges and adversities others face much better because of it – there's a quiet confidence built upon these experiences." The marathoners, he feels "are more extro-verted, they feed off other runners' energy", whereas trail runners are "more introverted, they feed off their own energy and just like to run, and are not so concerned with times at all."

Goals and priorities change over time. "In the first year", Tom said "I wanted to get better times. At some point you think about the training – what's more important – to accomplish a better time, or is it something else, like run more marathons?" Clearly, for Tom and others, running more marathons is important. When you think of the total experience that running more marathons provides over time – the friendships, the travel and the places, it's no surprise that in this instance, more is seen to be better.

It's continuous as well, whereas a short-lived physically intense experience to run your fastest time will not enhance the extent of your happiness for the rest of your life. In fact, such a pursuit could lead to serious injury and regrets, and could limit someone's distance running career and the extent to which new experiences can be acquired and new friends made. Letting go of 'the' PB fast time can help create a wider openness and willingness to embrace whatever experiences and opportunities emerge.

One of the goals Tom set himself over the years was to run a marathon on all seven continents. He came very close to achiev-ing that goal a couple of years ago. In 2008 he was on a glacier in Antarctica when, at Mile 4, he slipped and broke his pelvic bone. He didn't know this at the time of course. He tried to walk it off – walk a mile, jog a mile – but by Mile 10 he knew he was in trouble. He was actually bleeding internally. Back on the ship the doctor correctly diagnosed the problem, which was reconfirmed when he returned to his home in Chicago. Tom plans to go back in 2011. At the time of the accident Tom also had a streak of running a marathon every month for 140 months. Tom may have to wait a year or so, but he is probably the only runner who can claim a title of 6½ continents.

The influence of people such as Tom in social networks is enabled by the various 100 Marathon Clubs around the world. These clubs are the glue that binds the messengers and their social networks together.

One of the more formalized 100 Marathon clubs is the United Kingdom 100 Marathon Club, which has its own constitution and elected officials. The club is managed by a committee comprised of a Chairman, Secretary, Treasurer, and up to three other members. It has 204 members who have completed one hundred marathons and ultras or more and 30 'wannabees' who have completed more than 50 but who have not yet reached the one hundred mark. There are also 100 Marathon clubs in Japan (with 160 members who have run 100 or more), Australia (32), New Zealand (15), Germany (250), Netherlands (50), Poland (40), Czech Republic (20), Denmark (22), Sweden (35), Norway (20), Finland (190) and the North American Marathon Club for the United States and Canada (269), based in Washington state.

The number of club members in each country who have run 100 or more marathons and ultras is a close approximation. New members are added all the time and some runners are no longer club members. Some runners are members of more than one club (Bob Dolphin, for example, is a member of the German club and 10 UK runners are members of the North American club). Of course, not everyone who has completed 100 marathons is necessarily a member of any club, although from the research for this book it appears these runners are a very small minority.

Nonetheless, the totals listed give a sense of the number of Messengers around the world. Based on the membership of these respective clubs, the total number of Messengers is 1,217. Even accounting for non-club members and other countries, the total number is still considerably less than the total of 2,700 climbers who have reached the summit of Mt. Everest.

Messengers are typically older. There are predominantly more males than females. In the North American club, there are 210 men (78%) and 59 women, while in the United Kingdom club there are 211 men (86%) and 33 women. The average age of the Japanese Full Hyaku club, founded in 1987, is 60. The full name of the Japanese club is Full Hyakkai Raku-Sou Kai, which translates approximately to 'Our goal is to run 100 or more marathons and enjoy doing so'. The 'Full' is there because in Japan races over 5km distance are named 'marathon', so the club members refer to the 26.2 mile marathon as the Full Marathon.

In terms of occupation, there is a diverse range in all the clubs; from professors, teachers, researchers, accountants, engineers, lawyers, doctors, race organizers, running coaches and business-men to pipe fitters, drivers, forklift operators, custodians and la-bourers. Some messengers do not work at all, such as those with families to raise. A large number of messengers are retired.

The clubs play a valuable role for the messengers. They provide a focal point. Statistics on members' achievements are kept up to date and the clubs share knowledge and experience with others and encourage all runners in long distance running. In the United Kingdom full membership is given to all runners who have completed 100 or more races of marathon distance or longer, while associate-like membership is provided to the 'wannabes'.

The United Kingdom club's constitution includes the following definition to address "When is an official marathon an official marathon?" The constitution states:

> Only races should be included. Training runs should not be included, whatever the distance run ... An official event open to all applicants (occasionally subject to entry limits or qualification restrictions), advertised beforehand in running press, on the web, by leaflets at other

races or some similar manner. Normally, but not always, competitive. Normally at least 3 participants. Normally results available. The runner must have completed the whole race entered and have run (jogged, walked) the whole course (unless misdirected by the organisers) for the race to count. For example, dropping out at the marathon distance in an ultra race cannot be counted unless this was advertised beforehand as part of the race rules. The declared race distance counts ...If a runner finishes a race outside a stated time limit the race should not count unless the race director is flexible in his [sic] interpretation of the rules and the runner is given a medal/certificate and/or appears in the result list.

The accepted distances are: 26m 385 yards (26.2 miles) / 42.195 K (42.2 kilometres) for marathons on the road or, for trail marathons, accepting that exact measurement is not possible, rounded down (i.e., 26m or 42 K). Races less than this marathon distance are not to be included. Ultra Marathons are those races longer than a marathon distance. Stage Races are defined as races over several days with a set distance each day. One of the stages must be of marathon distance or longer for the race to count. If two or more stages are of marathon distance or longer and results are published for each stage, then each such stage may be counted separately.

These definitions are commonly accepted around the world by other clubs. They also provide the parameters for organizing events *privately* without having to rely on the larger more formal 'public' races to be set up. There are a number of runners in the various clubs around the world who organize what some refer to as 'private' races – still advertised according to the rules above, but done so through their own initiative, as we'll read about later on.

Another club that is growing rapidly is the Marathon Maniacs. It is not exclusively for those who have run 100 marathons or more but it is focused on people who are passionate about running marathons and ultras and more recently, half marathons. Based in Washington state, in just five years its membership has grown to over 2,300.

The club was founded by three messengers; Chris Warren, Tony Phillippi and Steve Yee. Chris told me his first marathon was "extremely hard – the whole fear of the unknown … but an exhilarating experience to finish it." But he was still disappointed with his time. So then came his second marathon, and together with Steve and Tony, he started to run more and more marathons, being not only competitive within the runs themselves but also in terms of the number of marathons actually run. "Steve might say 'oh I'm going to do a marathon next weekend' and Tony and I would say 'oh yeah, we'll probably do one too, even though we might not have been planning to."

The Dead Runners Society email listserv the three were part of started to refer to them as "maniacs" and they were asked what runners had to do to become maniacs. They put together some very basic criteria – so basic in fact, as friends in the 50 State Club pointed out, that many runners had already achieved the levels. They re-thought the criteria and now have a range of membership levels in the club. Just like the messengers in the 100 marathon clubs, they gain a great sense of satisfaction hearing of relationships and friendships formed by club members.

Club structures, regular events and ongoing communication enabled by the Internet foster social connections around the world. The distance running movement is a social movement, and it's a global movement.

10

"When you're running outdoors and watch the sun rising,
the world looks very different
compared to sitting in your house."

Fenny Roberts

"Running helps me maintain positive self-esteem
and confidence and provides some direction in my life.
It has lifted me up when I thought I couldn't get any lower,
and it has been a significant part of my
overall happiness due to the friends and experiences
I've encountered along the way."

Dave McGillivray

The health benefits of running are innumerable, and are backed up with decades of scientific research evidence. Physically, running strengthens the heart and reduces the rate of heart disease. It's a simple form of exercise for which there are many inter-related benefits.

Our lungs pump oxygen more efficiently through our bodies. The stronger blood flow and pumping of oxygen and antioxidants through our bodies reduces the incidence of different types of cancer. Our bowel and bladder become more efficient systems as toxins are reduced with the improved functioning. The toxins are also reduced because our breathing improves, and we sweat during exercise.

Meanwhile, adrenaline is released and increases the flow of white blood cells. This fights diseases and immune substances in our body. Our bones are strengthened, reducing the extent of osteoporosis. Endorphins are released which counter pain and reduce stress (Endorphins also enhance our creativity, concentration, and problem solving). Our bodies may feel tired from the exercise, which contributes to improved sleep. Regular running helps stimulate healthier eating and helps reduce weight, which in turn places less stress on our joints, and on our heart, lungs and muscles.

With all this going on, our overall *self-worth* is enhanced, our 'spirit' feels alive, and the likelihood of depression is much reduced. The more positive self-image also enhances our perceived sexuality.

Our *self-esteem* increases. Self-esteem is the level of contentment we have with ourselves and the knowledge that we can cope with whatever is happening in our lives. It is a basic human need, essential to a healthy life. Generally, we believe the people we know approve of us, our words and our actions. Their approval, and our satisfaction with whom we are, also depend on the extent to which we feel we lead a good life, that we're good at what we do, and that we can face any challenges that emerge. One of the leading researchers on self-esteem, Nathaniel Branden, describes self esteem as "the experience of being competent to cope with the basic challenges of life and being worthy of happiness."

American psychologist Albert Ellis argues that a more accurate analytical concept than self-esteem is unconditional self-acceptance and unconditional "other-acceptance" – of others – which he details in his Rational Emotive Behavior Therapy.

Then there is *self-confidence*. Someone may not be particularly good at a given sport or activity, but they can still remain confident because they are not that concerned about the outcome of the activity. The key element of self-confidence is acceptance of the range of consequences, good or bad, of a particular situation. When you don't dwell on negative consequences you can be more self-confident; you worry much less about failure or the disapproval of others following a failure. If there is less concern about failure you are more likely to be enjoying life; thus living more in the moment. Self-confidence creates a comfort with whatever outcomes occur. Experience further solidifies the degree of self-confidence.

Another essential element of our make-up is *self-respect*. In other words, having respect for oneself, and believing that we behave with dignity and honor. "If you want to be respected by others", Dostoyevsky said, "the great thing is to respect yourself."

Canadian messenger Wally Herman explained that "because of running, I feel a greater sense of self-worth – and this translates in great measures into a better appreciation of fellow man."

Self-worth, self esteem, self-confidence, and self-respect. On the face of it, it sounds very introspective. But this is not the case. Marathon running helps people find themselves, or rediscover who they once were. It can be a catalyst for change; a re-birth. Indeed, George Sheehan wrote about his own re-emergence through running: "You have one life to live. How do you want to live it? And then I [came up] with an absurd answer: 'As a distance runner'. With that decision, I awakened that passion, relived my dream, recaptured my youth. I re-entered my life through re-entering my body."

Running offers an escape, an opportunity to be in control of the rhythms of our lives. Jim Fixx commented that "we can run where we want to. We can go fast or slow, hard or easy. We can run by ourselves or with friends. We can get out seven days a week or fewer. We can think or let our minds go blank. All these choices are entirely up to us: furthermore we can change them according to the minute-by-minute requirements and fancies of our minds and bodies." He wrote that runners have the ability to be with their own thoughts while running: "The kind of thinking I most like to do while I run, though, is just to let my thoughts wander wherever they wish. What is important is not what I think about, but the fact that we are free to think at all."

A recurring theme in many running books is the assumption that all runners are equal and therefore the returns of running are the same. In reality the returns are highly variable for every runner according to their life context – current mental state, emotional condition, physical health, spiritual comfort and so on. So for us to say a distance runner gets 'x' out of every run can be misleading, although the specific conceptual categories remain consistent. Bernd Heinrich wrote that "We're not all identical peas from the same pod who happen to roll in different directions. There are individual differences, and for one individual it might be relatively easy to train to run a mile in under 5 minutes or a marathon under 3 hours, while to another individual such feats are heroic. Heroism deserves credit wherever it is exhibited. To run a championship performance requires commitment and willingness to take risks, but the risks are greater when the talent is less. Those who seemingly show less greatness because they run in the pack may actually draw from a fount of courage."

If, as Oprah Winfrey says, running is the greatest metaphor for life because you get out of it what you put into it, then what do we say about running marathons?

Or running more than 100 marathons?

Tom Adair at the Umstead 100 mile race in March, 2007.

Julie Thorn, first Australian woman to run 100 marathons, finishing the Rotorua Marathon, New Zealand.

German Messenger Sigrid Eichner, most marathons run by a woman.

Jack Brooks and Jim Mundy centre, ready for Nashville Marathon 2009. Rich Holmes from North Carolina was also doing his 200th (left in the photo). Warren D'Rozario (UK) on the right.

Danish messenger Mogens Pedersen.

British messenger John Wallace (aka Clark Kent).

New Zealand messenger Dave Penfold, Great Forest Marathon New Zealand.

Dave Major at the successful completion of his 400th marathon, Mont Blanc 2010.

Steve Yee, co-founder of the Marathon Maniacs Club.

Tony Phillippi, flying in howling winds at Mile 25 of the Bellingham Marathon.

Australian messenger Jim Barnes.

Noriko Sakota completed her 700th marathon in Athens, and had run over 860 marathons by the end of 2009. To her right is fellow Japanse messenger, Shinichi Nose.

New Zealand messenger Robert Scott, finishing the 2007 Auckland Marathon (his 153rd).

Chris Warren, finishing at the San Francisco Marathon.

American messenger Bob Fletcher, 100th marathon, Houston 1986

American messenger Yen Nguyen.

Pam Storey
finishing 6
day race in
Gothenberg 2009.

Gil John during
Tooting Bec 24
hour race.

11

> "I'm not a gifted runner, but I have now completed
> 113 marathons. That's not the epitome of greatness,
> but it's what I wanted to do, and I did it.
> Forget excuses, ignore nay-sayers, listen to your heart,
> and trust your desires. Dreams are for having."
>
> *Elaine Doll-Dunn*

> "I always feel great, when running …
> of course I'm 56 years of age, and every marathon is 'heavy'
> once over the 30 kilometres, but I'm used to 'suffering' and
> every time I pass the finish line, each 'pain' is forgotten …
> especially after the shower and a big dark beer
> while chatting with my friends in the local cafeteria."
>
> *Belgium distance runner*

Running marathons is more than just the physical act of movement over 26.2 miles. Training for a first marathon is itself a transformational process. The time it takes to train, for one thing, takes
away from other parts of the runner's life. It's all about choice,
however, as everyone has the option of training or not training.

We can choose to train for many reasons. Over time, the body
develops the capacity for distance running; we all have a different
ability for how fast we will complete a marathon but the process
of change and the transformations required are essentially the
same. If we don't get injured in this process, it feels really good.
This "feel good" is magnified when the race is over, the medal received, the goal achieved, and the stories with old and new friends
shared. Self-worth, self esteem, self-confidence, self-respect and
the respect for others are further reinforced.

The positive social, mental, emotional, spiritual and physical attributes of the overall marathon experience are cause for the experience to be repeated. What for many individuals starts off simply

83

as a test against themselves, turns into an experience that instills happiness at many levels. With so many positive affirmations of the experience, it is little wonder that people go back to run a second marathon. Little wonder too that for many, like our messengers here, running marathons becomes part of their lifestyle. Roger Biggs, for example, who is a veteran of several hundred marathons and currently Chairman of the United Kingdom 100 Marathon Club observed in Runners World magazine, that running marathons is "an excuse to see the world ... I love the fact that I do a marathon and see the sights along the way, meet people and learn about the history of these places."

New Zealander Malcolm Gray has run more than 100 marathons since his first, Rotorua in 1988. He's been running marathons for 20 years, and although it doesn't sound like many each year, the numbers accumulate. Each year he goes through about five pairs of running shoes as he typically runs about 100 K a week. He regularly gets up three days a week at 3.30am to train for two hours. Silently he's out there, keeping the training up, maintaining his fitness and lifestyle. Fellow New Zealand messenger Robert Treneman fits his marathon training in during lunchtimes. As a retail grocer, he slip outs and runs 15 K during his break. For many messengers running becomes as much a part of their daily life as doing chores around the home, shopping for groceries, or mowing the lawn. As Jim Manford put it, "I enjoy running every day and it has just become such an accepted part of my daily routine that I don't even think about not doing it."

Some of the messengers start marathon running at a young age, but most come to it later in life. Australian Ken Matchett, a former teacher, started running the longer distances at age 57. He recorded his PB of 3:15 when he was 63 years old. By his early eighties he had run more than 120 marathons. These were part of a full life that, in his eighties, included more than 50 K of training a week, playing the piano, learning Latin and playing with his grandchildren. In an article in Ultramag in 2005 Ken was quoted saying that the secret for his running success was his continual monitoring of his physical condition throughout the race: "A favourite pastime is to 'study' my fellow runners. It's easy to do because there are so many that go past me!" He said his greatest satisfaction was the journey itself and finishing each race. He was an inspiration. On his running shirt he had the phrase "There's Life After 80." "If I can run marathons at my age", he said, "anyone can get out there and go for a walk."

Alan Morton ran his first marathon, the Slough Marathon in Buckinghamshire, England in 1978. "It poured with rain" he said, "and I missed the train home." Now in his late seventies, the Welshman has run over 400 marathons and ultras. Alan says his family and friends think he's mad doing all the running he does, which now typically includes about 20 marathons a year. He's also a frequent starter at the Yakima River Canyon Marathon in Washington state. He does his regular training with his dog, who he says "knows his own way home and leaves me when he's had enough."

London Ambulance Service worker Jim Mundy completed his 100th marathon in New Forest, England in 2007. Jim, or "Manic Mundy" as he's referred to, loves the marathon distance because, he says, "it's always a bit of a challenge." He started running marathons because he saw the London marathon on television, and it "looked like fun." He is a purist sort of marathoner, preferring to run with nothing but a watch, which only occasionally he'll look at. Jim says he loves the "freedom of it." He says "when it's right, it's like poetry in motion." Now in his late fifties, Jim had actually retired after 21 marathons in 2003. But he was convinced to resume his running after being nicknamed Manic by fellow messenger Jack Brooks.

Jim dressed as a Serf in the 2009 Nashville Marathon, and commemorated the 100th anniversary of the 1908 London Olympic marathon with fellow 100 marathon club members in 2008, running the original course dressed as his hero, Dorando Pietri. He once told a reporter that "running all these marathons makes me feel on top of the world … members of the 100 Marathon Club and Sutton Runners have made the journey really enjoyable and I've made some great friends." At the time of writing, Jim has run more than 200 marathons, including twice being part of the Brathay 10 Marathons in 10 days Challenge in the Lake District of England. He refers to the "romance of the road", which may partly explain why he has run the Brathay Challenge twice, over some spectacular romantic, poetic countryside.

Greg Walchli, an accountant for a property management company in Seattle, Washington has run more than 180 marathons and ultras since he first started running marathons in 1981. He told me he's inspired by Bob Dolphin. Now in his mid-forties, Greg averages twenty marathons a year, running them, he says, to stay in shape. At lunchtimes he runs along Puget Sound, but acknowledges that he would like to slow down and see more of the destinations he travels to for marathons. Regardless of how many marathons he runs in a year Greg says, "I'm always experimenting with distance, how to feel best – form, stride and so on. I still enjoy the challenge, and hopefully finishing well."

In 2007, Runners World reported on Dave Obelkevich, a 63-year-old retired music teacher who has completed 55 marathons and 150 ultras. Dave has also run 34 successive New York City Marathons. Dave decided to run his first NYC Marathon after watching the 1972 race on television, and is now one of just two people who have run every New York City Marathon since the race expanded to its current five-borough route in 1976. In 2009, he was asked by Liz Robbins of the New York Times why he ran marathons regularly. He replied "Why not? They're there."

Sixty-year old Collette O'Hagan has run more than 160 marathons, and as such is the most prolific female marathoner in Ireland. She started running to get fit, running a women's 10 K race in 1989. She thought "it was brilliant, a really super feeling." She then trained and ran in the 1990 Dublin marathon, found that "absolutely exhilarating, so brilliant to have done it" and hasn't stopped since. Collette runs about 15 marathons a year. Her training is consistent, running 4-5 times a week, with a long run always on the weekend. Collette is a foster parent, and works with an orphanage in Romania – "the kids love it" she said, "they love hearing about the stories about my travels." "Running has been good to me" she said, "it clears my head and helps me deal with life. Running makes you a stronger and better person."

For Dutch messenger Henk Sipers, distance running is his life. Now 52 years of age, he has been running since he was 23 years old. "I think the whole day of things that remind me of running. If I go on holiday or there is something else I always try to combine it. Running is the first thing in life and then there's the rest. I was running before I met my wife so she knows how I live. We have no children so I am free to do what I like." At one point he switched to ultra events as he was getting too many injuries in marathons and triathlons. "The ultra running people" he says, "are just one big family."

Welshman Gilbert (Gil) John was playing squash when he decided one day to get fit by running. He entered the Cardiff Marathon as a way of raising money for the Children's Hospice. He then ran a few marathons each year. Now in his fifties, Gil runs 5-7 miles every day because, he says, "he enjoys it." In the summer he may run five miles in the morning and another five in the evening. During his birthday week he will run a total of 100 miles "just as a bit of a check", he said.

Messenger Jim Scheer is a 67 year-old retired steel fabricator and industrial maintenance mechanic welder now based in Oregon. Jim has run well over 250 marathons since he ran his first marathon in Portland, Oregon at age 38. He started running marathons to maintain fitness. "During the 1970s running was the fad", he said. He added in his quiet, humble way, "At first it was the challenge, then it was the achievement and accomplishment. And it still is too, although now it's become a force of habit and getting to meet up with friends from all around the country." Jim has documented all thirty years of his running in detailed log books.

When fellow American messenger Don Lang retired at 50 he quickly put on 40 pounds. He recognized that the sedentary life was not healthy, so he started walking. Walking turned into running, which turned into training for, and completing, the Los Angeles marathon in 1992. In a newspaper article he was quoted as saying "running marathons isn't something I ever dreamed I'd do ... but there's an almost out of body feeling I get, regardless of the country I'm in." By the age of 71 he had completed more than 400 marathons in more than 40 countries. In fact, he completed 300 different marathons around the world, and completed at least four marathons in every state.

American Bob Hildebrandt explains that when he started running again as an adult, he wanted to lose weight and improve his health. At the time he had no idea what those goals would lead to. It started with 5 K and 10 K runs, which led to longer races and eventually to the Snowgoose Marathon in Alaska in 1993, which he completed in a time of 4:29. The travelling to marathons turned into opportunities for family vacations. His two children became marathon runners, with his son, Dietrich, joining the 50 States Club in 2005. In a 100 Marathon Club North America newsletter in 2007, Bob wrote "Along the way I have had support from many people. Number One has been my wife, Patsy. Without Patsy's help I never would have made it … I may have run more than 100 marathons in all 50 states, but the journey is far from over."

12

"There's more to marathoning than the races and running.
It's the fellowship and friendships
that are formed that make it so great."

Lenore Dolphin

"You can run a portion of a marathon
with someone and be friends forever.
You can have 2-3 hours of bonding,
and yet there's still so much more
to learn about one another too."

Carol Dellinger

American messenger John Bozung is a member of the Fifty States Club. When I talked to John in late 2009 from his home in Montana, he was on a 174-month unbroken streak of running a marathon each month (14½ years). It could have been 186 months, but in 1995 he ran two in one month and not in the next. It's hard to imagine for most people; running a marathon every month for fourteen and a half years. But for John, obviously, it's become very much a part of his life. And he wants to continue; he said, "I want to be 70-80 years old and still be on this streak."

A streak like that doesn't come easily, and can be stopped with the simplest of injuries or accidents. A year ago, for example, about a mile into the Top of Utah marathon John hit a speed bump, tripped and did a face plant. He stood up, his knees buckled over, and blood was streaming down his face. This was marathon Number 235. He was embarrassed and angry with himself that he'd fallen but he wanted to finish the race. It took 29 minutes to do the first mile, 19 of which was getting bandaged up by the Paramedics. John's wife Marcie ran alongside, keeping a close eye on him.

He completed the marathon and discovered he'd broken his nose, split his lips and cut his forehead. He required 34 stitches – 14 for his forehead and 19 for his upper lip. It was, John said, "an emotional finish."

He's now run more than 290 marathons, including 44 ultras. When I talked to him he and Marcie had just completed the Inca Trail marathon (27.5 mile trail run) in Peru, which finishes at the spectacular Inca site of Machu Picchu: "it was the most incredible experience ever", John said.

John is used to making records and achieving his goals. He ran 52 marathons in 52 weeks at 52 years of age (in nine weekends he had to run double). In 1997 he was the first American to run a marathon in all seven continents in one year. In fact, at that time he became only the ninth person in the world to do so and one of only two people to have done all seven in one calendar year. "It was worth every cent", he said, "for I saw and went to places I had only dreamed of seeing, and others I had never imagined of going to."

John met his wife Marcie four years ago at the St. George Marathon Expo. Mutual friends George and Suzie suggested John should meet Marcie. They met up and drove together to the start line for the marathon. Other friends, Clay and Karen, invited John to go to nearby Zion National Park afterwards. John invited Marcie and she said yes. This was in the middle of John's year of 52 marathons in 52 weeks, and it was Marcie's ninth marathon in ten years. Marcie had four children aged 19 to 9 from a previous marriage.

John has run all of Walt Disney World's marathons. He and Marcie ran at Disney together – 30 feet from the finish line he asked Marcie to stop. He took a small box from his fanny pack and presented a ring to Marcie, asking if she would marry him. He put the ring on her finger when they crossed the finish line, and they were married a year later.

One year later Marcie's number of completed marathons rose to

19 – she'd run another 10 marathons since she had met John. Since then she runs about 4-5 marathons each year. "There's a common bond there", says John.

For the last of his seven continents he chose the Mt. Everest marathon. John said they arrived at the village of Darjeeling, which is famous for its tea. From there they could see Kanchajunga, the fifth highest mountain in the world. Darjeeling is also the starting point for the Himalayan 100-Mile Stage Race. The Mt. Everest Challenge Marathon was held on the third day of this five-day stage race (from Sandukphu at 11,856 ft. to Rimbik at 6,345 ft). With the average altitude more than 11,000 ft for the first twenty miles, it is the highest annually held marathon in the world. John won the Mt. Everest Challenge marathon. On the same trip he was also able to experience Agra and the Taj Mahal.

Fellow 50 States member Susan Daley, a lawyer from Chicago, has a similar affinity for travel and marathons. Although Susan has run 400 marathons she has only done the 50 States once. Instead she has been around the world, including exotic marathon locations such as the Great Wall of China, Singapore, Rio de Janeiro, London, Paris, Stockholm, Dublin, Ireland, New Zealand, Madagascar and Rome. Susan has been to Antarctica three times. The first time she could only do the half. The second time they couldn't run on shore so they ran around the ship for 26.2 miles, and finally, on her third trip, she was able to complete the course, on land.

Susan said "When I started in 1991 I would think, yes, I could run faster, improve my times and qualify for Boston. But over time it's more that I just want to finish the marathon and have a good time. One criteria for selecting races is to go where I've not been before. Some are quite enticing … different cultures … but you experience these places with like-minded people." Marathon Tours, a travel company in Boston specializing in marathons, for example, arranged a Turn of the Millennium tour, where a group went to New Zealand. Susan and others ran a marathon in New Zealand, tried sky-diving and went bungee jumping at the first ever original bungee jump in the Kawarau Gorge in Central Otago. Running marathons was a bit of a secret for a while at work, Susan said, "but then the small suitcase would keep appearing on Friday afternoons", and soon it was known that this signified Susan leaving later in the day for another marathon experience.

I was sitting beside 44-year old Dave Bell at breakfast the day after the Yakima River Canyon marathon in Washington state. Lenore Dolphin said I should meet Dave and tell him about this book. I'd never met Dave before but knew he had run more than 100 marathons. We were both looking forward to a huge breakfast, and it was a good feeling sitting there with a tired body knowing I was about to refuel. We talked about running, of course, and the race the day before, which just added to the magic of the moment. When I told Dave I was writing this book he said he wasn't sure he could help out. He said he enjoyed running marathons but "that's about it really." We had fun talking in any case; he's a friendly, unassuming, humble kind of guy. At the table also was Sean Meissner, who I discovered later is one of the most passionate long distance runners you'll find, and one of the top trail runners around.

Lenore came over and wanted to make sure Dave and I had connected. She explained that Dave is actually on his third cycle of the 50 states. In other words, he'd already run a marathon in every state twice, and was heading towards three times. Dave had failed to mention this to me, but I found it remarkable. And still do. He's probably well into his fourth cycle now.

Dave explained that he got to his 100th marathon by virtue of his quest to run marathons in all 50 states. In about his fifth marathon, he saw the 50 states tee-shirt and knew then that that was what he wanted to achieve. "It's the most expensive tee-shirt I have", he said.

Three "Fs" underlie Dave's philosophy about running so many marathons: Fun, Fellowship and Finish. "The social side of running", he explained, "is the number one reason why I do it so much – the friendships I've fostered over the years with the same mindset." He adds that "I have no rest of my life. I've done so many marathons sometimes I have difficulty remembering why I enjoy it so much." It's become part of him. A very big part.

When Dave's not running marathons, he's planning to run them, using a spreadsheet to cover the key logistics such as travel, registration, and accommodation. About a year after we talked, as so often happens, we met up by pure chance at the Valley of Fire Marathon in Nevada. And this is what happens to Dave every time he runs a marathon; reconnecting with those he knows will be there and with those who may just show up. Running 26.2 miles is merely the backdrop for the fellowship, friendship and nurturing of social connections.

13

"The camaraderie is incredible …
you may not see them again for months,
then meet up and begin exactly where you left off."
Big Dave Carter

"We are a tribe."

Jeff Galloway

Runners tend to be happier and healthier through the simple act of putting one foot in front of the other. The physiological effects are complemented by psycho-social benefits. Runners have a positive outlook, and long distance runners especially, exude a self-confidence that comes from pushing themselves beyond what they may have believed to be their limit. These benefits are significant for those who run long distances as a central part of their lifestyle. What may start as happiness driven by achieving goals of fitness and personal best times actually evolves over time into happiness based on something quite different, something that has less to do with the act of running and more to do with the social connections made with other distance runners, and the desire to embrace new experiences.

The pursuit of the 100 marathons and beyond, the lure of running the long distances, becomes stronger and stronger. The runners' *state of being* in the total marathon experience (more than just the actual run) does something for their spirit and soul, and it makes them a happier, and they believe, better person.

Happiness, as a concept, is both simple and complex. It's multi-dimensional when we take into account factors such as love, contentment, satisfaction, engagement, positive emotions and activities, meaning and pleasure. If someone asks me if I'm happy, I'll respond quickly without talking for hours on its meaning and sub-contexts. Philosophers describe happiness as living a good life, which would be self-defined, again on the basis of the individual's context. Researchers, especially in the past few years, have been busy collecting scientific evidence to identify the key attributes of happiness. The strength of the evidence is generally mixed or limited as to what variables are stronger than others, but some recent data clearly indicate what does make a difference to someone's level of happiness.

Recent research suggests that our *genetic predisposition* plays a significant role in our level of satisfaction with life. Having collected data on 4,000 sets of twins, David Lykken of the University of Minnesota, concluded that about 50% of our life satisfaction is due to genes. Other research shows that once basic needs are met, additional income does not significantly change our level of happiness.

Older people, it appears, are more satisfied with their lives than younger people. Religious affiliation appears to be associated with happiness although it's unclear as to whether that is because of the religion itself or the sense of community that religions foster. Researchers, such as psychologist Martin Seligman, have identified *optimism* as a trait associated with good physical health, a longer life and happiness.

By far the most significant association with happiness is having a *connection with others* – our friends and their friends especially. Seligman identifies three core components of happiness: pleasure, engagement and meaning. Of these, engagement with others and with hobbies and interests is the most important, followed by meaning – finding ways to make your life meaningful.

Another key concept in the research on happiness is *adaptation*.

Richard Easterlin of the University of Southern California points out in a 2003 paper explaining happiness, that our 'set point' for happiness changes over time due to changes in circumstances. It makes sense. What makes you happy today might not do so several years down the road. And a change for the worse in the near future is also likely to make you re-evaluate what is important to your happiness.

But it is the connection with others that recent research suggests is the strongest contributing factor to our happiness. James Fowler and Nicholas Christakis conducted a substantive body of research on almost 5,000 individuals over a 20-year period between 1983 and 2003. Their research, most comprehensively detailed in their 2009 book *Connected*, shows that people who are surrounded by many happy people are more likely themselves to be happy in the future. They assert that people's happiness depends on the extent of the happiness of the other individuals they are connected with. Significantly, the happiness of one person is associated with that of another up to three degrees removed; that is, the happiness of your friend's friend has a bearing on your own happiness. And, they write, "once we control for the emotional state in one's friends, we find that having more friends is not enough – having more *happy* friends is the key to our own emotional well-being." In other words, a group's happiness has a bearing on our own. Equally important is the fact that the existence of such social networks suggests that people's health is also interdependent.

We are social animals. We are socially connected. We tend to look for, and mix with, others who share common interests. The conscious or unconscious activity of associating with others who are like ourselves is known as *homophily*. Having reviewed over a hundred studies on homophily Miller McPherson, Lynn Smith-Lovin and James Cook concluded in 2001 that homophily has important implications for those within a social network in regard to the information they receive, the attitudes they form, and the interactions they experience.

There are very strong connections between this research and the world of long distance running.

14

"Marathon running changed my life.
It's given me so much self-confidence.
I didn't have that before I started running marathons …
I'm very consistent, but slow …
but I enjoy the time I have by myself – time to think."

Lois Berkowitz

"Running the long distances means freedom for me.
The freedom to follow the road or path ahead,
not to arrive exactly, but rather to experience the changes
around me in nature and those internal ones, which range from
the joy of the smooth, swift transition of the best miles to the
relentless determined pounding of the toughest ones!"

Jim Mundy

Social connections are enabled by the marathon clubs around the world. One of the clubs is the 50 States Club in the United States. The 50 States Club has over 2,000 members from the United States and 11 other countries. Collectively, the members have run more than 100,000 marathons.

One 50 States Club member is the quiet and unassuming Brenton Floyd. Like our other messengers, he too has run well over 100 marathons. Brenton's story is significant in two ways: that he is the youngest person to have completed 100 marathons, and the way in which he reached this goal. It was made possible by his grandmother who believed that giving Brenton the gift of the marathon experience would put him in good stead for the rest of his life.

Brenton's grandmother, Betty Mae Burrell, had raised him in their home state of Tennessee from when he was a young child. She was encouraged by her brother to bring him to a one-mile running event. She wrote once, "I thought, look at this bunch of lunatics out here … crazy people." But there was something enticing about running and 'Ma Betty' as she was called, returned, with Brenton entering in 5 K and 10 K races. And then, up in distance they went to marathons. They walked these together initially but then Brenton started running them. As a child, Brenton would run with a beanie hat that had a propeller on top. Over a 12-year period they travelled throughout the United States running marathons regularly.

Brenton completed his first marathon in 1995 at the age of ten. He ran his 100th at the age of 15 at the Ocean State Marathon in November 2000, becoming the youngest person in the world to do so. At 16 he had completed his first circuit of the 50 States. In 2003 alone, he completed 52 marathons or 50 K races, racing on both a Saturday and the Sunday 17 times. He celebrated his 21st birthday by running the Umstead 100-miler, which he completed in a time of 25:45. As of July 2007, at the age of 22, he had run more than 368 marathons, with a PB of 3:44. And he's still going.

Ma Betty completed 114 marathons and 8 ultras. She had walked marathons in each of the 50 states by the age of 57. Later, she would stop entering the races but would still drive Brenton to the events, volunteer and sometimes take a nap while he ran. Sometimes she would drive up to 15 hours each way to an event.

Ma Betty passed away in Harrison, Tennessee in October 2007. She once wrote, "one of my favorite things is to meet people and see friends. And that's the biggest thing I can say about running – the wonderful people I've met, the friends I've made all over the world." Marathon running became her life and was Brenton's life for many years. "I'm just an ordinary nomad person", she said, "Most of these marathoners are doctors or lawyers or they run companies. It's an expensive hobby, let me tell you. I have not a penny any more. All of my savings, all of my retirement, has been totally invested in marathoning. The way I look at it, he [Brenton] may not get an inheritance when I go, but he'll have a lot of memories."

Leslie Miller is a research scientist at the Institute for Systems Biology in Seattle, Washington. In 2008, at 28 years of age she became the youngest woman in the world to have completed 100 marathons when she completed the Crescent Forest Trail Marathon in Gig Harbor, Washington.

Leslie used to run 5 K and 10 K races in Kentucky, where she grew up, then ran her first marathon in 2002 at the Cincinnati Flying Pig Marathon. She moved to Washington state in 2004 to go to college. In the summer, she took classes and had a job but wanted to do something different. A friend of hers with leukemia had heard of *Team in Training*, so Leslie helped her friend run. He successfully finished the race and Leslie really enjoyed the weekend. She wanted to do more, and knew the conventional wisdom recommended running just 2-3 marathons a year. After joining a running club in Seattle, she met runners from the Marathon Maniacs club and discovered that it was quite possible to run *many* marathons in a year.

Leslie found four races she wanted to run but they were on consecutive weeks. She ran them all anyway, and felt great doing so. So she extended the streak to seven in seven weeks (seven being her favorite number). Because she wanted the streak to continue, she set up her own certified marathon in the fifteenth week, which kept her streak alive.

In 2007, Leslie ran 47 marathons. In 2008 she ran 54. When we talked near the end of 2009 she told me she had only run 15 for the year, and felt "like a total slacker." As at the end of 2009 she had completed more than 135 marathons and ultras with a marathon PB of 4:03.

"It felt so good", Leslie explained, "knowing I could go out and run 26.2 miles any time." Co-workers approached Leslie, worried that she was doing too much. But to Leslie it was her life "and you get to know so many people from around the country. A lot of people want to beat times, but for me it's the total experience. I like the races with friendly volunteers. I like the runner's high."

Society, she explained, can be superficial and materialistic but when you're running, everything is stripped away. Running is an escape, "you don't have to do anything else, and nothing gets in the way. But it's a healthy escape. Right now I feel I'm in the best shape of my life."

"I feel like I've been to cities and towns I never would have gone to otherwise. And I see and do as much as I can when I'm there." On race day, she wakes up feeling excited, "I've got a race today … you get tired, you push things, it's an accomplishment. When you run every single weekend it just alters your whole state of mind – it's a huge part of your life. You're always planning for, racing in, or returning. All the time I have a great sleep and I never have to train during the week." "It's who you are", she said, "it's exciting to challenge yourself."

"Running marathons has helped me focus on what's important and to focus on what I do... it transfers through to other things you do; it gives you more confidence … it tells you …I'm tough." Leslie wasn't planning or aiming to run 100 marathons. "I didn't look for getting 100, too daunting. I wanted to run weekly but only planned two months out. I was having so much fun, it's what I am, it's what I do. Getting to 100 is just another bonus. I can't fathom that I've done so many, now I'm here thinking about it."

And the connections, the social side of the marathon experience, are all important to Leslie. "The 100 Marathon Club brings people together who otherwise wouldn't meet, a chance to share our experiences... It's like you're all family ... sweaty and smelly-like but it doesn't make a difference. People who don't run don't understand it. I've another group of friends outside runners … sometimes it gets uncomfortable"!

Brenton and Leslie are at the younger end of the age spectrum of the messengers who have embraced marathon running as a lifestyle. At the other end are messengers who were running marathons well before the rest of the world knew much about the event. One of these older messengers, and one who is particularly admired by Brenton Floyd, is Ray Sharenbrock.

Born in 1933, Ray has completed nine circuits of the 50 States. He ran his first marathon in 1982 at the age of 49 in a time of 3:34 (which is still his PB), having been an avid cycler for many years previously. "Somebody told me I couldn't run a marathon", he commented to a journalist. When he retired as a school teacher in South Milwaukee, Wisconsin in 1996, he was able to commit more time to marathons. He has run all over the world and run marathons on all seven continents. In July, 2008, at the age of 75, he completed his 600th marathon at the Kilauea Volcano Marathon, Hawaii (in a time of 7:12). Ray finished the race with his friend, 58-year old Henry Rueden – Henry's 557th marathon.

Ray runs marathons for the health of it all, the stress relief and the friends he meets along the way. "You meet some wonderful, wonderful people ... you know, you can run two or three marathons on ego, but it hurts too much to continue beyond that. There's got to be something else." In the September 2006 newsletter of the North American 100 Marathon Club Ray wrote "I run for the Joy of Life, thankful always that God has given me chances and the guts to get out and get the job done --- knowing that we have a job and a responsibility to be an example for those around us. I feel so very lucky. I still think the greatest thing I get from running is the chance to meet wonderful people and make treasured friendships." The following year he wrote in the November Newsletter, "I feel that the joy of the marathon and ultra finish line is a gift from God. I am especially excited as I approach the start of my diamond jubilee of life in the coming year. I just feel so lucky to be able to follow a very active life. God has been so good to me." Ray says he has no problems with his knees, back or hips, and according to his physician, he has the "knees of a man half his age." When he can no longer run he says he'll walk. And when he can't walk, he'll crawl.

A similar attitude is expressed by fellow American messenger Norm Frank, who ran his first marathon in 1967. He's a large man at 6 feet 2 inches, and 175 pounds. Born in 1931, for his working years he ran his company - Marathon Lawn Service. Norm calculates that he's run over 86,000 miles (training and marathons) since then, which is like running around the world at the equator three times. Norm ran his 900th marathon in 2005, and as of the end of 2009 had run 965 (790 marathons and 175 ultras). For an 18-year period he ran at least one marathon every month. He ran 30 consecutive Boston marathons (1967-1996) and has a PB of 3:20. Between 1994 and 1997 he was listed in the Guinness Book of World Records for most marathons run by an individual.

Before he took up running he played racquetball and squash, and in high school he played basketball and football. It was a chance meeting that led Norm to run in the first place. He was jogging as part of a warm up for a paddleball game. "A much older guy was out running", saw Norm and suggested he try running a marathon – the Boston marathon, in fact. With no training programs or books in 1967, "no one really knew what to do", Norm said. He ran almost every day for a couple of months, including a 16-miler, and then headed off to Boston. "I fell in love with the marathon from the very first time. I couldn't wait to do the next one. I wanted to do better", he said, although he ended up running a slower time in his second race. "I never got good at it time-wise, I just enjoyed them. It became more about going places than the races themselves."

He told one reporter he knew "I was never going to be a world record-holder of any kind … I just did them to participate, and I enjoyed it. I wanted to do as many as I could, for as long as I could afford to. I haven't, for many, many years, thought about it as being important to me. It's just participating, that's the main thing."

The goal of completing 1,000 marathons, Norm says, entered his mind more and more only after friends and family kept bringing it up after he'd reached 900. He said to one reporter in 2007 that "I had no goals in all my years of running, until I hit 900, and then everybody's on my ass."

He enjoys the challenge, keeping fit, doing the best he can and visiting the place itself – "it's great to visit new places. It's been an enjoyable 42 years", he says, "I don't regret one bit of it. I have a lot of really good friends; that's about the best thing."

It's not all been easy running either. Norm had open heart surgery in September 1998, at age 67. Doctors rebuilt part of his aorta with a cow valve. He was back running marathons in October. Then in 2003, at age 72, he was being chased by a dog in a marathon, fell and cracked a few ribs. But he got up and continued running the remaining eighteen miles. Then in 2007 he had problems with asthma. These days, he says, he's become "more of a fast walker or a shuffler. But I try to stay on the same pace the whole way." In 2008 and 2009, he had a number of strokes and an infection around his heart.

At 965 marathons, he is itching to get out and complete the remaining 35 to reach 1,000. But he's just had a stroke so he's unsure as to when that will be exactly. "I'll do the thousand even if I have to use a walker" he told me, and started laughing. He's spritely and enjoyable to talk to. Inspirational. "He's a honey", says one Race Director, "he's everybody's favorite grandfather." As for all the medals, Norm says "I've never cared too much about the medals. I've got most of them but I've given a lot away to the school kids I've gone to talk to. I've kept the Disney medals."

One of Norm's friends is Don McNelly, who lives in Rochester, New York. When I last talked to Don he commented that even though he's 88 years old, he asks himself … "how much longer can this go on? But I see no sign of it ending yet." Like Norm he has been running marathons since the 1960s. In 1968, a close friend the same age as Don who lived in the same town "just up and died one night of a heart attack. No warning." Don made an appointment to see his own doctor, who advised him to lose weight, eat better and get some exercise. "I went down to the track and I could barely make it around once, but I was hooked. I'm addicted, but it's a positive addiction." His son, who was at the Massachusetts Institute of Technology (MIT) in Cambridge, Massachusetts, showed Don some photos of Boston. Don decided he would try and run the Boston marathon. In 1969, he ran his first – "my first of anything", as he put it.

Don has now completed more than 700 hundred marathons and ultras. He holds the record for the most marathons run by anyone after the age of seventy (436). He also holds the record for most marathons run after the age of 80 (166) and after age 85 (43). He completed his 100th Ultra at the age of 85.

Before he retired, Don worked in a job where he travelled all over the northeastern United States in charge of a box company. He could coordinate work with running marathons. The company knew what he was doing, he explained but they were proud of him being out there 'doing it'. "Running marathons forces you to go places you wouldn't normally go to", Don says, "It's broadened me a lot, I know a lot more about the world, I have friends all over the world." Another attraction for Don is the freedom it provides; the mental space to be with yourself. "Your brain goes into neutral. We're disciplined right now as we talk, but when you're running all sorts of things go through your mind. A lot of stupidness, a lot of good ideas. Where else do you get to do that these days? Running is the one place where you can be within yourself."

Don limited his running after surgery for prostate cancer in 1988, although he still competed in marathons while in recovery. He also began walking them. He now walks every race, but always to the end and no short-cuts he says; "no cheating, because you only cheat yourself."

The first time I talked to Don was when he appeared as a panel participant at the Niagara Falls marathon. Also on that panel was Rick Rayman, a 62-year old dentist from Toronto, Canada. Rick has not missed a day of running since December 10, 1978 – he runs either three miles or thirty minutes, whichever comes first, every day. It's a remarkable streak to say the least. He's combined that with more than 200 marathons. "No matter how many you've run", he says, "it's a long way and so many things can happen." He noted that in the mid 1990s he slowed his pace to 3:30 on average, and then it went down to 4:00, then 5:00, but, importantly, he says, "Yes I'm running slow but I'm meeting more people and I love it more than when I was winning trophies. I'll keep on running until I don't have that fire inside me anymore, and hopefully that will never happen."

Alongside Rick was another panel member, fellow Canadian messenger Wally Herman. In his later running years, Wally has hooked up with Don McNelly and Norm Frank and has run many marathons with these friends. When I last talked to Wally he had run 716 races, 150 of which have been ultras, including 16 100 K races and three 6-day stage races. Although Canadian, he was the first runner ever to complete the 50 American states. It actually took him longer to run in all the Canadian provinces and territories than the 50 U.S. states because the only marathon in the Yukon was held on his wedding anniversary every year. He says it took a while to convince his wife that he should run it, but eventually he did. He finished the 50 states two years before he finished all of the Canada provinces and territories.

He has also run a marathon in 99 different countries, and for many years it looked like he would be the first to have run a marathon in 100 different countries. But he's in no hurry to reach 100, even though friends such as John 'Maddog' Wallace have offered to run with him and have encouraged him to do so. Maddog was in Ottawa recently and they both ran in the Ottawa Fall Colours Marathon in 2009. Maddog told me he had tried to convince Wally to run that one hundreth country. But Wally told me later that "I'm not pressing it. If it happens, it happens … I just take marathons as they come. Every day is a great day. Every marathon is a great marathon."

Wally started running marathons because he always had a latent interest in endurance. He didn't start running until he was 50, although before that he was hiking and cross-country skiing. Like many others, he got interested in marathon running in the 1970s, spurred on, in part, by Frank Shorter who won the Olympic marathon gold in 1972. In his early fifties, he chose to take early retirement from his civil servant job in the Canadian federal government department of Industry, Trade and Commerce.

Wally's first event was the Kitchener-Waterloo Octoberfest marathon in 1975. He thought he'd run one marathon and that would be it; he'd get it out of his system. "I was hooked" he said. Over

700 hundred marathons and ultras later, it seems that his system is a slow one. "From day one", he told me, "I've put the mental benefits of running marathons ahead of the physical … each marathon is an experience – there's always something different."

With his early retirement he was able to devote more time to running marathons. "I was interested in travel and I had the time." He was able to run many of his 50 states with a 10-day greyhound bus pass. He'd regularly buy a pass and coordinate running two marathons within each ten-day period.

Like many other messengers, Wally has kept meticulous notes about each race he's run, including who he ran with, how he got there, the weather, times and how he felt. Flipping through his notes while we talked, the memories started coming back on different races. The accumulated knowledge of 35 years and more than 700 races is always worth tapping into. In that regard, he's similar to another friend of his, Horst Preisler from Germany, who also happened to be on that same speaker's panel at the Niagara Falls marathon.

15

"The bond is there,
we know what it feels like to go the distance."
Tony Phillippi

"Each run is a meeting of friends."
Horst Preisler

I first met Horst Preisler in Hamburg, Germany where he lives. I'd been invited over to run in the Elbe Tunnel marathon (which not unsurprisingly is run in a tunnel under the Elbe River in Hamburg), and to meet members of the German 100 Marathon Club. Fellow club member Juergen Kuhmley picked me up at the airport, and we then picked up Horst from his home and headed to the nearby mall for some dessert and conversations about running marathons. Horst speaks English but it's not as good as Juergen's, who acts as an interpreter for Horst and me. Although Juergen is no couch potato, with more than 300 marathons and ultras completed, we focus on Horst's running. I'd be talking to Juergen on other occasions.

Horst has run more marathons and ultras than anyone else in the world. You wouldn't know it from looking at him, and the juxtaposition of sitting in the middle of a suburban Hamburg shopping mall eating crepes with the world record holder for the most marathons was striking. Horst is quiet, humble, modest, and proud. He's in his mid seventies and looks very fit and healthy.

I wrote in an article in *Marathon and Beyond* that his world record is almost beyond comprehension. Over dessert, he matter-of-factly talks about some of his experiences running what now, at last count, is more than 1,670 marathons, including ultras.

Since 1990, he's run more than a marathon *every weekend*. If he never runs another, I would need to run a marathon every weekend for 30 years to equal Horst's number. Between 2000 and 2007 he averaged 75 marathons and ultras each year. He shows no signs of slowing.

His first 200 marathons were run, on average, in under 3:30 (with a PB of 2:54). The numbers almost start to lose meaning here, but he's also finished 615 marathons in under four hours, and he's finished in under five hours 1,100 times. Most of his times now are between 4:30 and 5:00. Of his total number of races, more than 340 have been ultras. His best time over 100 K is 8:15 in 1986. His best distance in a 24-hour race is 214 K. He's run the Spartathon and several multi-day races as well.

As we were talking, Horst showed me his book that contains the details of all his races. A few months later, he sent me his excel spreadsheet with the details. When you combine his training with all his races, he has run over 200,000 kilometres; about the equivalent distance of running around the planet at the equator five times.

To say running marathons is a lifestyle for Horst is a gross understatement. He's run in more than 50 countries, with most of these races being in Germany, the Netherlands, Switzerland, Denmark, France, Finland and Sweden. He doesn't drive. When he and his wife Christa first talked about raising a family they felt they needed to choose between a family or a car. They chose a family and his running career has focused on public transport and rides with family, friends, and other runners. Horst said that one day Christa told him he was "putting on too much weight around the waist." He started running. At 39 years of age he ran his first distance event – the Unna/Westfalen 100 K race, finishing in a time of 15:48.

Although now retired, he worked for 27 years as a human resources manager for hospitals in Hamburg. He balanced running with his work. "I had a really good boss" he said, who allowed him to make up time if he had been training or away at races.

Although it's easy to typecast Horst as a machine, he has a very simple underlying philosophy to his running; he enjoys it. To Horst, it's about meeting people, making new friends, and keeping in touch with the countless friends he has made over the years.

Apart from the world record number of races, there's nothing noticeably different about Horst when compared to other runners. He leads a normal life, including volunteer work with a social services organization, and spending time with his wife, children, grandchildren and friends. He does not have a special diet. Horst says that although he often leaves his wife Christa alone, she is also very active. She is a gymnast in their local sports club, and has other hobbies which, he says, give her fulfillment. They have raised three children, two boys and a girl, and now have five grandchildren, including an adopted boy from Africa, who is nine years old. There are hundreds of running shirts once owned by Horst, donated, and being worn in parts of Africa.

The main reasons Horst runs are written on his personal business card: Translated into English it says:

Each run is a story!
Each run is an encounter with a landscape and its people!
Each run is a meeting of friends!

Put all together, Horst says he loves the new experiences that each marathon offers. He believes running with others helps to break down barriers between nations and cultures, "The world would be a better place", he says, "if we all took the time to meet and learn from one another." Running the long distances builds relationships and long lasting friendships. Horst and the other messengers make and develop enduring connections locally, regionally, nationally and internationally. The social geography of long distance running is all about interconnectedness.

On the other side of the Atlantic, Team Dolphin – Lenore and Bob Dolphin – are pivotal in building and sustaining connections among the distance runners in North America, as well as internationally. Lenore and Bob come from previous marriages. They met at a school reunion in Ellensburg, a small town near Yakima in central Washington state, and within the year Lenore had started going to races with Bob. Lenore once wrote "Little did I know 17 years ago when I met Bob Dolphin and started going to races with him a year later, that my life would change so much. Supporting him at his marathons and meeting wonderful friends through these events became our way of life."

Lenore does not run, but maintains her "full-time support status", always with a smile. And if you're lucky enough, a hug at the finish line. Several years ago, someone said to Lenore "I bet you've been to at least 200 marathons yourself." So Lenore started counting. The North Olympic Discovery Marathon in Port Angeles, Washington, in June 2008 was where Lenore celebrated her 300th marathon volunteering.

And she does all this despite having had a series of major health issues. Lenore found out a few years ago that she was "a walking time bomb with her heart condition." In one recent 19-month period, she'd been in hospital for five angiograms, two angioplasties (getting stents to correct a 95% blockage of a coronary artery), and had open-heart, triple by-pass surgery.

Fittingly, when Bob joined the Marathon Maniacs club, he commented that Lenore had volunteered or been a support person at over 200 marathons. The Main Maniacs gave Lenore membership as the only "non-running" member of the club … half of "Team Dolphin, #32."

Bob's first ever race was as a 15-year old running a 3.5 mile race on paved roads in Worcester, Massachusetts. He finished 4th out of 50 from four high schools, which earned him a letter for his school sweater. Bob's first race as, he says, a "middle aged runner" was the Human Race, a 10 K race in Columbia, Missouri, in 1980. His first marathon was the Heart of America Marathon in 1981. It "wasn't a fun day", he said, "with six major hills and hamstring cramps in the last 10 K. There was, however, a sense of accomplishment at the finish line."

Bob says he "became a runner" at age 49, after his supervisor, a runner, loaned him his copy of Jim Fixx's *Complete Book of Running*. Around the same time Bob's car wouldn't start one day, so he decided to walk the two miles to his office. He enjoyed the walk and kept doing it instead of driving. After reading Jim Fixx's book he started running the distance each day.

Bob now runs 18-20 marathons a year. His next major goal is to complete 500 marathons, and he's well on his way to achieving that goal. "What I do for fun is study natural history and physical and biological sciences. I try to identify plants and animals and learn something of their life history. I do this while running and walking also." If Bob has no marathons scheduled for a few weeks he tries to run for an hour every day. He enjoys wearing headsets and listening to the news and country music while he runs. Otherwise, he rests in between, walks, mows the lawn... basically, he keeps moving.

Bob has run more than 450 marathons since he first started running them in 1981. His 80th birthday party at the Portland Marathon in 2009 reflects the centrality of the Dolphins. Dozens of visitors came to their Hilton hotel room. Lenore had t-shirts made for the occasion, which she handed out to everyone. Several runners ran the last portion of the race with Bob. "Marathoners" says Lenore, "are the nicest people in the world; they are the nicest people to be around ... we're blessed to have so many of them we can call friends."

One of these friends is Yakima resident Jeff Hagen. Jeff and his wife Joyce live about a mile from the Dolphins. Along with Bob and Lenore, Jeff is a member of the Hard Core Runners club in Yakima, appropriately named since it's the apple growing center of North America. Jeff has run more than 100 marathons and ultras over the past 30 years, with most of these being ultras.

His first long race was a 50 K run in 1979 in Yakima. In the fall of that year he ran his first marathon, also in Yakima. In 1981 he ran "my first 100 K race to see if I could cover 60 miles on foot in one day like my grandfather had done in the early 1900s while looking for a job in Minnesota." Around 1905 his grandfather walked and ran from Belview to St. James, a distance of 60 miles. He started at 4:00 am and arrived at 10:00 pm, carrying his shoes in a bag so they wouldn't slow him down. The story motivated Jeff. He went back to Minnesota and did the route. While his grandfather covered the 60 miles in 18 hours, Jeff ran it in half the time.

Jeff never planned to run 100 ultras and marathons. "I just ran one race at a time without counting them, until people started asking how many I had run", he said. He compiled a list and discovered he was close to 100. Jeff said, "I definitely got into the 100 Marathons Club the hard way, with 83 ultra marathons and 17 marathons. Now I have a total of 85 ultras and 18 marathons. Total race mileage for these 103 events equals 8,429.41 miles, or an average of 82 miles per race. Dividing the race mileage by the marathon distance of 26.219 miles gives an equivalent of exactly 321.5 standard marathons. Just thinking about those numbers makes me tired."

He runs ultras because "they are great fun." Many of his races have been within easy driving distance of the homes they've had in the states of Washington, South Dakota, and California. He and Joyce also like to combine races with visits to their families in Montana and Minnesota.

Jeff is known for his minimalist training. "Typically I train an average of 15-20 miles per week, and my highest mileage prior to a race has been 33 miles per week for a tough 100-mile trail race. My theory is that proper pacing, eating, and drinking during an ultra or a marathon is more important than training mileage."

His low miles approach has been a bone of contention; initially some observers wondered how he could be winning all his races with such little mileage in training. To this, Jeff observes that "A low key approach to training provides balance. It also provides longevity." Importantly, he says, "I have had very few injuries in the 28 years I have been running ultras and marathons, which is probably due to my low training mileage. And I don't treat it like a job. If you do 100-200 miles a week, it's a job. My low-key approach to running inherently provides balance, because training and racing don't take up a large proportion of my time." He also enjoys backpacking, skiing, climbing, cycling and has recently, over the past couple of years, taken up golf. At age 62 he is recently retired as a dental consultant for Indian reservations. And he's still winning distance running events.

When he was 50 years old Jeff broke the American 50-54 age group ultra record by running 216 miles in a 48-hour race. Five years later he broke seven American 55-59 age group records within a 16-month period (for example, 100 miles in 17:56, 127.5 miles in 24 hours, and 214.25 miles in 48 hours). At the Across the Years 48-hour race 2008-2009 he won the open event outright with a distance of 180.5 miles. He completed his 100th marathon/ultra in September 2006, at the Cle Elum Ridge 50K in Cle Elum, Washington. By the start of 2011 Jeff will have completed 100 ultras.

Just twenty-one minutes ahead of Jeff in that same Cle Elum Ridge 50K was 35-year old Van Phan from Maple Valley, Washington state. It was part of a remarkable year for Van. In 2006 she ran 53 races: 29 ultras and 24 marathons. In 2007 she ran 51.

Van told a reporter in 2008 that she started running because she was "getting a little soft." She added "Running is a quick and easy way to exercise. You just need a pair of shoes and hit the road. I love the trail running best. Trees and earth all around you. Totally in tune with your surroundings. That's the best."

In just six years of running, Van, also known as 'Pigtails' because of her long black hair tied into two pig-tail twists, completed 119 races (51 marathons and 68 ultras). Van used to hate running, finding it hard to keep up with her husband. But when she ran at her own pace and trained for the longer distances it was quite different. When I talked to Van she said her life is pretty hectic and her job as a Physician's Assistant can be stressful. The running, she says, helps her to put everything into perspective. "My husband is very supportive and we don't have any children. I make exercise a priority. We all should."

Part of her de-stressing is the camaraderie with the other runners; "I have more friends now than I used to have. When I started, I didn't know there was a social side to running… I'm surrounded by friends at races now. When you go to ultras, the runners are so easy to be around. We all suffer through it – we all relate; it's quite a bonding experience."

Running long distances has become an integral part of Van's life. "It's a very humbling experience" she says. "People are down to earth. Everyone has suffered in some way. Ultra-runners really try to grasp what life is all about; for example, being healthy and being humble. I haven't found any other activity that makes my body go into a higher level of function. It really makes me feel alive … ultras even more, trails even more than that. The listening, the breathing – I consistently feel in synch."

Most of 35-year old Oregon-based messenger Sean Meissner's long distance events have been ultras. Sean ran track in college, moved up to marathons and now concentrates on ultras. "I got hooked" he said, "especially the trail runs … I'm definitely a competitor but I really like the social side." At the breakfast in Yakima that I had with Sean and Dave Bell and others, Sean was quietly happy having finished third in the marathon the day before in a time of 2:44, breaking his PB time by seven minutes.

Based in Sisters, Oregon, he drives to, and camps at, most of his runs. "Ultra runners" he says, "are pretty laid back, outgoing … willing to do a lot for each other – there's more of a sense of community in the trails."

"Running breaks down the barriers" he added, "no matter how fast you are, you're still doing the same thing. I don't let it [running] rule my life, but it's a huge part of what I do and it's what I love to do. I make running a priority. You make time in your life for things that are important to you."

As of the October 2010, Sean had run 115 ultras and 47 marathons. I asked him how many he'd won and he said it was the first time he'd ever checked that – Sean's won 37 of those races and placed on 31 other occasions.

Another elite ultra-runner is Australian Kelvin Marshall. At 45, he has run over 230 ultras and 138 marathons, including 24 successive Melbourne marathons. In 2006 he was the Australian Ultra Runners Association male runner of the year. He has run Badwater, came 10th in the 18-day 1154 K Trans Gaule ultra run across France in 2006, ran the Deutschlandlauf 1,205 K race in 17 days in Germany in 2007, and has run across the Simpson Desert in Australia. Each year, he plans his life according to the marathons and ultra events around the world.

After his first marathon at age 22, Kelvin said "I'll never do that again." After his tenth marathon, in which he ran a sub-3:00 hour time, he said to himself, "well I've done it, so I better see what else there is." So he turned to ultra running. His first ultra was a 4-day, 63 K race up and down Mt. Bogong (the local Aboriginal word meaning *bigfella*): "I got dragged around by an experienced ultra-runner. And then you meet people and they say 'oh, you should try and do this [race] and do that one'." He fell in love with ultras and decided that from that point on he would run marathons for speed work.

Kelvin never wears a watch (he did have one once in a race, he said, but kept it in his bumbag). He doesn't take a drink in his training, but will in races because "that way it seems like a bit of a treat, makes it easier in a race. Probably toughens you up", he said. Kelvin is infamous for his navigation ability. "I carry a compass but I'm not sure what I'd use it for."

For 23 years Kelvin worked as a data analyst and computer programmer, but now he can "afford to be in semi-retirement." On top of some occasional contract programming work he combines his training with delivering catalogues and pamphlets and stocking shelves in supermarkets; "I get paid to do my gym work", he said.

**

It's well known that ultra-runners form a close knit, friendly, humble, compassionate community. The number of ultra runners is small compared to the number of marathon runners in the world. Close bonds form very quickly and are sustained over the years. It's easy to understand why. An ultra event is typically run on a trail and always over long distances. It can be a lonely experience with little interaction with others for many hours. In most cases, events go on for a full day, or two or three days. With the potential for many things to go wrong, extreme weather conditions, wild animals, fatigue, falls, blindness, getting lost and so on, the runners always look to help each other out. Stage races, completed over several days, will also test the physical, mental, spiritual and emotional limits, especially when there may be 30-50 miles to cover each day, sometimes in knee deep snow over poorly marked trails, or in the blistering heat of deserts.

There are countless stories of long lasting friendships made from running a single race together, even just one part of a race. Through the shared experiences of the challenges faced and the hardships endured, the runner's soul is often bared and their innermost thoughts revealed. The cumulative effects over time are increased self-worth, self esteem, self-confidence, and, importantly respect for others and for oneself.

Jeff Hagen, at Mile 152, at midnight in the 2009 Across the Years 48 hour race. Jeff was the overall winner with 180.51 miles (at the age of 61).

Joyce and Jeff Hagen when they're not out on a trail somewhere.

Kelvin Marshall, Australia, at Badwater (courtesy of Francine Alex).

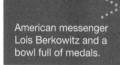
American messenger
Lois Berkowitz and a
bowl full of medals.

Leslie Miller,
running the Mt Si 50
Miler in 2010.

Horst Preisler, World Record holder for most marathons
ever run. 1,660 and counting.

118

Lenore and Bob Dolphin, just after Bob completes the Portland Marathon, the day after his 80th birthday.

American messenger Pam Reed. Photo courtesy of Luis Escobar.

119

American messenger Dave Bell with some of his 270 medals.

Sean Meissner as Richard Simmons running the Hagg Lake 50 K, February, 2009.

Canadian messenger Evan Fagan, at the 2009 Victoria Marathon.

16

"It's such a profound thing for two human beings
who were strangers hours before to bond because they have
this common denominator of running a marathon."
Carol Dellinger

"Marathon running has helped me see the world
and I've made some good friends.
The great thing about it is that you don't have to be brilliant
– all you need to do is be able to run."
Gina Little

As of 2010, 57-year old Australian messenger Bob Fickel had run 200 marathons and 60 ultras (he's also run more than one hundred half marathons). Like everyone else, that's a significant achievement, but the fact that he lives in Australia makes it even more impressive because there are simply not as many distance events that you will find in other parts of the world.

Early on in his running career he decided he wanted to run 40 marathons by the age of 40. He completed his 100th marathon in April 1998 in Canberra, 17 years after his first marathon. His first 100 marathons were all completed in less than four hours; he has a PB of 2:56, from the 1991 Gold Coast marathon. He ran his 193rd marathon – the Wagga Wagga Trail Marathon – in a time of 4:57 on a tough trail course that included styles to climb over, bridges to cross, tunnels to clamber through, kangaroos to avoid, and drizzling rain throughout the race.

Bob is a truck driver and forklift operator at a fruit and vegetable market in Sydney. Prior to this job he was a milkman. An Australian reporter once observed, "I was a dockhand in a milk depot when I knew Bob. He was always quiet. A 'please' and 'thank-you' man with a certain dignity about him."

Bob has been running long distance events since 1981. He ran his first marathon the year after he had run his first City to Surf 14 K in Sydney. He has now done 30 consecutive City to Surf races, and in 2009 finished in 70:19. Bob says he runs the long distances for the challenge of the distance, to meet people and renew friendships, and for the enjoyment of travelling to different places. But when it all comes down to it, he simply has fun doing it. "I got the bug", he said.

In 1999, Bob's marriage broke-up. Finding himself single again, he travelled for five years around the Australian marathon circuit. Along with his mates, he started "to chase 100. Somewhere in there we decided to start a club." Today, Bob runs the Australian 100 Marathon club and is President of the Southside Masters Running Club.

Bob acknowledges that his running was a contributing factor in the divorce from his first wife. "My wife thought I was mad going out running all the time", he said to a newspaper reporter. Although he cancelled planned runs in an effort to save his marriage it was still not enough. But several years later, through running, he met his second wife Anni. They met in the 1994 City to Surf run. Bob asked Anni out for lunch and in the following year they got married.

Bob met his best friend, Dennis Cunniffe, through running. As Dennis and his wife are deaf, Bob and Anni learned sign language, and the couples often would go away together camping, and running. Dennis also went on to run more than 100 marathons. As far as anyone knows, Dennis is the only deaf person in the world to have run 100 marathons. A running magazine in Australia referred to Bob and Dennis as "the Forest Gumps of Australian running."

Bob says his greatest achievement is running the Westfield Run – the 1006 K race from Sydney to Melbourne – in May 1990. The first Westfield Run in 1983 was won by the legendary Cliff Young, a 61-year-old potato farmer. Cliff inspired runners and captured the imagination of the Australian public. A vegetarian batchelor who lived with his 91-year old mother, he would run 20-miles every day in gumboots. Rather than run in the latest running gear, he preferred to run in modified traditional farmers clothing.

For the 1990 Westfield race, Bob became a science experiment – a human laboratory. Five post-graduate students and three former runners comprised his Team. They monitored his physiology over the 199 hours he was running. His first wife and their children moved out of the family home so he could be completely focused for the race. Bob finished 14th out of a starting line of 32 competitors, only 19 of whom completed the distance. Legendary Yiannis Kouros won the event in a time of 144 hours (Yiannis won five of the eight Westfields between 1983 and 1990).

Another good friend of Bob's is Grahame Kerruish, who lives in Sydney. "Mountain Man", as he is known, because of his lumbering running style, recently completed his 300th marathon. He started running marathons in 1984 at the age of 45 and has averaged about 15 marathons a year ever since. On top of that he has completed more than 80 ultras, including the Westfield Sydney to Melbourne race. At 65 years, he's retired from his job as a clerk. He considers himself to be a "marathon junkie." "I love the challenge of it and the social side as well" he said to a reporter. Like other messengers he runs for worthy causes. He participated, for example, in Relay for Life, a fundraising event for the New South Wales Cancer Council. His cause was personal; he had five close friends who had cancer and he himself had a malignant melanoma removed from his back.

When Janet Green finished the Victoria Marathon in British Columbia, Canada, long time friend and running partner Evan Fagan, himself a 100 plus marathoner, was there with a bottle of champagne to celebrate what was her 200th marathon. Friends and family were there too with flowers and congratulations. It was fitting for Janet to run her 200th marathon in Victoria as this was where it all started for her (her boyfriend at the time suggested that she could probably run a marathon). In the early days Janet ran about five-six marathons per year. But she started seeing the events for more than just the runs, and instead found enjoyment in their total experience, which included visiting new places, meeting up with friends and meeting new people.

Janet is a family physician on Vancouver Island, British Columbia. She runs in the early morning before she starts a very hectic practice. "Running gives my life a balance because most of my running friends are not doctors. I'm not running anywhere near my best times now, it's for all those other reasons", she said to me.

Like many other messengers she accepts that her best running times may be in the past; that the personal best times are not going to improve. At the point of "letting go" of PBs and performance, there is an enlightenment of what the marathon experience truly means. It's much more than the physical goal of running fast. It's what running long gives the messengers – it's the width and depth of life, not its length.

In the United Kingdom, messenger Gina Little said she never had a marathon running lifestyle until later in life. "I started the sport quite late, she said, "but once I was bitten by the running bug I couldn't stop. Marathon running has helped me see the world and I've made some good friends. The great thing about it is that you don't have to be brilliant – all you need to do is be able to run." I've met Gina, who is now in her late sixties, a few times, the first over lunch outside in London on a hot summer's day. We talked running; an easy, interesting and enjoyable thing to do. Gina is of short and slight build; you would not recognize her as a top runner at all. Humble and self-effacing, like many messengers, she's curious as to why I'd want to talk to her.

Gina started running at the age of 41. "I saw the London marathon go past at the end of my street – Christchurch Way - and thought 'I could do that'." She only intended to do one. "My husband joined me at the beginning but whereas he didn't keep it up I got the bug and have been running ever since." When I asked her what 'the bug' actually is, Gina replied "I think invariably that it's the people that you meet – you get awfully nice runners."

Gina has worked in social services administration for Greenwich Council for more than 30 years, and has two children and four grandchildren. She's raised over $40,000 for charities over the years.

Gina reached her 100th marathon in November 1997: "It just happened", she said. What's also 'just happened' is she now has run over 320 marathons and ultras (40) since 1983, and has run more marathons than any other woman in the United Kingdom. It turns out that Gina is also actually quite fast. She regularly places in her age division and sets age group course records. She was once the third woman to finish an 80-mile race and the first woman in the over-50 age group at a World Trail Marathon championship.

There's no special training, no tempos, no speed drills for Gina. Her goals are simply "to keep well, and keep going on all the trips." The trips with other runners to events in different countries cement social connections that are already strong from the shared experiences of the events they've run. Add to that the shared experiences of new places, new sights, new cultures, and it is little wonder the messengers keep looking for more events to run.

And the re-connections with others can occur by pure chance. I met Gina again at the Yakima River Canyon marathon in Washington state, for example; neither of us knew the other would be there. And I had no idea her friends, fellow messengers from the United Kingdom, Roger Biggs, Carla Hayes and Jack Brooks would also be there. Just minutes before the race began we were lining up at the start-line. I saw Gina, and then the others. I went over and said a quick hello. We connected later at the post-race banquet. By chance, I'd actually met Carla at a race in England the year before. We ran together for a few miles in that marathon. Afterwards, as the runners sat on the grass with their friends and family, basking in the accomplishment and reflecting on the race in the sun, Carla and I met up again. Turned out she was good friends with friends of mine. I'd also met Roger and Jack before as well, and had kept in touch over email. A small world; two degrees of influence.

Jack 'Dasher' Brooks was there at the Yakima marathon with

Carla, Gina and Roger. Jack's been there before and has a number of friends living in North America thanks to running. Yakima's a great place to meet up with everyone. Jack ran his first marathon at 41 years of age and had only started running a year before that. He "started running marathons as much as anything because when I first mentioned the idea a number of people told me that I wouldn't be able to manage it." Now in his sixties Jack has run more than 230 marathons and ultras, and has the distinction of being the second runner ever from the United Kingdom to have run a marathon in every American state.

Running is now so much a part of his life, he says, that it's difficult to envisage what life would be like without it. Jack typically trains 4-5 days a week; with up to ten miles a night. He's also the Secretary of the United Kingdom 100 Marathon Club. Marathon runners, he says are "nice, hospitable, friendly, and social folks. Even at the top level most marathon runners are not stuck up or pretending they're important, they're pleased you're enthusiastic about the sport. I've met so many fantastic people."

Like others, there are multiple benefits to Jack that derive from his marathon running. Most of his friends run so it's a huge part of his social life. It relieves stress and gives him an opportunity to clear his mind and think through problems. He said that "when it's going well running gives me a sense of well-being and euphoria that is difficult to explain to non-runners. I believe that running has made me a generally more resilient person and it has certainly given me a great sense of personal achievement and fulfillment." Importantly to Jack, running has enabled him to raise money for a number of charities he cares about; "it's an extra feel good factor."

Over the years Jack has run and travelled with 'Big Dave' Carter. I was told "that to meet him I'd think he was a skinhead, but he's a larger than life character, a great guy." I asked Big Dave why he's "Big Dave", "I'm very tall and very big boned", he said, "especially for perceptions of what a marathoner is suppose to look like … and then there's several Dave's…." The name has stuck, and he's known around the world.

His first marathon was London, England. "I use to sit and watch the London marathon every year on television. At the time I was 23 stone (322 pounds), and I decided I wanted to try the marathon the next year." He starting running, just a little at first, and began watching his diet. After completing the London marathon he came home and said that was going to be it. But a neighbor told him about another marathon that was coming up, so Big Dave decided to run that as well. He enjoyed it. The next year he ran eight more marathons.

Now, 20 years since his first marathon, he's run 734 marathons, ultras and stage races. If others ask him how many races he's run he simply says "I've done quite a few." These days he is more interested in orienteering (off road trail races), the 100-miler events and stage-races, which may be up to six days long. "I'm now more into the self-sufficiency stuff", he says.

Dave runs for the challenges that the races present to him. "It's a challenge", he says, "that only involves myself. If I fail it's because of me. You get a pair of shoes on and away you go. And you ask yourself 'can you do it', because there's so much that can go wrong. Even after seven hundred I still feel that way at the start-line. You have to respect the distance, respect the challenge; you can't ever take it for granted."

It's clear from talking to Dave that he lives a full life, and is passionate about his total running experience. "Marathon running is a great leveler; whether you're a laborer or a banker, you're out there and the job means nothing. To be honest, the drinks afterwards – it's all about the running – the camaraderie is incredible. You may not see them again for months, then meet up and begin exactly where you left off."

Dave is covered in tattoos, including three marathon tattoos, from the Marathon of Britain, the Augrabies marathon in South Africa, and the Yakima marathon in Washington state, directed by Lenore and Bob Dolphin. A few years ago, Lenore and Bob arranged a hotel for Big Dave and the others he was traveling with. The manager of the hotel was a big fan of tattoos and it got back to Dave in England that if he had a tattoo done of the Yakima marathon logo, the three rooms they booked for two nights would be free. "Why not", thought Big Dave. So he went to his own tattooist and had the Yakima logo put on his thigh. True to his word, the hotel manager gave them the free nights' accommodation.

One of the travelers on that American visit was Roger Biggs, the President of the United Kingdom 100 Marathon Club. Roger is a frequent traveler to the United States and has crossed the Atlantic many times with Jack Brooks. Roger is also known as 'Basher' in the Dasher vs Basher chronicles that have been written about their race rivalry.

Although he had always been a runner, it was watching the London marathon on television in the early 1980s that made him try it for the first time. "When I saw a lady about 70-years old doing it I thought if she can do it, I can do it." Prior to his first marathon he'd only ever run an aggregate total of 38 miles in races before.

So at the age of 36, Roger ran his first marathon. Then he tried another soon afterwards. For the next few years he ran two-three each year but gradually the numbers increased. Over the last few years, he's run at least 40 distance events every year. Aside from amassing 559 marathons and ultras since he ran his first marathon in 1984, Roger is the first person outside of the United States to have run a marathon in all fifty American states.

Roger has accumulated a wealth of knowledge on the United States and a passion for the American national parks. He has celebrated each of his 100, 200, 300, 400 and 500th marathons in the United States. Another goal for Roger is a marathon in every Canadian provinces and territory, of which he's run in only two.

Running is his life. Roger has also run over 180 10-mile races and 160 half marathons. In fact he was able to achieve an extremely rare feat of running his 100th 10-mile race, his 100th half-marathon and his 100th marathon in successive races. That said, Roger also adds that "I can remember the day when five miles used to feel like running to the end of the earth." When I last talked to Roger, at the beginning of 2010, he was on a streak of 60 marathons in 60 weeks.

In addition to running the races and his role as Chairman of the UK 100 Marathon Club, Roger often makes the travel arrangements for many other club members. He communicates with several American friends regularly, including Lenore and Bob, with whom he's stayed with several times.

Regardless of the quality of a run or the location, Roger comments that "I've been, and I have an opinion, and I'm glad I went." Travel broadens the understanding of people and place. "Running marathons", he says, "is a way to see the world, you get to know people." Roger's words remind me of a comment from Daniel Boorstin, the prolific American social historian of the 1960s: "the traveler was active; he went strenuously in search of people, of adventure, of experience. The tourist is passive; he expects interesting things to happen to him; he goes sightseeing."

Roger says he has become much more knowledgeable and tolerant of other people; things that he used to be concerned about no longer bug him like they used to. "I'm more interested and respectful of others", he says. "The marathon is an amazing leveler. I run with other runners who can't pay me for their race registration fees for several weeks, as well as run with millionaires, but we're just the same in the race and we all get together afterwards."

Roger has been retired for three years, which now makes his distance running lifestyle much more possible. For many years his career focused on production control, but he moved into computers when he was made redundant in 1984. He then worked as a programmer, team leader and manager until his retirement. Now, he says, "there's no way I could do what I do if I was still working." I asked Roger what his goals were now, with so much accomplished. Most immediate is the desire to continue his streak of running a marathon every week. He also has plans to raise money for charity by running a marathon in each of the 26 counties in Ireland, one a day, along with Peter Ferris, an Irishman who is also a member of the UK 100 Marathon Club.

It's a small world. Roger asked if I knew who Peter was. I replied that Peter and I ran most of the spectacular Connemara Invitational marathon together in the west of Ireland, not far from Galway. The invitational race was small, held the day before the main Connemara marathon, with only about ten of us running. So we carried our own supplies. Occasionally a support vehicle would drive by and ask if we needed anything. Over a three-hour period I got to know Peter fairly well. At Mile-18 we stopped at a pub in the middle of nowhere to get some water as we'd run out.

We were hot and sweaty as we walked into a quiet roadside bar with half a dozen people drinking, I'm guessing Guinness. The conversation stopped and mouths opened. Peter explained what we were doing – running a marathon – and asked if we could we fill our bottles with some water. With their mouths still gapped it was clear we were considered crazy, a point 100% confirmed when Peter explained he'd run more than 300 hundred marathons.

It is often a bit of shock and awe when the messengers tell non-distance runners how many races they've run. Big Dave's answer of "a few" perhaps best exemplifies a common response by messengers when asked. Messengers are not out to broadcast their achievements to the rest of the world. That's not what their passion is about. The benefits are far more intrinsic than that.

**

Our 'humanness' and our 'happiness' is to a large extent predicated on our social interaction – our relationships with other people. The more you look at the distance running world the more you see it's very small. While the physical long distance is significant, the *social distance* is very short. You could perhaps argue that the longer the physical distance (that is run) the closer the social distance among runners.

17

"People say life on the road can be lonely,
but I say that it's been the best part of 18 years for me."
Bob Fickel

At the individual level it is the interplay of the mind and body that attracts the runner to the longer distances. In *Why We Run* (2001), Bernd Heinrich writes that "The key to endurance, as all distance runners know, is not just a matter of sweat glands. It's vision. To endure is to have a clear goal and the ability to extrapolate to it with the mind – the ability to keep in mind what is not before the eye. Vision allows us to reach into the future ...." Similarly, George Sheehan observed that "I look for answers on the road. I take my tools of sight, hearing, touch, smell, taste, and intellect and run with them. I discover a total universe, a world that begins on the other side of sweat and exhaustion."

While most long distance runners may not have the extreme physical endurance of the Tarahumara Indians in Mexico, East African runners or the Tendai Monks in Japan, they still exhibit many of the same characteristics. If you've run more than 100 marathons you know what it's like to endure through less than desirable conditions. You've likely felt pain, pushed yourself in some way beyond what you would typically do, experienced adverse, sometimes dangerous weather conditions, and seen many others who, with less experience, have suffered at the measure of the 26.2 mile distance. But you've accomplished something, and likely repeatedly, through running. Bernd Heinrich wrote, "The cup is full. It contains what I had put into it. Like catching an antelope, the best things in life that we can experience are served on the challenge to endure and to overcome in the long run."

Daniel Leiberman and Dennis Bramble reported in their 2004 *Nature* journal paper on fossil evidence that humans are designed, and have evolved, to be long distance runners and walkers. This, they say, was essential for basic survival needs. And as Bernd Heinrich and later Chris McDougall (2009) in *Born to Run* point out, the scientific and anthropological research increasingly indicates that humans were, and still are, the best adapted of all animals to run long distances.

It makes sense. Sharon Kaye, a philosophy professor from John Carroll University in Cleveland, Ohio points out that we essentially still have the bodies of hunters and gatherers. She writes: "If we compare our biological history to a single 24-hour day, we are hunter gatherers from the wee hours, past dawn, through the morning, all afternoon, and into the night, until about five minutes to midnight. Farming changed our entrenched lifestyle suddenly, radically, and recently – so much so that there has not been enough time for it to have any significant effect on our physiology. Only roughly 500 generations of humans have lived and died as farmers."

Jim Fixx wrote about this possibility in 1978: "As runners, I think we reach directly back along the endless chain of history. We experience what we would have felt had we lived ten thousand years ago, eating fruits, nuts and vegetables, and keeping our hearts and lungs and muscles fit by constant movement." Little wonder then that if we're ideally suited physiologically for running long distances that there is something more intrinsic, something more mental, emotional and spiritual but yet less definable about the activity that we are drawn to.

Experience is a great teacher. Aldous Huxley said in 1956 that "experience is not what happens to you; it is what you do with what happens to you." The ability to continue through hardship or adversity in life has its parallels in marathon running. Some people have amazing resiliency and can endure extreme pressures in their lives while others have trouble facing up to, and getting through, the challenges that come before them. And challenges will and do come; it is part of life. Overcoming challenges makes you stronger. It's no surprise that enduring the marathon distance – with the stresses self-imposed on our physical, mental, emotional and spiritual well-being, helps runners in their everyday life.

18

"I've not found any experience which bestows the high level
of satisfaction, accomplishment and self-respect
as one receives from finishing a marathon – at any speed."

Jeff Galloway

The year 2010 marks the 2,500th anniversary of Pheidippides
making that epic run to Athens to break the news of the victory at
Marathon. That was in 490 BC. Socrates was born just 21 years
later in 469 BC and lived until 399 BC. In that time he established
himself as one of the founders of western philosophy. But he was
a critic of Athenian society and spoke of the need to improve
Athens' social justice. He was there when Athens encountered a
humiliating defeat to Sparta in the Peloponnesian War. He was
found guilty of corrupting the minds of the young in Athens and
sentenced to death. Although he had opportunities to escape, he
chose to die instead, which he did shortly after taking hemlock,
upon which he kept walking until he could walk no more and the
poison that numbed his feet moved up his body to his heart.

One of those corrupted youth was a student of his, Plato (428-348
BC), who produced numerous writings on philosophy, logic, math-
ematics and other subjects that continued the Socratic dialogues.
The most famous of Plato's students was Aristotle (384-322 BC),
who also went on to strongly influence western philosophy and to
tutor Alexander the Great.

Alexander continued the spread of Greek thought and culture around the Mediterranean and beyond, in a time known as the Hellenistic period (approximately 300-150 BC). It was in this period that the concept of *apathy* took on greater significance. Not as we define the word apathy today but rather, in a quite different conception – one that nevertheless sheds some light on the messengers in this book.

The philosophy professor Richard de Witt comments in the book *Philosophy and Running*, "In the Hellenistic concept [of apathy] one does not merely have apathy; rather, one acquires it. And acquiring apathia can be a long, involved process. And importantly, one cannot acquire apathy without first having pathos, that is, without first being passionate. One must work, and work passionately to understand the universe and to understand one's place in that universe ... the key central idea behind Hellenistic philosophers is that if you are passionate about such study [of philosophy], you will come to understand the universe and your place in that universe. And it is this deep understanding of the universe, and your place in that universe, that leads to peace of mind, to mental tranquility, mental unperturbedness ... one's passion eventually leads to apathia, the right sort of apathy – an unworried state of mind."

After having talked with more than one hundred and twenty long distance runners, each of whom has run more than 100 marathons and ultras, one of the most common recurring themes is their sense of the unworried, both during their runs and in their everyday lives. It is as if they are well on the road to Apathia, if they haven't already arrived there.

19

"Your health is the most important thing you'll ever have,
so make sure as you get older that you have some
positive things in place. If you don't have your health
you've got to wonder what the big circle of life is all about."

Ray James

"Marathons are not about running from Point A to Point B.
They're about the mental strength to run a marathon.
Anyone can do the physical."

Ron Fowler

"I run because I find it therapeutic for mind, body, and soul."

Andrew Kotulski

Running long distances has created an opportunity for individuals
to transform themselves. The word "transform" sounds huge and
significant but that's exactly what has occurred for a number of
messengers. Through running long distances they have changed
the way they live. Sometimes it has been through life changing
circumstances. Other times, it has been the realization that they
are on a path of self-destruction. And for some messengers it
was simply a choice between life and a premature death. What's
achieved in the transformation is a celebration of the human condition – a reminder to all of us that resilience, tenacity, courage,
perseverance and determination can make for new beginnings
and a better life.

I first met Jose Nebrida at the Yakima River Canyon Marathon
in 2007. Jose has a wide booming smile which seldom leaves his
face. Standing just 5 feet 2 inches tall, at 67-years of age he is
now retired from his social worker and school administrator jobs
in Chicago. Jose was distinctive at the marathon because he ran
the entire distance carrying a huge American flag. He received an
immense ovation from everyone at the post-race dinner as race

director Lenore Dolphin asked him to come up to the stage and receive a special award. He walked slowly, backwards, up the stairs, always smiling. It had been a long, tough run. Not surprising given the size of the flag he was carrying. Jose and I have met a couple of times since and we talked over the telephone in the fall of 2009. At that point he had carried the flag in 57 marathons in 35 States.

Originally from San Juan, Philippines, Jose immigrated to the United States in 1975. He completed Masters degrees in social work and education, but in his mid-forties, he said, he was depressed. He smoked two packs of cigarettes a day, paid no attention to eating properly, and was drunk every weekend. He left his wife and two teenage children, and for a nine day period he lived in his car. On top of this his family had a history of heart disease. His father died at the age of 72; his brothers died at 47 and 58. The writing was on the wall; either he did something or something would happen to him.

Jose's friend Ernie Billups, came to his aid. As Jose said, Ernie became his drill sergeant, and determined that the first thing Jose needed was discipline. Ernie made Jose get up at 4:30am every morning and walk a block and back. The point of this was habit reversal – Ernie, a marathoner, was trying to instill the positive addiction of exercise to replace the negative addictions of drinking and smoking, as well as the negative feelings Jose felt. After a while Jose started to run. He increased his distance each week and soon ran his first 5 K run. Then he ran a 10 K. The distances increased. Later that year, 1986, he ran his first marathon, Chicago, in a time of 4:52. Ernie was waiting at the finish line. They shared emotional embraces, tears and much jumping up and down for joy and celebration. They had both come a long way.

Several years later Jose ran his 100th marathon, also at the Chicago marathon. He has now run more than 170 marathons and ultras. Joes told me "we're getting old and slowing down, but we keep on going. What we have is sheer determination. Because of goals we just keep on going ... those who run more than 100 marathons, we all have the same sort of philosophy."

Jose's currently running about one marathon every month. It's not about running a fast time, it's about all those other things that make up the marathon experience, especially the friendships. "We don't have any control over age. We run and pray that we will finish it. We're old. What's time to us"?

As I talk over the telephone to Jose he's walking around the marathon expo area of the Patriot's Run event in Kansas. He interrupts our conversation as he sees his good friend Eugene, another 100 + marathoner who has come from out of state to run the event. I'm listening to their conversation as I wait for Jose to get back on the phone; they're clearly pleased to meet up with one another. Within seconds, I'm introduced to Eugene and he and I talk on Jose's cell phone. They talk some more and promise to meet up later in the day.

It was great talking to Eugene – I feel like I know him well already. We're all friends. Jose and I continue our conversation. "It's just wonderful to be in the company of the likes of Eugene", Jose says.

In 2002, Jose had a heart attack not long after the Oklahoma City marathon. He required emergency triple by-pass surgery; one artery was 100% blocked, the others 95% blocked. One doctor advised him to stay in bed and rest. Another cardiologist said to get running again. The doctors told him he would have been dead years ago had he not been running marathons. A few months of rehabilitation later, and he was running marathons again. A few years later, he had another heart attack. Doctors put stents in to keep open an artery to his heart.

In 2002 the *Des Moines Register* had an article detailing Jose's visit to one of their schools. Jose was quoted as saying "they are so enthused... every time I go to one of the centers for the gifted I take a medal to show them. The younger ones put it around their necks and shout 'I'm a winner'. Many of our children are from the shelters and barrios and they are looking for positive role models. They can say 'here's somebody who's doing something good, not like the bad things they see every day ... When I had a heart attack they sent cards they made themselves. They said 'you are our hero' and 'please run again'. Every time I opened one I started to cry … If the people really do care, the least I can do is believe I can do it."

The American flag. Jose is passionate about the United States, it gave him his life. Running a marathon is a significant achievement. Running 100 is truly remarkable. Carrying a huge flag in 57 marathons may perhaps be beyond description. Especially after two heart attacks. Jose has been referred to as Captain America and is often heard calling out "God Bless America."

The flag running began soon after the events of 9/11 in 2001. The first scheduled marathon after 9/11 was the Air Force marathon, but it was cancelled due to the terrorist attack. So Jose decided to carry a flag at the next one, in Lake Bristol, New Hampshire. At that event he ran with a large school flag. There were only 174 runners in the event. It was hilly, windy and quite desolate. There was little support to be seen. Jose was asking himself "what was he doing" throughout the run. He decided it would be his first and last carrying the flag, but at least he had done it once to commemorate the fallen.

As he came to the end of the race, he saw the event was pretty much being closing down as he, the last runner, was coming in. But a fire engine came out of the finish line with Jose just 385 yards away from finishing. The firefighters had come out to cheer him on, calling out "God Bless America."

Then the Police emerged. They presented arms with their batons and formed a gauntlet under which Jose ran. The firefighters then took him back to the hall where the after-race gala was taking place. As he entered the hall, all the runners and their friends and family rose to give him a standing ovation. He knew then he would continue and keep running with the flag at other marathons.

The flag itself, however, changed. When Jose was at his favorite race, the New York marathon, which he has completed 12 times, he went to St Paul's Church where a man in a wheelchair called out to him – he'd recognized Jose as the flag carrying marathon runner and made a request. The man had been a firefighter who was injured, now paralyzed, from the events of the day at the World Trade Towers. He had created a flag on which are sewn all the names those who died in 9/11. It's a huge flag – 8 feet by 5 feet, and weighs about 25 lbs. He asked if Jose would carry the flag he had made. Jose, quite honored, said yes. He runs with this flag now when there are no limits on finishing times. If there are limits he runs with a smaller 3 feet by 5 feet school flag.

On the day I talked with Jose over the telephone his flagpole had broken and he was getting a new one made at Ace Hardware. He was preparing to run the Patriot's Run which would be held the next day, September 11, 2009. It's an ultra-marathon dedicated to the heroes and victims of the terrorist attack of 9/11. Jose was going to run for 9 hours and 11 minutes, carrying the flag, honoring the fallen heroes and victims. Last year the Patriots Run called and asked him to participate, saying that he could run at his own pace. Last year in this ultra, he did 27 miles, and was awarded one medal for the marathon and another for the ultra. After hearing Jose being interviewed by the media, a number of people came to the event to see him and to run with him, including children after school, and adults after work. Some ran with him for a few miles, some up to nine miles.

Jose Nebrida: inspired and an inspiration. Passionate and enthusiastic for life.

Rory Coleman was in a successful design and print career in London, England. Like many in their early phase of their careers, he had pushed himself to the limit; working hard, playing hard. The long hours at work were counter-balanced by a partying lifestyle in which his health didn't get much of a consideration. As Rory told me, "At 31 years of age and 15 stone in weight, I had the revelation that a daily diet of 40 cigarettes, 12 pints of beer and an extremely stressful job equaled a much shorter life span." He said he "was the original couch potato. I was very unfit, very unhappy … an unhappy marriage – nicotine and alcohol got me through the hard times. By 1994 I felt toxic. I was surrounded by people who enabled me to get drunk every day – completely out of control. I decided to clean up."

On the 5th January 1994, he stopped drinking and smoking and dramatically changed his diet. He started running. "I almost collapsed at the beginning." But he was able to run a half marathon in April 1994, and built up to run his first full marathon in November that year – the Telford Marathon. Rory used the Telford race as training for the 1995 London Marathon, which he'd dreamed about doing. It was a proud day at that London marathon when he was able to watch himself on television crossing the line.

In 1998, Rory completed his 100th marathon. He discovered that his personality was well suited to longer distances, so he started doing ultras as well. He has now run over 550 marathons and ultras (with a PB of 3:24 for the marathon). He has set nine Guinness World records for treadmill endurance running, including one record of 283.65 miles completed in seven days, and has plans for a tenth. In 1998, he broke six treadmill records in one day.

On the 5th of January every year Rory sends himself a birthday card to celebrate his rebirth, "I'm 14 this year", he said. He has long since left the work world of printing and design and has created a number of fitness and running events over the years as well as developed a personal training career, always seeking to help others transform themselves. He has a diploma in Personal Training and is qualified as an Advanced Level Three Instructor with qualifications in Nutrition Management, Ante/Post Natal, Obesity, Training in Special Environments and Health Screening. He notes on his website "fitness has bought me great happiness and is a fundamental part of my daily life."

"The spiritual journey of going 26.2 miles is fantastic", Rory said. He explained that people are now looking for life experiences – they're running away or running towards something – life turning in some way. "People started asking me what I was doing next, so I started encouraging others to come and do it." A CEO came to one of Rory's event and said "don't ask me questions just tell me everything I need for a change." Life to Rory, he says, is about helping others achieve their goals, and building relationships is fundamental to achieving this. "I shake hands with everyone who finishes my events. I would trade all of the world records I have for those moments."

In December 1989, Englishman John Dawson owned an engineering company, making parts mainly for the transportation industry. He was an accountant by profession, but through career moves had found himself in the engineering world. In his earlier years, work and looking after his two daughters had taken up most of his time. Exercise was not high on the agenda. But the consequences of also being a heavy smoker (80 cigarettes a day) would soon change that.

He had been driving all day when he had his heart attack soon after he got home. "I must have reeked of tobacco", John said. The doctor asked him if he smoked, and he said "no." With disbelief the doctor asked when had he quit and John replied "an hour ago." John said "I knew then I would not smoke again." He was told by the doctor to walk a lot. This "cheesed him off" because he lives in a small village and people would wonder why he was walking all the time. Two years after his heart attack, he started jogging. He saw an advertisement for the New York marathon about eleven months before the event, and knew that it would motivate him to do it: "you can't buy fitness in a shop", he said.

Two weeks before the New York race, he got shin splints, so he alternated between walking and running during the race. Then he ran the London marathon, and then Los Angeles. Twelve marathons later, and he was hooked. In 1999, he met an Irishman at the Rome marathon who had run 42 marathons. This was another turning point in John's life, as he discovered that people were running marathons regularly; and seeing new places, meeting old friends and making new ones. Since 1999, John has never run less than 20 marathons in a year. He reached his 100th in 2003, his 200th in 2006. In 2007, at the age of 73, he ran ten marathons in ten days in the Lakes District of England to raise money for charity, and, of course, to simply see if he could do it.

He ran his 300th in Connemara, Ireland in 2009. I ran and chatted with John for a while during his 300th. He's known as the "metronome" because he keeps a steady pace from beginning to end. His best time is 3:54, but typically he finishes between 4:20 and 4:30. "There's always a feeling of satisfaction finishing a marathon. When you see people finishing, they've all got that look of achieving something – that's what it's all about. Gradually over time you get into a different set of friends and have these lifestyle changes – the running friends are extremely supportive, as is my family, especially my wife."

These days, John goes to the gym, gets a regular massage and sees a chiropractor every few weeks. He says it pays to assist the body when you can. One of the reasons he goes to the gym is to train others in their running. One of these individuals is 41-year old Simon Beresford, who has worked at McDonalds for 16 years.

Simon has Down Syndrome and for the past two years John has set about helping Simon fulfill his dream, his goal, of running a marathon. Specifically, the London marathon.

Down Syndrome (DS), also known as Trisomy 21, is a condition in which extra genetic material causes delays in the mental and physical development of children. It affects about 1 in every 800 babies. While some children with DS may need a lot of medical attention, others lead healthy lives.

I talked to Simon's mother, Marie, about her son's running. She said that the family all watched Simon's brother run the London marathon in 1984. Then his father, Dave, ran it a few years later. Simon never mentioned wanting to run a marathon but he started running, and with Marie, he ran a 10 K race. A few years later he came home from the health club and announced that he wanted to run a marathon. He had a friend there, he said, who would help him train for it. Marie met with John, and then he and Simon set about training for the 2007 London marathon. They applied for an entry place, as you must do with London, but were unsuccessful. Instead, they decided they would enter and raise money for charity. They set a goal of raising one thousand pounds. They ended up raising 10,000 pounds.

Simon and John ran together on that day, a hot day, completing the marathon in a time of 6:15. Simon came running down the Mall finishing strong. The Down Syndrome Association in England couldn't believe it – a first for anyone with DS. "They made a big fuss over him" Marie said. Simon and John were invited to 10 Downing Street, the Prime Minister's residence, and word began to spread of Simon's achievement. In addition to the positive attention, the training and accomplishment has made a positive impact on his physical and mental health in all the ways typically associated with running.

In Germany, Anita Kinle, who has a young son with DS, heard about Simon's achievement. Inspired by Simon, she started a running club – *Laufclub Down Syndrom Marathonstaffel e.V.* – for those with DS in Germany. Anita contacted Simon and John and invited them over to Germany for a race. Several other members of the UK 100 Marathon Club went with John. It was quite an emotional run for many of the 100 Marathon Club members. Anita's club has a growing number of DS runners and several coaches. Although they are not running marathons, they are running longer distances and achieving goals that the individuals, families, friends and organizations had not really thought was possible just a few years ago.

On March 21, 2010, the fifth World Down Syndrome Day, Anita's club organized the Ultra Marathon Relay (100 miles) for Down's Syndrome at the location of the former Berlin Wall, 21 years after its fall. Those who do not have DS ran the 100 miles. Those with DS ran as part of the relay team. '21' is also the lucky number of the Marathoni, as it represents *chromosome 21*. Anita acknowledged the efforts of her English counterparts in correspondence about the 100 mile event "[And] last I thank you Simon Beresford, John Dawson and all the English Friends for bringing us together."

For John Dawson, coaching Simon and others has been a significant part of his running career. John has been able to give back to others and make a difference in their lives. As he said to me one day "you need the motivation to keep running. I have it because I've got these commitments; I've got these responsibilities and commitments to keep."

John's act of support has led to Simon to push beyond what he thought were his limits. John's own transformation through running has inspired others to run, and for Anita to form the German DS running club. This in turn has inspired others with DS and their families, and many other runners, to reach for the impossible and to make a positive difference in lives. But John's influence has spread much further beyond that of Simon. He continues to run marathons in his quiet, unassuming, modest way. I have been told repeatedly in the course of many conversations that he is a source of inspiration to many. In 2009 alone, he will have completed close to 50 marathons and ultras. But it's not the numbers that inspire, it's the way the individual takes on the challenge and relates to others in the process.

As John and Simon continued their training after the successful London marathon in 2007, messenger Holly Koester was inching closer to her 100th marathon in the United States. In fact, she went on to race her 100th marathon at the Buffalo Marathon in New York on May 25, 2008. Later that year in Juneau, Alaska, at the Frank Maier Marathon, she became the first person ever to race a marathon in all 50 States and DC in a wheelchair.

Holly's transformation began in 1990. She had been a captain in the airborne division of the United States Army for nine years at the Redstone Arsenal in Alabama when she was called up for Operation Desert Storm. Driving to the base to report for her post, her vehicle tipped over on a temporary road. Holly injured her spinal cord, was paralyzed from the chest down, and lost the use of her legs. She underwent treatment and rehabilitation at the Cleveland, Ohio VA Medical Center, and began the process of learning how to live life using a wheelchair.

Holly is bubbly and enthusiastic as we talk over the telephone. Before the accident, she had been heavily into sports – softball and volleyball especially – and had tried out for the Army volleyball team. She also ran with her group in the army and with her twin sister, who was also in the military at another base. "I was pretty active as a runner before I got hurt", she said.

Holly needed to build her upper body strength for everyday activities such a showering, and moving from beds to chairs, cars, toilets and wheelchair use. "Even pulling up your pants in a wheelchair had to be learned. I was the only female on the ward. I had to ask the guys how to do all this. It was kind of like we became one big family. And runners are just like that – one big family."

"When they told me I would never walk again, I really didn't know what to think. I didn't think I could do anything. Then I just saw some of the other guys and they would come into my room and show me how easy it was to get into the chair and get back into life. I have to credit the guys at the hospital where I was recuperating. They showed me everything they could do – and I said, 'if they can do it, I can too'."

Her rehabilitation therapist knew she was very involved in sports and told Holly about the Veteran's Wheelchair Championships. Holly participated in the games, entering several field events. In some cases, what would take others two or three minutes, would take Holly up to 20 minutes. This included falling out of her chair. "I'm not gonna give up", she said. Holly won two gold and two silver medals at the games, and in 1996 went on to win the Games' overall Endeavour Award, which is given to one athlete for their spirit, enthusiasm and achievement. She now regularly wins a number of medals each year.

Holly then entered a 10 K wheelchair event in which her sister ran/walked with her. This was without a racing chair, which made it even more difficult. As a veteran, she was allowed to purchase a sports chair, however, and this changed things for her significantly. A friend in a wheelchair started going to races with her and her sister made sure she would get to the race. Holly completed a couple of half-marathons and in October 1995 entered the Columbus Marathon. It was quite the moment, she said, to be on the start line with Para-olympic champions and to hear the conversations (what pace, let's work together…). She finished in just under four hours, but it was the start of something that hasn't stopped.

Holly did the Columbus marathon for the next couple of years as well as some shorter distances. The first marathon she did outside of Ohio was in Florida, about five years after her first race. She started to race in more and more marathons. She joined the 50 States Marathon club after meeting with Paula and Steve Boone, who ran the club, at the Houston Marathon. She had been invited to Houston by the Texas chapter of the Paralyzed Veterans of America organization. The Boones explained that they did not have any wheelchair members but encouraged Holly to join – once she had raced in at least 10 of the states, which was the club's eligibility ruling. At this point Holly had raced in seven, but now she had a new goal. "If I got the 50 states, then great", she said, "but if not I'd still get to see and do a lot."

Holly continues to race in marathons all around the United States. "I plan all my trips anywhere around doing a marathon", she says. The challenges of travel are magnified when you're in a wheelchair. "Racing the marathons is one thing, but apart from all that I still have to get in and out of the chair and get to all the events – either flying or loading my chair in and out of my van.

One time during a race I had to push 17 miles with a flat tire." Like many other wheelchair competitors there's the ongoing concern of getting shoulder injuries due to the continuous pushing of the wheels on conventional chairs (push chairs and crank chairs are becoming increasingly popular ways to avoid such injuries). Part of the reason she enters marathons is the endurance element, but there's also the pragmatic consideration that it takes some setting up in a racing chair, and "once I'm in it I don't want to get out straight away again." At the start of the race, Holly estimates it usually takes her about three miles to warm up. Even at track events, she enters the longer distances.

Holly's most challenging race to date was the Mount Rushmore marathon in South Dakota. Originally planned to finish downhill into Rapid City, the course was changed to an uphill finish into Crazy Horse. Quite the difference in a wheelchair. According to a local newspaper article, when she crossed the finish line after over seven hours, and after the last runner, the people who had waited were in tears. Quoted in another article Holly said, "I was so happy to cross the finish line, and it was so cold and my heart was warmed to see people still waiting for me. I was totally blown away and didn't expect the reception, and it was family and people that didn't know me."

A big part of the marathon appeal to Holly, however, is what she calls the "whole experience." Marathoners, she said to me "are one big family – the main goal is to finish – get your medal – tell the story." On top of that, traveling around the country and experiencing new places is an incredible experience, despite the challenges in the logistics of getting to some runs. The support is wonderful; from her own family and friends, to the friends she has made in the marathon running world. Holly met Lenore and Bob Dolphin at the Yakima River Canyon marathon, for example. Lenore found Holly a residential house to stay in for the weekend that was wheelchair accessible. The Dolphins also encouraged her to join the Marathon Maniacs club, which she did, and also to join the North American 100 marathon club when she reached 100! Which she also did.

Holly has developed several "rules" for herself. First, complete the marathon. Second, do the best she can. Third, try and place. Fourth, have fun. She has been a source of inspiration to many, runners and non-runners alike. "Mom still thinks I'm crazy. She thinks driving 26 miles is a long way. My friends and family are really proud of me, but they still think I'm crazy." Holly is one of 12 veterans who are wheelchair athletes pictured on a Cheerios cereal box that came out in March 2008. She was also an Olympic torchbearer, volunteered at the 1996 Paralympics in Atlanta, and is the sports director for her Paralyzed Veterans of America (PVA) Buckeye chapter in Cleveland.

In her non-running world, Holly is a supply teacher for grades K-8 in Ohio. She likes to teach children about not being intimidated by people who use wheelchairs, and talking to and supporting those who are newly injured and facing life in a wheelchair. Her life is focused around marathons, educating children and educating others who live with a physical disability. But her message is much broader than that group of people. As she said to one reporter; "I think if we don't get them when they're newly injured, they end up lying around and often become hermits. We (the PVA Buckeye Chapter and local VA therapists) try to get them out there and get them educated. I tell them, 'you have to be here (at the Games)... you have to go and hear the cheering, and do it for yourself!' We all want to be productive, and these Games encourage you."

The first time American messenger Jerry Dunn ran a marathon, it was "to see if I could do it." In the early days it was part of his recovery from alcoholism: "I swapped one addiction for another", he said. Jerry told me of his "drinking issues" between the ages of 23 and 37 as he progressed through college, three years of military service and beyond. Despite going to Alcoholics Anonymous, the issues still remained.

Jerry grew up in Indiana but now lives in Spearfish, South Dakota. He started running recreationally in the mid-1970s while living in Sarasota, Florida. Although running helped him move away from drinking, he was still drinking *and* running for seven years. "I was established as a drinker but was becoming a runner. Most people on the outside wouldn't have known that."

The turning point came when he passed out on his 37th birthday. He woke up the next day and decided he needed to do "something else" with his life. In the back of his mind he had the memory of his father, who, he said, was an overweight smoker who died of a heart attack at age 47. Running became a bigger and bigger part of Jerry's life. But the positive addiction of running almost became a negative. As Jerry explains, "it basically ruined my marriage in 1993, well it was one of the reasons for it, and I was away all the weekends – I didn't take care of the relationship side of things."

Jerry wasn't able to quit drinking completely until he totally committed himself to running long distances. This he did, as if he had something to prove, and a lot of catching up to do.

In 1991, Jerry ran across the United States. In 1993, he ran 93 marathons - "93 in '93" - breaking the world record of 87 in one year (held by fellow messenger Steve Edwards from the United Kingdom). He said that his 93 in 93 was probably when he was in the "deepest part of his running addiction." He then heard about someone who had done 101 marathons in a calendar year, so he increased his goal to 104 in order to break the record.

Jerry told me he ran this huge "tour" of marathons because it was his 47th year, and each run was in memory of his father. While on his tour he made stops at hospitals and rehab centers to tell his story, which essentially boiled down to this: "there are other ways to live, and there is life after alcohol." In 1996, he ran the Boston Marathon course 26 days in a row. This was the 100th anniversary of the Boston Marathon, and Jerry's way of celebrating the occasion. In 1998, Jerry ran the Los Angeles Marathon course 14 times, because that race was 14 years old, and then ran the New York marathon 29 times, since it was 29 years old.

But, like many other messengers, he was continually looking for new goals; new challenges with which to re-set their focus. And so, with the new millennium coming, Jerry set out to run 200 marathons in the year 2000.

In one of our telephone conversations Jerry said to me "In the last few years my self-confidence has improved – things are coming together for me. I used to compare myself to other people, but in the last year or two I've realized I'm who I am. I don't have to be perfect before I tell my story and get others to hear it and think about it. I'm just another human being walking around the planet like anyone else and I've just chosen to run. Running endurance – it's what I picked to do." We'll come back to Jerry's story later.

Meanwhile, Australian messenger Ray James, a family lawyer based in Sydney, was going through similar torments with alcohol.

In 1997 at age 48, Ray woke up one morning, looked out the window and saw his friend's car in the driveway. Ray had been driving it the night before and he could see it had been damaged. He had no idea why, but he had a huge hangover as he thought about it. Time for a transformation. As he explained to Kelly Baker in the Australian Runners World in 2009, back then "I knew that I'd hit the stage in my drinking where I was a danger to myself and to other people. I thought I'd better sort my life out before I did something really stupid."

His drinking, he said, had been "out of control" for six years. But it was "private drinking" and his family, wife and three children knew little of it. Ray said "I was drinking every day, but always alone. That was the really sinister thing about it. When I went out anywhere I would always drink water, but that was because I always had enough alcohol beforehand to get me through."

Ray's brother-in-law also had a drinking problem, but his was well known. Ironically, some people suggested he should try and be more like Ray. In 1996 Ray's brother-in-law stopped drinking, but nine months later, without a drink, he was diagnosed with terminal cancer. Ray's brother-in-law stayed sober despite the diagnosis. Surely, Ray thought, he himself could stop drinking!

So he stopped. And felt better and healthier. Although he visited a doctor at rehab monthly, the doctor wasn't convinced it was enough. He wanted Ray to go into rehab. Ray said he didn't have the time. In December 1996, Ray started drinking again. The resumption of drinking gave him even less self-respect, and he drank even heavier than before. After the car accident though, he did finally enter rehab.

One of the principles of rehabilitation programs, formal or informal, as we saw with Jose and Jerry, is to reduce or eliminate the negative elements of life and focus on building the positive. Running is a positive element. Ray asked if he could get out of the rehab centre to go running, which they agreed to. He started running early each morning. After six weeks, he left rehab and hasn't had a drink since. But he's kept running. Later that year, 1997, he ran in the Cities Marathon in Sydney. He'd run four marathons many years earlier between 1982 and 1984, but felt he was now, again, up to the challenge. It went well and he ran another the following year, recording a time of 3:16. He kept running marathons.

According to Ray "alcoholism was only a 15-year romance, and we parted ways … I was lucky." He attended Alcoholics Anonymous for a while but stopped, he said, when he realized he had returned to who he once was. He and his wife have had a family law practice for 25 years of their 40-year relationship. Over the past ten years, he has mixed that practice with teaching an undergraduate course and a post-graduate course on family law.

In April 2009, he ran his 100th at the Canberra marathon, in a time of 3:17, which, as a 59-year old he was very happy with. He has run all his marathons in Australia, the majority in New South Wales. As of September 2009, he had run 108 marathons, with a PB of 2:58.

A friend convinced Ray to run in an ultra event. At first he didn't think it would be possible, but those little conversations, as often happen among runners, sparked something in his mind. He decided to give it a go. He's now run one 100 K run and five 100-mile races, and eagerly awaits each ultra season at the end of the year in Australia.

"I don't feel sixty", Ray says. He doesn't take any medications and doesn't see his doctor; he has trouble remembering their name. "Your health is the most important thing you'll ever have, so make sure as you get older that you have some positive things in place. If you don't have your health you've got to wonder what the big circle of life is all about."

Helen Klein started running at the age of 55. In an interview with a sports journalist, she explained that "growing up, girls were not taught to do anything like that [running distances]. They were taught knitting and sewing and cooking, all the things that would make them good housewives and mothers." It wasn't until her husband was challenged to run a 10-mile race, and he talked

Helen into doing it as well, that her running career began. She said, "We trained for 10 weeks and did the race and never stopped. It gave me a good feeling, even though I wasn't aerobically fit." Although she had been smoking most of her life, she seemed to have a gift for running.

That 10-mile race was 32 years ago.

Helen's first marathon was in Miami in 1980. She ran her first ultra in Mt Vernon, Washington the following year. In 1989, at the age of 67, she completed the ultra Grand Slam of the Western States 100, Vermont 100, Leadville, and Wasatch, and Angeles Crest – five challenging 100-mile trail runs completed in a 16-week period (only four are needed for the Grand Slam). These included over 175,000 feet in elevation change.

At last count, she had run 66 marathons and more than 140 ultras. This tally includes 280 miles in the Sri Chinmoy 5-day race (1986), the 370 mile (9 days and 4 hours) Eco Challenge Utah, the 145-mile stage race in the Himalayas at age 70, the 145-mile Marathon Des Sables stage race across the Sahara Desert in Morocco (two weeks before the Eco Challenge race) at age 72, another 140-mile stage race in the Andes at age 74, and, at age 81, the Tahoe Triple (three marathons around Lake Tahoe in 3 consecutive days in a cumulative time of 18:05). In 2002, she set a marathon world record time for the 80 to 84 age group in the Sacramento California International Marathon with a time of 4:31. At age 85, Helen completed the Napa Valley Marathon in a world age-group record time of 5:36.

Helen has been a recipient of the Arete Award which symbolizes courage in sports. At the age of 76 she was elected to the USA Track and Field Hall of Fame, and was elected into the Road Runners Hall of Fame (2004). She is one of the four ultra-runner inductees in the USATF Masters Hall of Fame. She has held American and world records in 50 K, 50M, 100 K, 100M, 24 hours, 48 hours, five-day, and six-day runs.

Helen is in her late eighties now, a retired nurse, and a legend in the ultra running world.

It's as if her last 32 years have been spent catching up for the lack of running in her first 55 years. Off the trails she is equally inspirational. With her husband, Norm Klein, she has directed many marathons and ultras, including the Napa Valley Marathon, the Western States 100, and the Helen Klein Ultra events. Helen has been quoted as saying that "ultrarunners are goal-oriented and we have a great sport characterized by sportsmanship, camaraderie, and a great deal of integrity on the part of our athletes." In addition she coaches runners whose goal is to raise money for diabetes research and education.

Helen is proof that anything is possible if you set your mind to it and believe. But running is just one part of her life. She has four children, nine grandchildren and three great-granddaughters. Helen says she is disciplined, determined, and dedicated. If she starts something, she will do her best to finish it. Her mother taught her the value of discipline, while her seventh grade teacher taught her self control. Her husband, she adds, has confidence in her ability to excel. Helen believes she is "nothing extraordinary. I was – and am – just like you are. We all have tremendous potential, but potential is an inactive state. Potential must be turned to realization. And we realize our potential by tapping it. But tapping it can transform our lives…and it doesn't have to be running we're talking about."

Helen leads by example, working to inspire people to live healthy lifestyles. "I would rather wear out than rust out", she says. "It is great to slow the aging process through physical exercise." Helen gives motivational speeches to all levels of students, the most rewarding ones, she says, being those at the elementary level. "I do motivational speaking at elementary schools, at middle schools, at senior citizen centers ... I guess I haven't learned to say no. You know, our children are so overweight now it's terrible. One in five children are overweight and that is so sad. That's the main reason I still do motivational speaking, to get the message out there ... In order to be healthy, you have to have exercise. It's what I base my life on. I don't sit. I enjoy a physical lifestyle. I'm not a sitter. This is a healthier lifestyle. It's healthy physically and mentally, as well."

Motivation and inspiration have also been a central theme of life for fellow American Jim Ottinger. Jim ran his first marathon at the age of 54 in Birmingham, Alabama in 1987. He ran his 100th in Mercedes, Alabama 20 years later, at age 73.

Jim's a large man at 6 feet 2 inches and 205 pounds, and has always been athletic. During a boxing career in his younger days that totaled 39 wins and 6 losses, he won a Golden Glove boxing title and an Olympics trials silver medal. He almost went professional, but was offered a job in Chicago at Emerson Electric, along with a place on the company's fast pitch softball team. He went to Chicago and won the World fast pitch championship in 1959 and 1961. It's said he could pitch a softball at 90 miles an hour. During his career he had 50 no-hitters and seven perfect games.

Jim was a motivational speaker at Emerson Electric, retiring from there after 44 years. He met his wife Jaye while he was conducting motivational talks. It was a blind date which ended with Jim being rushed to hospital for an emergency appendectomy. Jaye would visit and sit with him during his recovery. They now have five children and twelve grandchildren, further inspiration for Jim's running and attitude to life.

But it was in the 1980s, when some health issues emerged, that Jim decided to bring back some of the old athletic spirit into his life. His story is a familiar one. At 53 his doctor told him he had mitral valve prolapse, a form of heart disease. Jim also needed to lose at least 50 pounds, put on as a result of pushing exercise to the side and throwing himself at his work. But the biggest motivator for changing his life through marathon running was his son telling him that by not looking after himself he was 'stealing years' of his life away from his grandchildren. And so at age 54, Jim ran his first marathon. Jim was quoted as saying "I will do it one time, and then I'll quit."

Not long after his first marathon he ran his second, the New York marathon, with his two sons.

Jim and Jaye have travelled extensively around the world. His belief is that you need to make and keep goals for yourself. "It's all about accountability", he said, "If you don't tell other people your goals, if you keep them to yourself, you can fudge. Running means consistency, persistence and accountability."

As he closed in on his 100th marathon, Jim encountered other medical problems. In 2004, he was diagnosed with prostate cancer and had a radical prostatectomy. He had hernia surgery in 2005. In 2007 he experienced atrial fibrillation, a condition where the heart muscles of the atria quiver instead of making coordinated contractions. While this is not life threatening in itself, it does significantly increase the risk of a stroke. Despite this, his doctor told him he was as healthy as a 30-year-old male. Jim said in an article about his running, "I might have died a lot faster or longer ago if I had not been running."

Jim is known to make his own mottos ("Live with passion, run with Pride", for example), which he wore on his shirt for his 100th marathon. On the front of his red shirt in the 2006 New York marathon he had *Jim, Jim, Jim* which he would point to and get the crowds chanting, while on the back it read "Vintage 1933." Although he says he's not a fast runner, his PB is 4:32, he has been fortunate, especially given his size, to have avoided any running injuries. "I don't have problems with my knees or ankles", he said, "That's the Lord's work. If God made the earth in six days, He can take care of my knees. I pray about it all the time."

Jim has spent his life motivating and inspiring others, but finds his own inspiration from his grandchildren. One of his grandsons was born with his feet backward and his toes touching the back of his calf. He's had several surgeries. In the last one they cut through the bone, twisted and pinned it. At the Mercedes Kids Run, Jim ran with his grandson. "He has been through so much – he's an inspiration to anyone." In an article in *Runners World* Jim was quoted as saying, "I live my life like I'm going to be here forever." One of his goals is to live to 100 and run the New York marathon.

On the other side of the Atlantic, English messenger Keith Scrivener saw his own life transformed through running in more ways than one. Keith had "been plagued with Epilepsy" for all his younger life. It ended his RAF career, and by 1981 at age 39, the seizures had become so bad he had been revived several times. It was "crisis time", he said. He had a large mortgage, his wife Meryl, and three young children to support.

Keith's doctor was the father of David Warren, a British middle distance Olympic runner. Through these connections, Keith's doctor was friendly with Sir Roger Bannister, the first sub-four-minute miler, who also happened to be a leading neurologist. Keith was sent to Roger Bannister, who proceeded to diagnose his condition by causing him to have over 30 fits in an hour on what Keith described as a "fast twisting torture rack complete with flashing lights and loud noises" while being attached to numerous electrodes and recording machines. After Dr. Bannister examined the print outs, he gave Keith the choice of going on drugs for the rest of his life (and no longer having a driver's license), or trying out a "new radical treatment" he had devised.

The alternative to the drug regime was to start running or doing a similar energetic sport every day for the rest of his life. The idea was to make his heart beat very fast every day, which, it was theorized, would stop the electrical connections in his brain from creating the massive debilitating seizures. As well as running, Keith was put on a strict diet, with no alcohol, meat, tea, or coffee; just water, vegetables, pasta, rice and so on.

At the time, Keith was living a sedentary lifestyle, with little activity at home or work. Despite having to drastically change his habits, it was far better option for living than to be an invalid for the rest of his days.

He kick-started his new lifestyle with a twelve mile run, which kicked him right back. He was sick in a ditch and had to walk the last few miles home. He could barely move for days afterwards. But he persisted, and kept running. After a few weeks he ran a half marathon. Not long after, he ran his first full Marathon in the mountains of North Wales.

More importantly, once he had transformed his life he stopped getting the seizures. Roger Bannister was so pleased he asked Keith if he could use his case in medical books and lectures.

Keith was running every day but getting bored with doing the same thing all the time. So, in addition to running, he took up canoeing, cycling and swimming, always ensuring he got his daily heart boost. This led him into what was then a new sport: triathlons. He moved up in the triathlon distances to the longest, the Ironman – a 2.4-mile swim, 122-mile cycle and a 26.2-mile run. He won the British Ironman over-50 championships. He then graduated to the Diamond Man distance in Quadrathlons, which are like the Ironman but with a longer 3.2 mile swim and the addition of a 12-mile sea kayak. He represented the United Kingdom in his age group in three World Championships and three European Championships. At his best, he was ranked number three in the world.

But after years of transporting his 20-foot long kayak and racing bike through airports and getting them stored in foreign hotels, Keith finally decided it was "too much." When he retired from work at 60, he also retired from multi-sports. But he joined a running club for the first time ever, and got exposed to a wider range of running events.

Unfortunately, he faced another medical setback in that same year. He contracted Weil's disease, a relatively rare bacterial infection that humans may get through contact with water, food or soil containing urine from infected animals. The disease destroys the kidneys and liver and can be fatal. Fortunately, Keith's doctor recognized the symptoms and treated him with the strongest antibiotics available, although he was not able to stand for weeks. At the same time, he developed a large cancer growth that needed to be removed through an operation. Ill health, of course, can be problematic for Keith if he cannot get the exercise he needs to counter the epilepsy.

"I still carried on running because I had to" he said, "but without a real goal to aim at it was hard to go out every day." One of his friends at the Great Bentley Running Club suggested he set his sights on 100 marathons. Although not running as fast as he once had, the goal served as his motivation and inspiration. To date, Keith has run over 108 marathons (PB 3:20) and ultras, completing his 100th in 2008.

A couple of years ago, Keith wrote to Roger Bannister, congratulating him on the 50th anniversary of his first four minute mile triumph and to tell him that thanks to him he was still clear of his epilepsy after 25 years. Roger Bannister replied, saying to Keith that it was the first time his two great loves, athletics and medicine, had came together as a treatment that worked. For Keith, quite simply, the treatment saved his life and changed his life.

When he was 46-years old fellow Englishman Robbie Wilson had one of those life-changing moments. He carried 15 stone of weight (210 lbs) on his five feet, seven inch frame. The weight had accumulated over the years through drinking about 15 pints of beer every day, along with Bacardi and coke chasers. "My stomach went from my chin down to my knees" he said, "a big fat face hidden with a full faced beard."

He was at the local cricket club in Surrey, England, where he was membership secretary, when he saw a man he didn't recognize. He went over to introduce himself and collect the member's fee. He discovered he'd been looking in a mirror. "A great beery, overweight slob", he said. "I needed a sport to save my life, and it had to be running." While Robbie took up running, his friends took up golf. "They're all dead now", he says. "There's no doubt I would be in my own grave now if I hadn't changed my ways."

He stopped drinking, got into running and lost 84 pounds (6 of his 15 stone). It didn't happen all at once of course, although the following weekend he found himself running in a five-mile cross-country race to help make up numbers for the event. He was only there, he said, to watch his son run. He explained in a later newspaper article that it felt like a lifetime going over boggy ground, hills, tree roots ... he raised his arms to celebrate crossing the finish line only to be told he'd only run one lap. He eventually finished and was "quite invigorated and had a sense of achievement." So he joined the Collingwood Athletic club.

Although now running, Robbie hadn't completely stopped drinking. Lunchtime drinking, close to where he worked as a Post Office manager, was doing most of the damage. So much so that he felt he was on the verge of being an alcoholic. The next biggest transformation for him was training for, and completing, the London marathon. He said "All the hardships in life are described as a marathon, so what an achievement if you could run one." He had a shower put in his office and he'd run to work and back from his home. He stopped drinking. The weight, he said, quickly disappeared. He went down to 133 pounds, which has been his weight ever since.

At 74 years of age Robbie 'Red Hat' has run over 320 marathons and ultras. He's called red hat because he has worn the same hat in every run. It's now almost in tatters and completely faded. One weekend in Spain, he lost it off a balcony, but fortunately found it in some garbage down the street.

It's hard for me to imagine Robbie at 15 stone because when I ran with him in England a couple of years ago he was a spritely, energetic runner who happily chatted away. "I treat most marathons now as a weekend away, so I look for an interesting location, or a foreign country that appeals to me", he said. He reflected on the past weekend: "That was great meeting my 100 marathon club mates, and having a drink afterwards with them, swapping stories en route; something to look back on. It's now a social thing. I always meet so many friends. An excuse also for a long weekend away. And I do it to keep fit and keep the weight off."

Robbie told me that he sometimes wonders how he does it. 'What with six grandchildren, and an allotment [small garden], even though I retired 16 years ago I still work as a gardener. When gardening in my two-acre gardens I jog with the wheelbarrow, stretch when doing various tasks, and think running and what I can do to improve fitness at all times. Don't waste a minute of your life. I enjoy all my training and running marathons. I try and have a great laugh and not take it too serious."

Although bettering his PB of 3:03 may no longer be possible, Robbie's main goal now is to become the oldest runner still running marathons. He's come a long way since his first marathon in 1982. More importantly, he's still alive and healthy, both of which would have been doubtful had he continued his previous lifestyle. He's even been able to run marathons with his granddaughter Ellie, which gives him a huge sense of accomplishment.

In 1978, at 28 years of age, American messenger Marshall Ulrich was living what he calls his "calculated, planned out, no-stopping, always-move-ahead, nothing-will-stand-in-my-way life." Marshall was working 12-hour days while starting up a byproducts business. He was married to Jean, also 28, and they'd been together ever since they first met in high school. Jean had graduated from law school the year before, and was now practicing. They had just had a daughter, Elaine. Suddenly, as Marshall wrote in Marathon and Beyond, "life began to unravel."

"Jean was diagnosed with cancer ... My blood pressure skyrocketed as Jean suffered and started fading away, so I started running."

Two years later, Jean died and Marshall was alone with their three-year old daughter. Running was his way of surviving. He said he was a confused, terrified young father. He ran and kept running – running harder and longer. He wrote: "I didn't know what I was running from or running to. I knew only that running was familiar to me. It was something I could control."

His running started small, with five and ten mile runs. But he jumped to marathons fairly quickly. In 1988, after his first two 100- mile races, he started to believe he had some kind of ability with long distance races and could recover quickly. Much of this could be attributed to his days growing up on the family farm in Colorado and the work ethic that went along with long, full, physical days cutting and baling hay, and working at night salting hides in his early days of starting a business. These days he told me, "instead of bales, it's just miles."

Marshall's physical toughness was built on these foundations, and he ran more often and further, always challenging himself and pushing to see whether he could achieve the new goals he kept setting. Deep down he was still running scared from his earlier suffering with Jean's death. Marshall said his running was compulsive, addictive behavior. In 2006 he wrote that "my attempt to be an island unto myself was hurtful to others." He remarried, and had two more children. But they divorced in 1992. He kept "running from reality" as he put it. "I hid my fear of dying, my fear of being hurt. I was still scared ... My fear of dying kept me from living."

But running was his life.

Marshall's endurance and extreme sports achievements speak for themselves. He has completed more than 120 ultras (averaging more than 100 miles each). In 1989 he completed all six 100-mile trail races in the United States in one season. He has won the 146-mile Badwater race, from 282 feet below sea level to the 14,494-foot summit of Mount Whitney, a record four times. Marshall has crossed Death Valley a record 21 times, including a 586-mile Badwater Quad (two out and back trips of the race), and also ran Badwater in a self-contained, unaided solo. In 2008, he completed a 3,063-mile run across the United States in 52.5 days (with an average of more than 58 miles a day, equal to 117 marathons). He set new Grand Master's and Master's records, and achieved the third fastest crossing ever on that route. He was 57 years old.

Marshall has also completed nine Eco Challenge adventure races. If that isn't enough, he has climbed the tallest summit on each continent, an achievement known as the Seven Summits, including Mt. Everest, which he climbed as part of a Russian team in

2004, fulfilling a dream he had as a five-year old, and managing his fear of heights in the process.

His goals these days still include endurance events but he has shifted focus to helping others achieve their goals and to raising funds for charities. He has raised over $850,000 for charities, including the Religious Teachers Filippini, a small religious order that has a mission to empower women and children in the poorest parts of the world through education.

Marshall said he had an epiphany in 2001 while he was running the Badwater Quad. He realized that he wasn't running for himself anymore, he was running for others – helping others by raising funds through his extreme sports activities. He'd found his true purpose. He had been given a gift – the ability to do extreme endurance challenges – and he is able to use that gift to give to others. "I still feel like I'm a normal, average guy", he told me, "there's many others out there who are doing much more significant things than me, and contributing to society. It's becoming more important to be socially responsible."

Marshall leads by example and speaks from experience. He believes we are all more capable than we think we are. As well as continuing his endurance activities to raise funds for worthy causes, he's become a motivational speaker, trainer, guide and author.

And he's keenly aware of the necessity for people to have balance in their lives. This is what he tells others now. "If the balance in my life goes to shit", he said, "my wife [he remarried] is the first to point it out.… Invariably she's right 99.9% of the time. It's part of why our relationship works so well. Her love for me … she understands it's a huge part of who I am." As Marshall himself wrote in 2006, "I realized that stepping outside of yourself and doing for others is the true essence of life. I have found a new purpose for life, a purpose outside of myself. Only this has elevated my quality of existence and has saved me."

**

Ray James, the Australian messenger we met earlier, has now run over 108 marathons, as well as five-100 milers. When I last talked to Ray he emphasized that we all need to have a strong mind; that we have a soft and a hard side to our mind. Our mind, if you will, talks to itself during a long distance race, just as it does in life. When you've faced alcoholism head on and taken a positive path, you've built that stronger side as it's overcome the easier path of having another drink. That builds an inner strength that can be taken into distance running. "I enjoy exploring the limits", Ray said, "if there's pain, then so be it." There is an inner confidence about yourself and your capacity to cope, to overcome whatever is in your path. The pain endured in a run pales in comparison to pain endured with alcoholism.

The longer runs, the ultras, require a much longer time for your mind to face the challenges encountered. "They're like marathons in slow motion. With all the things going on in your mind. That's where the challenges lie; not in the 'physicalness' of the distance itself, but in the mind."

Alcoholics often lose their self-respect, which is an important contributor to happiness. For runners who have overcome the challenges brought on from alcohol addiction, opportunities emerge to regain self-respect. This is especially apparent when people read, hear or meet runners such as Ray, Jerry and Jose, and are inspired by what they have accomplished in their lives and how this carries over into the running world. This inspiration – the seeking of advice and the ongoing interaction further improves these messengers' own self-respect. As Ray pointed out, "[with alcoholism] you lose your self-respect, but with people respecting me for what I do, I'm getting it back." This, he says, transfers into different attitudes in other parts of his life as well, such as a more positive approach to work, and improved relationships with friends and family.

While running is not *the* panacea for all that ails, it is a catalyst for positive change, one that is reinforced by the positive approach to life that many marathoners share.

20

"While running a marathon is far from damaging,
it should be respected for the physiological stress
inflicted over its 26.2 miles."

Jake Emmett

"Distance running has a higher injury rate
than most other sports."

Ross Tucker and Jonathan Dugas

It is estimated that you take somewhere between 30,000 and 50,000 steps as you cover the 26.2 mile marathon distance. That is a great deal of repetition; a great deal of continual impact on your muscles, bones and connective tissues. You need to spend a significant period of time, typically several months, to adequately prepare your body for the stress and strain that accompanies a long distance running event like a marathon.

Ross Tucker and Jonathan Dugas explain in their 2009 book '*The Runner's Body*' that every time our foot hits the ground there is a force of two to four times our body weight moving upward through our lower leg, knee, thigh, hip and pelvis and spine.

They liken these forces to the seismic activity of an earthquake moving around the walls of buildings. And like a building, some areas of the body are more susceptible to damage, to injury, than others. Importantly, they write, that "with repeated stress *and recovery*, bone adapts by becoming denser and stiffer, thus more injury resistant; novice runners have not yet achieved the adaptations that take many months and perhaps years of consistent running to develop."

Tucker and Dugas go on to note that several studies have shown that experienced runners who have trained for several years are significantly less likely to become injured than new runners. A major reason for this, they say, is that over time the experienced runners' connective tissues become more durable and their bone density increases.

On the one hand, if you run more you will strengthen the durability of your body but, on the other hand, too much running, and at too fast a pace, increases the possibility of injuries. The trick is to find the right balance – and to learn how not to push your body beyond its limits that could result in serious injuries.

In a 2007 article in *Marathon and Beyond* Dr. Jake Emmett asked: Just what does running a marathon do to your body? Dr. Emmett, who teaches exercise science class at Eastern Illinois University, writes "running a five-minute-per-mile marathon requires a 15-fold increase in energy production for over two hours. Even runners who finish in over four hours maintain a 10-fold increase in their metabolism." Our cardio-respiratory, endocrine and neuromuscular systems are all under considerable stress for a long period of time.

In endurance events such as marathons the body requires a constant flow of energy to maintain performance. It requires glucose, which is found in the blood supply and as glycogen in the liver. This glycogen comes from our consumption of carbohydrates. If we don't have enough glycogen stored then the body will instead convert its own fat for fuel. When the glycogen reserves are used up the transition to burning body fats for the necessary fuel is known as 'hitting the wall' or 'bonking'. At this noticeable point, everything, it seems, becomes extremely difficult and performance takes a significant downward turn.

While there are many health benefits to training for, and running, a marathon it still warrants close attention to potential damaging effects, especially if a runner has a history of heart disease in their family, has high cholesterol, or is a smoker. Doctors should be consulted first if these conditions exist, and most certainly if the runner is over the age of 45 and contemplating running a marathon. Dr. Emmett cites research evidence from a number of studies in his article. For example:

- If a runner does not consume carbohydrates during a marathon, liver glycogen depletion can occur within two hours (Noakes, 2003).
- Muscle damage and inflammation can remain for seven days after having run a marathon (Hikida et al, 1983).
- Taking carbohydrates during exercise helps prevent hypoglycemia and improves performance (Tsintzas and Williams, 1999).
- The repair of muscle fibers can take three to 12 weeks (Warhol et al, 1985).
- Higher levels of training decrease the risk of knee injuries but increase the risk of injury to the quadriceps and hamstrings *during* a marathon (Satterthwaite, 1999).
- Twenty-nine percent to 43% of runners develop injuries during training.
- The muscle damage incurred from running a marathon can divert some immune cells for muscle repair and weaken others, leaving the immune system less able to protect against upper respiratory tract infections (Nehlsen- Cannarella, et al 1997).
- The risk of sudden death is greater in marathon runners who have a positive family history, elevated cholesterol and warning signs such as angina, nausea, and epigastric discomfort (Noakes, 2007).

Despite these effects on the body, Dr. Emmett notes that the actual running of a marathon, once the recovery process is complete, will contribute to a stronger heart, and stronger bones and muscles. On top of this are the many emotional, mental, spiritual and social benefits.

The key for any runner is to ensure they have an appropriate level of training for the energy they anticipate expending in the long distance endurance event itself.

Jeff Galloway is a messenger who has dedicated his life to training individuals for marathons and other running distances. Jeff writes in 'Marathon You can do it!', one of over a dozen books he has written on running: "The marathon is primarily an endurance event. It is only secondarily a race and should not be an ordeal. This isn't to say it should be a walk in the park, but you should be able to finish a marathon, enjoy the sense of achievement it gives you, and look forward to running your next one." Jeff goes on to say that he ran his first 60 marathons "hard." But now after more than 50 additional marathons he runs "within himself." "I've received the same satisfaction, sense of achievement, and internal glow from all the slow ones as I did from the fast ones. The main difference is that I could appreciate the satisfaction and celebrate the achievement on the slow ones. I wasn't very social for very long after the fast ones."

Running within oneself. It is a key phrase that explains just how the messengers are able to run so many, over such a long time period, without significant injuries; all the while feeling stronger mentally, socially, emotionally, spiritually, and, physically.

The UK 100 Marathon Club vets 70+ picking up the prizes. **Left to Right:** Colin Poole, John Dawson, Ray Bennett and Robbie 'Redhat' Wilson.

Holly Koester, coming up the last hill in Alaska.

American messenger Marshall Ulrich (courtesy of GoLite).

Linda Major, Simon Beresford and John Dawson at the end of the marathon in Furth, Germany.

Englishman Roger Biggs at his 500th marathon. The first non-North American to complete the 50 states.

British messenger Jack Brooks celebrating completion of the 50 states.

Elaine Doll-Dunn.

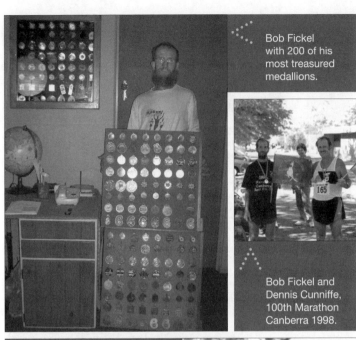

Bob Fickel with 200 of his most treasured medallions.

Bob Fickel and Dennis Cunniffe, 100th Marathon Canberra 1998.

Ray James, at age 58, finishing at the Gold Coast Marathon, Australia, 2007 in a time of 2.59.40.

British messenger Keith Scrivener.

Australian messenger Bob Fickel's 200th Marathon, 2010 Macleay River Marathon. **Back:** Brian Glover, Peter Gray, Steel Beveridge, Grahame Kerruish, Ray James, Chris Stephenson
Front: Dennis Cunniffe, Bob Fickel, Bruce Hargreaves

Jose Nebrida, inspired and inspiring. Photo courtesy of Adrenaline Event Photography.

Marshall Ulrich in 1999, during his unaided, self-contained solo crossing from Badwater to the summit of Mount Whitney: 146 miles in 77 hours and 46 minutes.

21

"If we had known the time that the Greek soldier
had needed for the distance, we could have set up a record.
I, personally, claim the honour of sponsoring
the marathon trophy."

Michel Bréal, 1894

Marathon running emerged as a serious sporting event in the
very first modern Olympics held in Athens in 1896. Fittingly, the
marathon race was run from Marathonas into the Panathinaikon
Stadium in what is now downtown Athens – a distance of 25
miles. There were just 17 runners, mostly Greek. All the runners
walked at some point, and one of them cheated. The eventual
winner, Spiridon Louis, had a glass of wine at the halfway mark,
and received a kiss and a hug and some orange slices at mile 23
from his girlfriend, Eleni. He became a national hero overnight,
and is immortalized now in Greek language with the saying *Yi-
nome Louis*, which means '*to become Louis*' - to disappear by
running fast.

Why did they hold this distance race in Greece? Because in 490
BC the Athenians defeated a huge invading Persian army on the
plains of Marathon. Legend has it that immediately that victory
was won, the hemerodromoi – the messenger, Pheidippides – who
we met at the beginning of the book, was dispatched to Athens
to tell the news. The Athenians were preparing to burn their city
to the ground rather than have it overrun by the Persian army.

Pheidippides needed to get there as soon as possible to convey the news. He told the news of the victory as soon as he arrived, and then died.

It's a great story. But we don't *really* know what happened. We're not sure about his name. We're not sure if it was he who actually ran from Marathon to Athens. We're not one hundred percent certain about the route. We don't know if he did collapse and die when he arrived in Athens to give his message. And why were horses not used instead of runners, especially over what is typically believed to be the route? And the story itself has been passed down, literally, through the centuries, first by Herodotus, who wasn't even alive at the time of the battle and who only wrote about it 40 years later, and then by Plutarch and Lucian. The story was modified each time it was told.

In his 1979 paper 'The Dubious Origins of the Marathon' in the *American Journal of Ancient History*, FJ Frost raises doubts about the authenticity of Pheidippide's run. Frost writes, "For all we know, every great battle in antiquity eventually attracted anecdoctal embroidery like this, with a runner arriving at the gates of the victorious city, gasping out the good news and breathing his last."

But it's still a great story.

Hundreds of years later, the story caught poet Robert Browning's attention and inspired him to write a poem about it – *Pheidippides* – in 1879. Browning was the son of an abolitionist father who had a personal library of over 6,000 books. By age 14 Browning was fluent in English, French, Greek, Italian and Latin. He secretly courted Elizabeth Barrett, who became a renowned poet in her own right, and in 1846 they married and quickly fled to Italy where they remained for many years. It wasn't until much later in his life, after Elizabeth's death, that Browning wrote the poem that, as Roger Robinson put it in his book *Running in Literature*, "invented the Marathon."

Having researched the origins of the marathon, Robinson notes that "It is without parallel in being a major sports event that has entirely literary origins." He added: "The poem thus transformed a sport (long distance running) that in Browning's day was little more than a seedy gambling activity or a paper chase. It gave a symbolic focus to an idealistic movement for international unity that had not yet been born (the revived Olympics)." "With its dramatic pace and energy", he noted, *Pheidippides* is a compelling poem." Again though, like others centuries before him, Browning embellished or enhanced the story to romanticize it further – with a love interest, and the messenger actually fighting in the battle, for example.

The significant moment in the evolution of the marathon event came when Browning's little known poem attracted the eyes and mind of Michel Bréal, a Frenchman considered to be the founder of modern semantics. More significantly, the running world would say, he suggested to his friend Pierre de Frédy, Baron de Coubertin, the founder of the modern Olympics, that there should be a long distance race to commemorate the Battle of Marathon in which Pheidippides had made that legendary run to Athens.

In a letter to his friend in 1894, Bréal wrote: "If you go to Athens, you could try and see if a long distance run from Marathon to Pnyx could be organized (the current Panathinaikon stadium). That would emphasize the character of Antiquity. If we had known the time that the Greek soldier had needed for the distance, we could have set up a record. I, personally, claim the honour of sponsoring the marathon trophy."

In the first printed program for the marathon, the distance was said to be approximately 48 K, which implied a route over the mountains into Athens, but in the programs that went out with the invitations only 42 K was mentioned. In the end, on race day, the distance was 25 miles (40.24 K).

Baron de Coubertin had wide ranging academic interests, but his primary focus was physical education and the role of sport in schooling. He held an idealized vision of ancient Greece, which in part was responsible for the emergence of the modern Olympic Games. He also felt that men who had physical education would

175

be better fighters in wars. More importantly, he thought of sport as being democratic. He visited England twice, as a 20-year old in 1883, and again in 1886, spending time at Rugby School, where the game Rugby was invented after students picked up the soccer ball and ran with it, not realizing they had unleashed a new sport that would hold much of the world captivated less than a century later. Upon his examination of the English schools, de Coubertin came to the conclusion that organized sport could create moral and social strength. A modern Olympic Movement, through organized sport, could improve the education of young people. He saw the logic of the mind and the body working with one another to essentially make a better, more satisfied, happy and fulfilled individual. The positive addiction of sports would also occupy the individual's mind and time, and that would prevent, or replace, negative addictions from taking hold.

The ancient Greeks had already 'been there', of course, but watching the games of rugby, of which he became a great fan, reinforced de Coubertin's growing belief that education had forgotten what to him was self-evident – that physical activity was central to the development of the human character.

In 1890, he returned to England and visited Much Wenlock, Shropshire, where they had arranged a revival of the Olympic Games. Entranced by its success and similar revivals in Greece, along with archaeological finds at Olympia, he felt the timing was right to create something new and significant. To cut a long story short, the Olympic movement was born.

De Coubertin became president of the International Olympic Committee (IOC) after the Athens Olympics. He resigned after the 1924 Olympics, but was made Honorary President of the IOC until he died in 1937. Although buried in Lausanne (the official headquarters of the IOC), his heart was buried separately, as he requested, in a monument near the ruins of ancient Olympia.

The evolution of the marathon meanwhile, continued over the years, with the actual distance variable. The first Boston marathon was run in 1897 over a distance of 24.5 miles. It wasn't until the

Dorango Pietri – Johnny Hayes race in the London Olympics in 1908 that the marathon distance of 26.2 miles emerged. It was suppose to be 26 miles. The marathon event was scheduled to be started by the King at Windsor Castle on "The Long Walk" section of the grounds, and to finish after a clockwise run around the track at the Royal Box in the Stadium. Instead, it started at the eastern terrace of the Castle, which as John Bryant wrote in *The Marathon Makers* in 2008, "introduced yet another mystery into the problem of the distance." Bryant notes that modern day research that recreates the start of the 1908 race along with modern day measurement of the distance suggests in fact that the first mile was 174 yards short. He adds: "The mystery of the missing 174 yards and the question of who first suggested shifting the start to the East Terrace may consume sports historians and statisticians for the next 100 years."

In any case, the 55 competitors ran point-to-point from 'there' to White City Stadium (originally *The Great Stadium*) where the Queen was soon to witness one of the most dramatic finishes to a marathon of all time. It wasn't until 1921 that the International Athletics Federation finally ratified 26 miles and 385 yards (42.195 kilometres) as the official marathon distance. The reason for that is another story.

The rest, as they say, is history.

Women did not run in any marathon until the 1960s. Kathrine Switzer was the first woman to officially run the Boston marathon In 1967 she registered for the marathon as K. Switzer. It made world headlines because women at that time were not allowed to compete in the Boston marathon. When Jock Semple, the race director, discovered a woman was running, he tried to physically remove Kathrine from the course. It didn't work because her boyfriend at the time – a footballer – blocked Semple, who went flying. It was all captured in photographs. Kathrine Switzer went on to become a world class marathoner and dedicated herself to promoting women's marathoning around the world. She still does. Her concerted efforts, and those of others, eventually led to the first women's marathon event at the 1984 Olympics.

In the year 2010, it seems astonishing that it has only been since 1984 that women have had an Olympic marathon.

So the marathon origins are based on a battle in 492 BC, the details of which are sketchy and only brought to our wider attention through the pen of Robert Browning, who inspired Michel Bréal, who in turn influenced Pierre de Coubertin, who in turn got the support of the Greeks to host the event that would be known as *The Marathon*. It then took another 25 years for what, really, is an odd distance, to be ratified as *the* marathon distance. And half the world's population could not officially run marathons until the 1960s.

It's now estimated that there are around one million marathon finishers in the world every year. Over forty-one percent of these are women. More and more people are running marathons every year. The goal is common but the reason for completing a long distance race can be quite different from one person to another.

The marathon experience is a social movement. And where there are people involved, you can never be sure what can happen from one moment to the next.

22

"The fun stuff is when things don't go as planned."
Todd Byers

"On most weekends there is a funny story."
Linda Major

Some of the memorable long distance running experiences occur while training. Jeffrey Horowitz was out for a training run when he got stuck in a 'port-a-john' that was being taken away while he ran along the Charles River in Boston the day after the 4th of July celebration. 'Luckily, the driver heard me, stopped the truck, and let me out'. In England meanwhile, Robbie Wilson was out training with eight Collingwood club members; most dropped out over the run, so that by the time they were running through Oak Park there was just three of them left. Robbie had to go to the toilet, 'number 2', and said to the others to go ahead, he'd catch up. 'I didn't fancy them watching me do my business'.

As he was near a public footpath he had to go deep into the woods, against a wire fence, looking around at all times in case anyone was coming by. As Robbie explains from this point ... 'I was doing my business when, like a bolt of lightning, something was licking my arse. What was it? A bloody great big horse (there were two of them). What a fright. Then I ran out of toilet paper and I had to use leaves and suchlike. Off I went home, but something was still not right, it was uncomfortable running. It could be a couple of leaves doing a rub job. Home I arrived and straight up for a shower…. A great flow of twigs and leaves washed down the plug hole. Something was still wrong; something was still up there. After using the shower gel to loosen the object, down it came, with the help from my finger. There it was a great big acorn. Hence the story I often tell - *Two Horses and one Acorn'*.

It is often the logistics of getting to a distance run that becomes etched into the memory. More than one messenger observed that the actual running of an event is the easiest part of the total experience. John McFarlane tells the story of the time when he and a friend drove from England to Belgrade, Serbia to run in the marathon. They set out on the Thursday evening and arrived 36 hours later only to be given the wrong directions to register. By the time it was all sorted out the race had begun. So they got back in the car and drove to Munich, Germany where they entered and successfully ran that race, despite the lack of sleep. Then they drove back and were at work again Tuesday morning.

Jeff Hagen recounted the time while traveling to and from Yakima in Washington State to the 100th running of the Boston Marathon in 1996. The flights were jammed because of the 40,000 runners in the race. "My wife and I gave up our seats on four different flights and received $2,400 in airline vouchers. We arrived home exactly twenty-four hours late, but we used the vouchers to take our two daughters to Washington, DC, and had enough left over for a delightful trip to Hawaii."

Christian Hottas, Barbara Szlachetka and a friend ran an afternoon marathon in Neubrandenburg, Germany and then drove 700km to Viborg, Denmark for a 5am start. They stopped briefly in Hamburg for a shower and pasta, and Barbara needed to pick up her passport. They arrived in Viborg at 4:40am, just in time for the race, in which it rained all the time.

It's the same sort of "craziness" in North America. Larry Macon, for example, has a reputation of "almost flying" as he finishes one event so he can get back on the road as quick as possible to race another one the next day, or later the same day. Other messengers have referred to Larry as a "wild man." His ritual can include getting changed in the car en route. Dave Bell and a friend decided to run marathons in two days. They ran the first in Tennessee, and then drove to Kentucky in time for the second one. At least so they thought. They had forgotten about the time zone change and arrived at the race with runners already on their way. The Race Director "was generous and got them going."

Bruce Katter, who has since passed away, was well known to many messengers, and is remembered as "thoughtful and caring, talented, competitive, adventuresome, clever and full of surprises." One year he was Bob Dolphin's support person for the Western States 100. As told in a newsletter, "The night before the race, the two of them decided to stay in sleeping bags on a grassy area near the starting line to make sure they'd be on time the next morning. Good choice!! They were awakened several hours before the start when the automatic sprinkler system turned on."

Pam Penfield says she has been known as a task master. One season while doing a long training run for the Honolulu Marathon she started with a friend and her husband Gary. After getting ahead of them after about seven miles she discovered they were nowhere to be found. "After about an hour in the ritzy Kahala neighbourhoods I spotted an open house. I am not sure why but I went in the million dollar house and found the both of them schmoozing with the realtor and drinking coffee. It was really funny since I had thought they wanted all those preparation miles. They didn't."

Jack Brooks and fellows Brits Roger Biggs and Big Dave Carter stayed with Bruce Katter during their visit to run marathons in the United States. Bruce had two spare beds and a camp bed. Jack describes one evening: "It was obvious from the start that Big Dave and the camp bed was not a perfect pairing and I drew the short straw. Halfway through the night I visited the bathroom. Not wishing to wake anybody I crept there and back in the dark. Alas when I alighted on the camp bed the two ends closed in on me like a Venus fly-trap. It took some time to extract myself from this predicament. Everybody was highly amused at my misfortune as

I recounted my misadventure the following morning and I swear that even Bruce's dog was smirking."

In England Linda Major recounted a race when her running friend Colin found a pair of glasses in his goody bag. He decided to wear them at the post race celebration only to find that they belonged to the local priest, who had lost them in one of the bags he was helping to make up.

New Zealander Dave Penfold was running in a race huddled in amongst a group of other runners – the group had said to Dave that he should run with them; they'd give him shelter on what was a very cold and wet day. He said 'thanks' and was grateful for the respite. One woman, Sue Carr, who Dave did not know at the time, said she was trying to qualify for Boston. Everyone left at the end of the run and that was the last he saw of them.

Until he himself was running the Boston marathon. While running the course he got a tap on the shoulder: "Do you recognize me", a woman said. "No", replied Dave. It was Sue, who had also qualified. Dave and Sue ran to the finish line together.

Van Phan was been running an ultra with another woman. The other woman "went into a potty stop and came out and ran nude from there on." Jack Brooks ran the Cape Town Marathon in South Africa one year; he asked others where the toilets were only to find one toilet, no door. Everyone was able to watch. Still along the same theme, in a marathon in Australia, Jim Barnes saw the effects of the heat and distance: "I saw a fella in one marathon who went funny – he went into the bushes to have a crap and came out with his trousers down and started running in the wrong direction. He had to be caught and picked up and taken away."

Still in rural Australia, Dennis Cunniffe was competing in a marathon in the countryside when he came to a junction in the road – he went right instead of left – the race official on duty, not knowing he was deaf, shouted at Dennis from behind to turnaround. Dennis carried on running the wrong way. Finally, after not seeing an aid station for some time he began to realize he must have gone the wrong way, which he had. His marathon included an extra 16 K of distance.

New Zealander Robert Treneman ran a marathon in South Africa and finished in a time of 2:47. It felt like a good time so he was surprised to be beaten on the line by a woman wearing a knee length dress and running in bare feet. At Mile 25 of the Tri-city marathon near a golf driving range Carol Dellinger was hit in the left breast by a golf-ball. "It felt like I'd been shot. It left perfect dimple indentations. I'm a small B Cup but was a D Cup for the next three weeks. I still have the golf ball in my Trophy Case."

Jim Manford told the story of his experience at the Pennine marathon: "I was running along talking to a friend at the 23 mile mark of the race when I realized he hadn't replied for about 5 minutes. At first I thought he must just be out of breath until I was told by a cyclist that he'd been side-swiped by a caravan and left lying in the road about half a mile back." Jim added, "It isn't really funny but we both laughed afterwards"!

A few messengers described a marathon in the Netherlands a couple of years ago. There were less than one mile laps around a housing estate: "You'd think it would be boring but all the spectators had a list of the names of people running and were cheering you on. Plus with each lap you'd run through the middle of a pub." One of the Brits didn't run but instead fuelled up the eighteen 100 Marathon club runners, out of the one hundred who ran, when they required it. Physically the race went through one set of pub doors up a ramp through a courtyard and out onto the street. Each year the community changes the venue and theme.

A few years ago John Sturley was running the New York marathon. John was helping a British lady who was having difficulties during the last four miles. At the finish line "she leaned into me and I thought I was going to at least get a kiss for my troubles, but no. She promptly went white as a sheet and threw up right in front of me! Next time I see a runner of either sex in trouble maybe I'll not be so chivalrous, and let them struggle through to the finish on their own."

You meet some interesting characters in the race itself. John Zeleznikow, for example, ran a marathon in Florence, Italy when he saw a competitor running with a baby in her pram. And although no-one under 18 is typically allowed to compete in a marathon John spent most of the race running with a 7-year old. "It seems that the boy's Grandmother and mother and father and family were all running the marathon."

John Bozung had a less than humorous experience on his own Squaw Peak 50 Mile Trail Run. On the race's website there is an image of a cougar. It's a very personal reminder to John who had the unenviable experience of meeting one first-hand on the trail.

John and Ken Myers were working on the trail for the inaugural running of the race, and were coming separate ways to meet up and finish for the day. The race was due to begin in two days. John had just come off a patch of snow and heard a noise behind him. A cougar had slid down a snow bank onto the trail, about 20 yards away. The cougar sat there eying John up. After a minute the cougar stood up and started walking towards John. John in the meantime was thinking what to do. He remembered the movie 'Shoot to kill' starring Sidney Pointier. He thought of the Grizzly Bear scene – the actual real Bear, Bart, was trained nearby – and so he began screaming and looking 'Big'. He pulled his fanny pack off and started swinging it wildly. The only things he could throw at the cougar were snowballs. Slowly reaching down he rolled a snowball and threw it at the cougar. The cougar watched as the ball went by him. John threw another behind the cougar and it chased after it. As he did so, John walked back a few more yards and was able to get to a pine tree. He turned his head as he picked up a branch, taking his eye off the cougar. The cougar, seeing this, was now coming at him, getting ready to pounce.

The cougar stopped his charge when John set his eyes on the animal once more. By this point there were just a few yards between them. John used his branch like a baseball bat and was able to grab some rocks. The first one he threw missed the cougar … "nerves", said John. The second one hit the cougar in the ribs, making it jump in the air not unlike you'd see in a cartoon. He threw another that hit the ground in front of the cougar and another went past it. The cougar turned and went down a bank. John made a fast escape to put as much distance as possible between he and the cougar. It was now 8:45 in the evening and it would be getting dark at 9pm. He still had a few miles to go to get to his truck. John would run fifteen feet, stop and look. Run fifteen feet, stop and look. About five minutes later a Sage Grouse flew out of the bushes beside John, and he says his life flashed before him. Fortunately he didn't see the cougar again. As John says, "Had I not heard him slide on the snow he would've had me."

You will see costumes of all sorts at many races; some of which are worn by the messengers. Once a year, Englishman John Wallace, the original long distance runner superman, does a bucket run to raise money for charity. Children (and adults) love to drop the coins into the bucket. In one bucket run he collected 1,400 pounds. He gets 'immense satisfaction' from doing this. One year someone broke into his car and stole six buckets of coins, so he lost 1,000 pounds. To make up for it he organized a dance and raised the 1,000 pounds, again. John has raised over $100,000 for charities over the years, and gets sponsors through work and friends. He's raised money, for example, for Nightingale Hospice, Autism, Medical Centres, kidney transplants, cystic fybrosis among other worthwhile causes. Sometimes organizations contact John asking him if he would raise money on their behalf.

Fellow UK 100 Marathon Club member Osy Waye also enjoys raising money and donning the costumes. Over the years he's raised money for Guide Dogs for the Blind, Save the Children, the Centre for Cerebral Palsy, and a local Church Soup Kitchen, and he's dressed variously as a polar bear, a mummy, and a clown. "I'm keen to dress-up", he said, "it makes you feel like a bit of a celebrity. You cheer others along, wave to spectators, have fun with the children. You don't see many mummies out there; but there's lots of clowns though." Osy has also been part of the 'bucket brigade' in the London marathon. One year he carried two buckets around for people to drop their money in, but after just three miles he had to discard the buckets as they became too heavy. Osy, like many others, has approached corporations for support but it's hard he says, and often doesn't work, partly because they are always getting asked. What's important he says, is "that people are interested in giving to the charity and that they not see it as giving money to you."

Another 'unsung hero' as others put it, is fellow Brit, Big Dave Carter. Dave often runs his marathons wearing a jester's costume. He was featured in a Marine Corps Marathon program in 2003. When he was traveling for marathons one year he ran with a large flag that read 'Big Dave's World Marathon Tour'. He also dressed in his jester costume which had the British flag design incorporated into the garment.

Friendships are important to everyone I've interviewed for this book. Todd Byers told me of his chance meeting with Ken Saxton on a beach, through a mutual friend one year. The three ran along the beach as Ken talked about the virtues of running barefoot, which he did regularly. Todd decided to give running barefoot a try. "You were designed to run without shoes", he said to me, "so what we do is train our feet to fit our shoes. You have to do it properly, but if you learn how to do it right you'll have a good time Malcolm."

I've tried it; it feels great. While running with a new barefoot runner one year Todd looked over and saw the runner was smiling, a lot. Todd asked him why he was smiling and the runner replied that the barefoot run was ticklish on his feet. A few years ago a reporter wrote a skeptical article on barefoot running. Then months later he was asking Todd about it at a race and Todd explained it to him – "it almost felt like a forty-five minute seminar", he said. Todd didn't know at the time that the man was the author of the article, but by the time Todd had finished the author looked deep into Todd's eyes and said 'I was doing it wrong'.

Todd manages to run without any problems. He hasn't cut his feet on glass or nails or anything. "I heard someone behind me today say if 'he can do it without shoes, I can do it with shoes." In the middle of a marathon in Las Vegas one time he went into a casino, put on some flip flops, bet (and lost) $20, left the casino, took off the flip flops and finished the marathon. He's had a swim several times in the middle of a marathon. Runners and spectators stare at his feet almost in disbelief. Many runners want to get a photograph with Todd.

Todd is not the only barefoot runner. Jon Gissberg of Seattle, Washington, is known as Marathon Maniac Barefoot Jon. Jon ran his first marathon in Anchorage, Alaska, in 1977 and his 100th in the Seattle Marathon in 2007. Since 1990 he's competed barefoot in over twenty marathons, two Ironman races and one ultra, or in flip flops in two marathons and four ultras (including 50 Miles and 100K).

Tony Phillippi of Tacoma, Washington runs occasionally in sandals. And he's fast. Tony is one of the three Marathon Maniacs club founders. On the Internet he writes: "Well I had many couch years after school. When I finally got off the couch I ran the Sound to Narrows 12 K in 1996." Of his first ever marathon he said "It was the hardest thing I'd ever done. I was high for weeks and couldn't wait to run another!' ... and these days ... My life is consumed with running, it's what I love." Tony ran his first marathon at Portland, Oregon in 1998 and completed his 100th, also in Portland in 2005.

Tony told me that it was "The mystique of the marathon that intrigued me, the challenge was to see how far I could go, and how fast - it's the thrill of the accomplishment getting through those last six miles – it's a rush." In his first marathon running in sandals he qualified for Boston. His marathon PB is 2:53:37, and with that time he set a world record by running a race wearing sandals. He ended up running for the company – BITE running sandals. "No matter what shape I'm in", he said, "anything after 20 miles gets hard. But I'm a pretty neutral runner. I don't pound a lot and usually wear running flats in marathons." In fact he completed one of his six Ironman events in sandals.

In Germany Yen Nguyen and her husband Peter ran a 100-mile trail race with the route marked by white dots on trees. They lost their way and ended up in a small medieval-like village. They took a taxi back to where they were staying, re-thought their route, went back to the race, and successfully finished the course from where they left off.

Lynda Petri commented in an article that "Joan Benoit's jaw dropped when we talked and she found out I was running in every state. I replied to her that I can't imagine winning an Olympic gold medal." Jim Scheer told me about his chance meeting with marathon great Bill Rogers in a marathon in Oregon in 1981. Jim had to leave the course to relieve himself. He headed into the bushes and found himself in there with Bill. Seizing the moment Jim said "Bill, this is probably the closest I'll ever get to you." Two years later Jim was in Boston for the marathon and went into Bill's running store. Bill remembered Jim from the bush encounter two years earlier. "He's a really great guy", said Jim.

Bob and Lenore Dolphin met the Governor of Arkansas, and potential Republican presidential candidate Mike Huckabee, at the Marine Corp marathon when the Governor was a speaker on a cruise on the Potomac. At one point in his life the Governor weighed over 300 pounds. In 2003 he was diagnosed with type 2 diabetes and told he would not live more than ten years if he didn't lose weight. He lost weight. Mike Huckabee was amazed at the number of marathons Bob had run – at that point Number 368. He invited them for dinner at the Little Rock Marathon. Lenore gave the Governor her trademark hug after he finished the marathon, and gave his wife a hug as well. Mike Huckabee has now run several marathons. In the 2005 Little Rock Marathon he and Iowa Governor Tom Vilsack had an unofficial challenge, with Huckabee finishing in 4:38 ahead of Vilsack by 50 minutes.

Pam Penfield ran The New York marathon in 1999 with her close friend Denise McFadden. Denise made her vow that Pam would talk to her the whole way. "Well needless to say I only thought of one thing to say during the marathon and that was at Mile 11. She didn't berate me till the end but we laughed pretty hard about my lack of words."

There are always experiences around the marathon, as Dave Major has described in his upcoming book 'One for the Road'. He and his UK 100 marathon club friends were out on the Friday night before the Barcelona marathon near the main social area known as Las Ramblas. Fellow runner 'Badger' was pick pocketed. As Dave described it "unfortunately for the thief picking on six marathon runners was not a good idea. As Badger closed on him he threw the wallet in the road and made off with the cash. … No harm done just an expensive drink, but with all cards in the retrieved wallet, little issues."

The Jungfrau marathon in Switzerland is self-labeled as the 'toughest marathon in the world', and also the 'most beautiful marathon in the world'. The Swiss holiday resort, Wengen, is the host community, sitting quietly at the foot of the spectacular Eiger - Mönch - Jungfrau mountain range. There is no road leading to Wengen, where it is based, only a mountain railway. The village itself has few cars. Wengen is reknowned for its pure mountain air and lack of traffic noise. Full of old wooden chalets and sur- rounded by mountains, the village has all the charm and character you could want for a vacation.

And a beautiful marathon. Around town the first half, and then up the Alps for the second half. At the back are individuals on bikes with brooms – the 'sweepers', who, if they feel the runners are not able to compete the race within the time allotted, will effectively let you know your race is over. You receive, on the course, a cer- tificate and a black t-shirt, that say, basically, it's over, and you need to get off the course. Susan Daley from Chicago was handed these in the second half of the marathon. And in return she had to give the Sweeper her timing chip.

But Susan kept going. It got dark. People didn't know she was still out there. Meanwhile, as Susan explained, she was "prob- ably on the edge of my limits", and was seriously recognizing she might end up on the mountain overnight. She eventually made it to the finish line where everything was being packed up. Susan met up with the Race Director, who was surprised to see her. Rec- ognizing her achievement, the race director gave her a finisher's medal and a finisher's t-shirt. It's an unlikely combination, to receive both a finishers and a non-finishers t-shirt for the same race, but it exemplifies both the spirit of the race (race director) and the seriousness that must always be central (sweeper). And the persistence of the runner.

Indeed in the longer distances you can never be sure of what to expect. And for some runners, like Big Dave Carter looking for something different after over 300 marathons, it's the challenge of the unexpected that attracts them.

Dave told me about the point-to-point seven day 250 K Augrabies Extreme marathon in South Africa. It's run through the Kalahari with temperatures ranging from 40 Celsius (104 Fahrenheit) during the day to Minus 4 (25 Fahrenheit) at night. The actual route only disclosed to the runners the day before the race begins. Runners bring their own food and sleeping bag and the race provides the shelter and water and fire at night. In the morning, he said, "you have to take two litres of water away with you. If you get lost, get in shade and put a great big red flag out." He recalled one moment under a Joshua tree – "six guys trying to hide in the shade of one tree that has no leaves." In all, 30 runners started, and 14 finished. "You'd be running along and there would be giraffes or a huge pack of antelope running in front of you. The most dangerous though are the Ostriches ... sharp claws and beaks."

With his marathons these days ultra runner Kelvin Marshall says "its novel to finish a run in the morning that you started that same morning and be able to talk to others coherently." Like Big Dave Carter earlier in the chapter, Kelvin enjoys the Stage Races. Kelvin said he likes "waking up and having breakfast, 'go to work', get back, eat, and have a shower." It's still a challenge however. In his race across France there was "an awful camber for the first 400 K ... I walked into my dorm room and saw myself leaning as I looked into the mirror. But I was able to straighten up for the next 600 K." In that Across France race he averaged about 64 K a day. In the 2007 17 day 1205 K across Germany race he was the 3rd male finisher and 4th runner overall, averaging about 70 K a day.

In many respects, it's hard to imagine what it must be like to endure such distance, even for messengers such as Kelvin; "When you do the likes of Badwater" he said, which he's done twice, "it's hard to think of 'what next'."

One thing though, he told me, is that he would really like an opportunity to do a Stage Race across Australia. The Western States 100 is also "unfinished business", as he had DNF there. He had arrived in the United States on the Monday with a bad cold that got progressively worse by the Friday. On the run itself he was putting on weight and at the 50-60 mile mark the doctor pulled him – he'd put on 12 lbs. "I want revenge on that course", he said, … "and I want to run a perfect Badwater."

Anything can happen when you're on a run for such a long time in ultra events. At about mile 46 in the Wasatch Front 100-Mile Trail Race in Utah, Jeff Hagen was running hard downhill when his toe hooked a hidden rock in the trail. "I did a shoulder roll and came up running, but then I noticed a foot-long stick about the diameter of a wooden pencil coming out of my nose. I tried to pull it out, but it was apparently embedded very deep into the tissue, so I had to remove it with a strong yank. Then my nose bled profusely, but I stuffed my nostrils with toilet paper and finished the race while breathing through my mouth. By the time the race was done, my nose had healed. It didn't seem so funny at the time, but I will never forget the 'stick-in-the-nose' incident."

Ultra-running adversity is well known for Oregonian Sean Meissner. On the Internet Sean talks about his "most memorable" distance race. It was the Tuscarora Trail 252 mile Stage Race in 2003. It required running 30-50 miles a day for six days in "lots of nasty conditions, on a poorly marked trail, with sporadic aid, with twenty people I came to know extremely well, sleeping in a closet, trying to consume as many calories as possible at dinners, post-holing up to mid-shin on day 1 for 25ish miles, a complete emotional breakdown at the end of day 1, logistical nightmares for RD's Clapper and Horton, the nastiest day ever of running on day 4 in freezing rain for 40 miles … but I moved relatively fast just too stay warm, DNFing on day 5 after only 3 miles because of a stupid fall on day 2 where I banged my knee, then joining the thirteen other DNFers in a support role for the six studs who would go on to finish, knowing that only nineteen other people will ever completely understand what I went through."

Another ultra runner had all her teeth pulled about ten years ago. She now has to calculate how long she should run before she puts cream on for her dentures. She said that her "running actually got better when my teeth were pulled."

Peter Wieneke from Germany likes trying new races in new places. He and several other runners ran a marathon inside a prison in Wolfenbüttel, Germany, running together with the inmates. It was quite the experience he said. 'You felt sorry for the prisoners'. To get into the complex to run they had to first pass through eleven doors. The runners had taken on the event to help motivate and inspire the inmates. None of the prisoners finished more than 10 km.

Peter has also run two marathons in underground salt mines. Huge salt mines. The mine in Sondershausen Germany is 700 metres underground. It's a difficult run as you need a light on your Helmut and the temperature is in the range of 26-28 degrees Celsius. Incredibly you run just four laps of the mine, which gives an indication of the size of the underground complex. 'It was very good to have a beer afterwards' Peter said.

The other salt mine, Merkers, which is also in Germany is 600 metres underground. The marathon here only requires two laps of the complex. Underground there is also a Museum and an Orchestra room. If you want, you can get married there. A tourist bus takes visitors around the complex.

Peter has also run the Elbe Tunnel marathon under the Elbe River in Hamburg ten times and completed sixty-eight laps of a parking garage in Denmark in another marathon.

It was fellow German Christian Hottas who first organized the Elbe Tunnel marathon. Christian has run in the salt mines also and recalls finding himself running against horse-coaches on the

North Sea seabed (at low tide) between Cuxhaven and the island of Neuwerk.

Omaha Nebraska local Gary Julin has run over 160 marathons (112 marathons have been under 3 hours). He is another streaker who has run every day for the past twenty years. His twenty year old jeep has clocked 55,000 miles but Gary has ensured that he has clocked more miles himself – over 59,000 miles – although admittedly over another ten years). He said to one reporter "A couple times the odometer caught up with me ... so I parked it and didn't drive it until I got back ahead."

After Californian Jim Simpson took early retirement, his two children had grown up, and he and his wife went separate ways, he refocused his life on running long distances. As the Runners World wrote in a February 2009 article, Jim set upon a quest to "run marathons in all 50 states as many times as possible." As of September 2009 he had done so nine times. Since March 1988 he has run a combined total of over 650 ultras and marathons. Jim has also stayed in a Wal Mart parking lot in his Ford F-150 Camper, in all 50 states. "You might call me a budget marathoner" he told Runners World. "It's a simple lifestyle. I read mystery novels through the week and have fun with 50 States friends on weekends." His camper is fully equipped with a propane stove, microwave, fridge, computer set-up and a mattress. He takes any opportunities he can to shower at races, or in the hotel rooms of running friends, at truck-stops, or at the local Y's. He said to Runners World that "I'm having a great time out here ... People don't understand how beautiful America is, all the places to see and things to do. By driving and running, I'm experiencing it all."

In 2003 Paul Selby and five others, including fellow messenger Rory Coleman, raised money for charity by running 1,000 miles in 1000 hours around the London Marathon route. This was to re-enact an 1809 run by sportsman and Gambler Captain Robert Barclay who did it to win a bet of 16,000 guineas. He was assisted by supporters slapping him around to help him stay awake and two pistols to prevent gangs from mugging him. "He lost a lot of weight and lost his marbles", Paul said. Paul and the others ran one mile hourly in one hour segments every day and night for six weeks, which was the equivalent of running the London course thirty-eight times. "The blisters were unbelievable." But Paul discovered he copes quite well with sleep deprivation, and so embarked on more ultra events. The run was timed to end during the official London marathon. Unfortunately their achievement received little attention because the Iraq war broke out at the same time.

World record holder Horst Preisler sat isolated on a wall looking bemused at a piece of paper at an off-road trail race in England. Messenger Dave Major sensed the problem: each runner was given written instructions that they had to read to navigate their way around the course. Dave asked Horst "Can you read the English instructions?" He couldn't, so Dave and Linda Major asked if he would like to go around with them. They were greeted by a beaming Horst smile. Linda had invited a relative newcomer to running – Carol – to run with them also. Horst has his own style of running which to some looks hard work but he keeps going and going. Given his broken English the conversation during the race was minimal, but every time Dave looked around Horst gave him a knowing smile as almost to say, "thanks" and "I would have never done this without you".

With 24 miles in and few words exchanged, Dave politely asked Horst if everything was okay. Horst replied "Yes". Carol, who is not shy in talking, and not knowing about Horst's running feats, goes over to Horst and says "Keep going, only 2 miles to go…. You can do it … nearly there !!!" At that point Dave immediately asked Horst, who had said almost nothing for the whole time, "How many marathons have you done?" Horst's instant reply, in almost perfect English was "One thousand six hundred and seventy-six marathons". Enough runs to instantly floor Carol.

Nineteen years ago Steve Boone started a running program for children kids around Houston, Texas. It began at the local elementary school with the physical education teacher and fourteen children. If the children ran a total of 26.2 miles or more over the year they would receive a t-shirt. The teacher would sign off

194

as the students completed their runs. The program has proved so popular that there are now seven thousand children involved each year. Some children Steve said, even ran 90-100 miles last year. The twenty schools involved have each set up their own course; children get a dot on their arm each time they do a lap. Some schools provide a ribbon for 'x' miles accomplished along the way. Steve told me that in one school, everyone ran – the teachers, all the students, janitors, principal, nurses ... everyone; 937 people. The costs per t-shirt are nominal, but when added up the dollar contribution made by Steve, aside from his own time, runs into the thousands each year. "It's great that they get motivated", he said, "it gives me special pleasure." As does a neighbour of his who lost 85 pounds and who couldn't walk to the end of the block. He's now running marathons with Steve.

Steve inspires in many ways, as all the messengers do, whether they realize it or not. Opportunities are created and choices for how one leads his or her life are made possible. It starts somewhere.

23

"The carryover of training and running marathons
transcends into your life every day.
It's not obsessive or self-absorbent.
It's about constantly striving to better yourself,
resetting your goals and continually
learning about others as well as yourself."

Lynda Petri

"If you're going to do a marathon,
be grateful you are, and that you can."

Pam Reed

The messengers acquire a growing body of knowledge about the world in which they live and how they fit into this world. The world is made up of people and places, and a deeper understanding of both serves to make it a better place. American Andrew Kotulski said "If more people ran marathons around the world there would be less war."

Knowledge brings confidence in oneself. Confidence grows as an individual takes on the challenges and uncertainties associated with marathons and ultras. Nothing is ever guaranteed in a distance running event; a certain level of mental preparedness must exist for the experience to be a positive one. Overcoming challenges and uncertainty promotes the growth of self-esteem. Dave Major said "in general people have confidence in the certainty zone versus the uncertainty zone – some people are better in one zone than the other – you would find travelling marathon runners doing well in the uncertainty zone."

The experiences gained over time contribute to an individual's sense of self-worth and self-confidence, and to the happiness of others. Often, the messengers become a source of inspiration whether they know it or not. A source of inspiration for many, is American messenger Pam Reed. In one continuous stretch of almost 80 hours Pam ran 300 miles.

300 miles.

She then ran one more mile "just to be sure."

This one run, she said later, was "the highlight of all the running I've done." Pam wanted to achieve this almost unthinkable non-stop run, in part, she was quoted as saying, "because I'm a woman and I wanted to show how women multitask every day of their lives." The 300 miler is not all she's accomplished.

Pam has firmly etched her name in the distance running world with some incredible achievements. These include winning the Badwater Ultra Marathon twice as the overall winner, setting an American record in the 24-hour track run and running for the American team in the Netherlands in 2004 and in France in 2005. In May 2009 Pam became the female American record holder in six-day events after completing 490 miles in the Twelfth-Annual Self-Transcendence Six-Day Race in New York. She was awarded "Runner of the Year" by Competitor Magazine and has appeared on numerous TV Shows to talk about her running achievements. Much of this is discussed in her book *'The Extra Mile: One Woman's Personal Journey to Ultra-Running Greatness'*.

Pam had taken some time out of her day to talk to me for this book. Seven weeks ago she tore her hamstring. She had never been injured before so the experience was quite revealing. She's starting to run a little now, but only at sixty percent, she says. The typical day right now sees Pam riding a stationary bike for an hour when she gets up and then running for an hour. She does some work on the Tucson Marathon (she is the race director), and will then go for another one hour run. Later, she'll swim again and then run again. I'm getting tired just listening to her regimen. Then Pam casually adds "if I'm training, I'll do more."

Which is why she is one of the top ultra runners in the world. On top of this regimen she raises a family, with three boys and a dog to look after. The injury, Pam says, "has helped to put it all in perspective." Instead of running all the time she rides and swims in its place. "The injury might be a good thing, it resets everything." It's also made her more keenly aware of the negative effects of an injury. "You need to be careful and listen to your body; I should've seen the signs. It taught me a lesson."

Pam's personal goal is "to motivate people of all speeds and ages to do something for themselves and set a fitness goal that will encourage a healthier lifestyle." Pam acknowledges that she has been extremely lucky, as if "someone up there is watching over me" she says, but regardless, she trains hard and long and that is, in fact, what makes the difference.

Some runners, many people say, should be committed, because they're simply crazy to be running so many events. But completing 100 marathons is all about a different commitment, and is sometimes more striking when seen in some athletes than others. Holly Koester, for example, with more than 100 marathons in a wheelchair, or 'Blind Paul' in the United Kingdom, who has run more than 200 marathons.

Or messenger Jim Barnes, who lives in Perth, Australia, where there is simply not that many marathons in close proximity to run.

Jim has been chipping away at marathons over the years; it not easy accumulating 100 when you live in Perth. There are no major centers anywhere near Perth; there are only two marathons in Western Australia, and even a flight to Sydney – over two thousand miles away – will take four and a half hours to complete, as well as the $800 return air fare involved.

He has been running marathons since 1979, although he's run many more each year since he retired 11 years ago from his job as a butcher. Jim has kept diaries recording all his running since 1977. When he was in his forties he was running up to 160 K a week in training. It wasn't until he had run 50 marathons that he decided to try for 100.

Jim lives with rheumatoid arthritis (he has injections every week in the summer and tablets because his joints swell up so much) and hemochromatosis – whereby the body absorbs and stores too much iron. "I'm sure I'd be in really big trouble with my health if I didn't run." Jim's commitment is based on passion and patience. He said to me "When I've run a marathon I feel so good afterwards. I go on a high. It increases my self-esteem. If I could just encourage one person to take up running I would feel as though I have achieved something as I'm sure it would be beneficial to them."

Englishman Jack Brooks encapsulated a lot of what other messengers feel when he said "running is now so much a part of my life that it is difficult to envisage what life would be like without it. Most of my friends run so it is a huge part of my social life. It is also a great stress reliever and a time when I can clear my mind and think through problems. When it is going well running gives me a sense of well-being and euphoria that is difficult to explain to non-runners. I believe that running has made me a generally more resilient person and it has certainly given me a great sense of personal achievement and fulfillment. Last, but not least, running has enabled me to raise sponsorship for a number of charities that I care about so that is an extra feel good factor."

"To me", said Jim Manford, "the marathon still provides the challenge that no other event does. It's not just something you can get out of bed and do. It requires planning, self-discipline and sacrifice", qualities he feels are important in everyday life. Qualities that are essential if you want to complete 100 marathons. "Running", said Collette O'Hagan, "makes you a stronger and better person." Pam Reed told me that "it's easier to run now. I want to win, but if I don't it's not devastating. I'm not going to win them all, but I'm going to learn from them, and experience them more."

Looking back on his 100 marathons Jeffrey Horowitz observed that it was "The good and the bad all mixed together into a grand adventure." John Zeleznikow said that "anyone out there running needs to simply enjoy the moment." As Pam Reed put it to me: "be in the moment." She said that while completing a 2009 six-day event another female runner said to her "You have to enjoy the moment." So Pam "kind of let go and just really enjoyed it - I'm always thinking about the 'next thing' to do", she said, "but I know I need to embrace what I'm doing at the time."

To Jim Mundy, running the long distances means "freedom for me ... the freedom to follow the road or path ahead, not to arrive exactly, but rather to experience the changes around me in Nature and those internal ones, which range from the joy of smooth, swift transition of the best miles to the relentless determined pounding of the toughest ones"! Bob Dolphin noted that "for each race there is a meeting of a challenge, seeing the country, meeting friends ... there's never any sense of boredom." That may be what Dave Major was thinking when he said that the "runners brain is always active and aware – taking in new places, taking changes to the body, talking ... its always active taking in the surrounds – there's an anti-aging element to this – storing the data, and that can come back years later."

In his engaging 2004 book '*Feet in the Clouds*' which looked at Fell running in the United Kingdom, Richard Askwith falls in love with off-road running up and down mountains and hills; it might also be called an obsession. Importantly, having traced his own and others' fell running he determines: "The point is not the exertion involved: it is the degree of involvement, or immersion, in the landscape. You need to *feel* it, to interact with it; to be *in* it, not just looking from the outside. You need to lose yourself – for it is then that you are the most human."

The messengers make a passionate recurring connection to the long distances and share similar feelings. But they are not just in it for the landscape, they are in it for the *total experience* which includes the landscape, the culture, the friendships, the socialization, the build-up, the achievement, the reward, the travel, the logical challenges overcome, the acceptance of uncertainty and their confidence to overcome it, and the reflection of having set out to do something and accomplishing it. Little wonder they keep returning to the experience; and when that experience is differentiated by the location, the course, the different array of individuals, travel logistics and so on, such uncertainties only increase the likelihood that each total experience is even more magical. Chances are, if you have run 100 marathons you have accumulated a full spectrum of possible experiences. The messengers inspire, and are themselves inspired by others.

The messengers are drawn by the social connectedness, which is a huge factor in their overall happiness and well-being. Chances are, having spent that much time *with yourself*, you know yourself so much better as a result. You appreciate what you have. By regularly running long distances the messengers also contribute to the happiness of others.

Connectedness. New connections are continually being made. They can be made when runners pick up their registration kit for a race, at the pasta party the night before, when they run alongside one another during a race because they are going at the same pace, and when they sit together afterwards and share their stories. New friendships emerge, old ones continue. As one messenger commented, "you touch someone, who touches someone else."

These can be inspirational touches. The shared experiences bring into focus potentially new places to go, new runs to enter, different types of events to try, new people to run with, new ways to train …the touches open up endless possibilities – unknowns – for the future. A good example of this may be a conversation about new races. The decision to run ultras may come after talking with others who have already run them: "hey, if Sally can do it, I can at least try." The touches – the conversations – can be quite unknowingly transformational; they plant the seed of an idea. As Jim Barnes put it, "When you hear about exotic runs around the world, you want to go."

A number of messengers started running more and more marathons when they discovered that people can run a large number of marathons *every year*. Conventional wisdom suggests two-three marathons a year is best in order to optimize performance and reduce the risk of injury. But upon meeting others who may run anywhere from 10 to 50 marathons a year (or more!), they start to think that running that many can't be that bad for you. Without knowing it, Leslie Miller became the youngest woman in the world ever to complete one hundred marathons after she had met and talked with runners who were running marathons almost weekly. And Todd Byers, who tried running barefoot after meeting a friend's friend who ran barefoot, has since run eighty marathons barefoot, and inspired many others to try running barefoot as well.

In 2002, Peter Dodds, Roby Muhamad and Duncan Watts conducted a study that sought to test the 1960s six-degrees of separation theory once more. In the 1960s Stanley Milgram conducted a study that showed people are connected to each other by an average of six degrees of separation. In other words, your friend would be one degree of separation, and their friend would be two degrees from you. Milgram asked several hundred people in Nebraska and Kansas to send a letter to a businessman in Boston. No address was given and the participants had to contact people they knew in the hope that they might know the individual in Boston, or if not, send the letter on to someone who might. Eventually the letter would arrive to the designate in Boston. Many didn't arrive, but for those that did it took on average almost six different points of contact to do so; hence six degrees of freedom, which has been popularized and the basis for more research.

Peter Dodds and his colleagues tested the 'small world' hypothesis using email as the mode of communication. Over 60,000 e-mail users, mostly in the United States, tried to reach one of eighteen target persons in thirteen countries by forwarding messages to people they knew. Like Milgram and others earlier, they found that it took between five to seven degrees to reach the targets.

Nicholas Christakis and James Fowler went one significant step further. They tested the degrees of separation in their landmark research on 5,000 people over a 20-year period. They concluded that there is a Three Degrees of Influence Rule, in that everything we do or say will "ripple" through our own networks and will influence in some way our friends, our friend's friends, and their friends' friends. That includes our attitudes and feelings and beliefs and includes the nature and extent of our happiness.

So if we recommend a particular race, or talk about the possibility of running longer distances, or talk about how enjoyable it is to run with members of a club, these will influence others' attitudes, behaviors and actions. If we are positive in our outlook on life, that too will ripple through to our friends, and their friends.

Given that runners by and large are a very happy 'tribe' the three degree of influence effect is mutually reinforcing; runners enjoy the connectedness with other runners, and feel better off for the connections. Importantly, according to the research, their friends will also be better off.

The Three Degrees of Influence Rule helps us to understand the rapid rise in membership of the Marathon Maniacs Club, the Fifty States Marathon club, and the importance of the various 100 Marathon Clubs around the world. One could even argue that in the close-knit world of distance running, there may well be just two degrees of influence.

The messengers constantly influence their families and friends, other runners, and sometimes complete strangers, simply leading by example. Paul Allsop observed that "I am still working quite a lot and it is an effort to fit in the training and the running, but I guess that this is how life really is, we make space and time to do what we want to do. I now negotiate with my wife, who is not a runner, when and where I run. In 2006 I ran a marathon with my eldest daughter who was 38. I am now hoping that my 20-year old grandson will make it for a three generational marathon, possibly four generations at some time."

Similarly, Paula Boone said that she just has "such a great time with my friends, that's what it's all about for me ... where else and how often can you spend six hours with a friend in quality time like this." John Zeleznikow said that running marathons "makes me more relaxed, and I'm more capable of doing other activities … and it's a wonderful social way of meeting people all around the world." John Bozung was equally emphatic "Not all the marathons are fun, but the people and places are. Just the nature of the sport lends itself to instant friendships. I've got friends all over the world that I stay in touch with." John added that "my good times are behind me so it's more meaningful to help others get to the finish." One such runner was a young woman he helped to finish the race. When she went back to the car with her boyfriend, who had been waiting for her, her boyfriend proposed.

Siri Terjesen has run in many parts of the world, has won numerous long distance races and has represented two countries at international events. But Siri said that her proudest running achievement was in 2003 at her first 50 K at the AAA England national championships. She met Isobel Partridge at the start line of the event. On an Internet site Siri describes the event: "Isobel and I talked and ran side by side throughout the race. In the closing 200 meters, either of us could have made a sprint finish to claim the national title, but instead we held hands and finished together in the first tie in a national championship. We have been best running friends ever since."

Michaela Sanders said she enjoys "the conversations, companionship, the war stories and the friendly rivalries. You hear the stories from people, stories of adversity, that you'd never get watching something like 'wifeswap' on TV. Without the marathon running I wouldn't have been social, met up with friends, seen the places I've seen, I never would have done it otherwise."

Danish messenger Tor Rønnow, who has now run more than 200 marathons, says his "present madness evolves around running a lot of marathons, and his present grace is spinning around his children." Tor has a diverse background, including a doctorate in Chemistry, software development, and a lifelong learning in spirituality, philosophy and science. He writes: "For me, activity, play, love and Nature are the great things to enjoy each day, be it with your loved ones, your colleagues, your friends or alone." Tor has just had a book published with co-author Bente Klarlund Ped-

ersen titled 'ELSK AT LØBE - med Maratonbogen', which translates to *Love Running – with the Marathonbook*. It's a "unique
cocktail" he said, integrating the physiology of running with the
stories, facts and pictures from the major races.

Tor said to me that after a few races "you start to notice things you
haven't seen before, and the social side of the running experience
becomes more important … nature … travel …with a growing
number of friends my name gets shouted at almost every race
now." Larry Macon meanwhile, says he prefers to chat his way
through the miles. He's been quoted as saying "I'm addicted to
the social part of running … Runners have a lower percentage of
jerks than the rest of the population."

This resonates with the thoughts of Dave Major, who situates himself in the messenger mental state. "My friendships, my social life
and whilst I am running I am what I can best describe as 'at one
with myself'. I still try to work out exactly what this means but
for those hours I am running the whole world is such a great place
where nothing goes wrong and everyone lives with the same goal
and that is to enjoy life. Only when you stop and the buzz recedes
does life return to the moment."

Similarly, Don McNelly told me when running long distances
"your brain goes into neutral. We're disciplined right now as we
talk, but when you're running all sorts of things go through your
mind. A lot of stupidness, a lot of good ideas. Where else do
you get to do that these days? The one place where you can be
within yourself."

Yen Nguyen said, "I like to think; to have time to myself, it's
kind of relaxing." Linda Major highlights the importance of her
connectedness with the marathon 'family': "I have got some very
close friends [through running marathons] that you can depend
your life on. We are like a family and you know that if anyone was
ever in trouble someone would be there to help. This is one family
that you have the privilege of choosing who you want in it." "It's
a healthy lifestyle" said Pam Penfeld, "you make lifelong friends."
John Sturely considers marathoners to be a "special breed" of run-

ners, and that this is "the most important aspect of training and running marathons."

Part of the reason for being that 'special breed' may be the natural bonding that occurs. Van Phan said that "running long distances is a very humbling experience. People are down to earth. Everyone has suffered in some way. Ultra-runners really try to grasp what life is all about, for example, being healthy and being humble. When you go to these ultras the runners are so easy to be around. We all suffer through it – we all relate; it's quite a bonding experience."

And inspirational also. Tor Rønnow echoed many messengers' thoughts when he said that "marathons can show you that you are capable of putting out the mental and physical activity if needed." Runners feed off the stories and dedication and the superhuman feats; which although they appear superhuman, are not. They are, however, passionate achievements of endurance and courage. Sometimes they are feats that pull the body to the edge and beyond. The mind takes over. That people can go well beyond what would typically be 'possible' according to the general norms is becoming of increasing interest, as evidenced by recent books such Maria Coffey's Explorers of the Infinite, and Cecil Kuhne's Near Death in the Mountains.

In the distance running circles the feats of Yiannis Kouros are what legends are made of. And they are why he has been labeled variously as "Ultra-marathon God", "Immortal Legendary Greek Ultra-distance Runner", "Superman", "Bionic Kouros", "Miracle Man", "Master of Mind Games", "Poet of Endurance", "Poet in Motion" and "Superhuman."

It is difficult, if not impossible, to truly report on all his running achievements in such a short space. But here goes …

Yiannis Kouros was born in 1956, in Tripolis, Arcadia, Greece. By the age of twelve he was writing his own poems and melodies. From age sixteen and on, he focused more on sport. In 1990 he migrated to Australia, and has lived there ever since. He studied Greek literature, music and poetry when he completed his undergraduate and Masters degrees at La Trobe University in Melbourne. He had more than 150 world records as of April 2006. As one commentator put it, he has had "decades of mythical and unbroken World Records."

While clearly passionate about running ultra distances, he is also passionate about music, literature, and poetry. He's also taken part in singing competitions. His goal, he says, is to inspire and many around the world look to him for motivation. For he not only leads – well, wins – by example, his remarkable running prowess reflects dedication, resiliency, tenacity and mind over body. Yiannis believes in the ability of the mind – our inner power – to bring, and extend, our own personal improvement, which in turn can act as a catalyst for unity, friendship and harmony. To Yiannis, this happens through two routes: deprivation and learning.

He ran his first marathon in 1977, on the Athens course, in a time of 2:43. By 1982 his PB was 2:25. This was just the beginning. The longer distances seemed more attractive to him. By 1983 he had completed about 25 marathons and ran his first Spartathlon (246 K between Athens and Sparta). He won decisively, finishing over 3 hours ahead of the second runner. Race officials and runners could not believe it as at this point in his career he was a relative unknown. He was only able to get in the race as a late registrant, and only after other runners agreed to let him do so. He won the event again in 1984, 1986, and 1990. His record time of 20:25 in 1984 is still two hours faster than the second fastest runner ever to complete the course – American Scott Jurek, who won the event three times (2006-07-08).

Between 1983 and 2000 he won 53 ultra-marathons, making distance running, as many observers said, look easy. In the 1984 New York 6-day race, alone, he broke 16 World Records. In 1987 he won the Sydney to Melbourne race, covering the 875 K (544 Miles) in 5 days, 14 hours, 47 minutes. In 1995 he won the prestigious invitation only Surgeres 48 Hours in France in May, setting a new world 24-hour track best of 285.362 kilometres (177.3 miles) before reaching a final 48-hour distance of 470.781 kilometres (292.5 miles), also a world record. According to Adam

Chase in the April 2006 issue of *Running Times* when he set his 24-hour record of 303 kilometers (188.3 miles), he averaged a 7:26 mile, with a sub-three-hour marathon split. And in the 2005 Cliff Young Six-Day Race in Australia, at age 49 Kouros broke four world records and broke his own records that he had made 20 years earlier. In the 2005-06 Across the Years race over the New Year's weekend in Phoenix, he won the 72-hour event, winning that by 60 miles.

His running may look easy, but the challenge he says, is the ability of the mind to overcome pain and tiredness and move into a more transcendent form of self. As Yiannis himself said in his book *The Six-Day Run of the Century*, "when the body has given up the ghost, only through willpower it can be mobilized." In the Year 2000 *Runner's World* magazine proclaimed him as the 7th best runner of the Millennium and as the best ultra-marathon runner of all time. At the heart of it all though is his *passion*, and a belief that what he has been able to achieve has been less about his body (which must be unique all the same) and much more about his mind. The mind, Yiannis says, must be cultivated. He was quoted by Adam Chase in a 2006 issue of *Running Times Magazine* that "Like a tree that grows stronger with more branches and roots, you need to find more and more ways to be inspired." Kouros says his strength comes from his "hard-working carpenter father" and his "mother who was also a tough character" In addition, his "grandfather's strong discipline left an indelible mark."

Yiannis says that there is a separation of mind from body during his races, although it is the mind that commands the body. "The pain is the reality but your mind can inspire you past it. I look to the countryside, music, and art, to help inspire me. We have ups and downs in life and the same is true in ultramarathons. I need those ups and downs to go back to my childhood, memories, and past experiences." Because, he says, "we gain more and more life impressions as we age, the older you are, the better for ultrarunning because mental experience is much more important than physical speed."

***

The messengers have all in their own way, found "something." They may not all be poets. They may not all be elite runners. They may not talk eloquently about running. They may not talk much at all. It doesn't matter. They have found something; and they keep returning. They are in a better place, Apathia, or whatever you want call it, because of running the longer distances.

And it is addictive, a positive addiction, or more accurately, a 'passion', which is why many of the messengers are adamant they will run the longer distances for as long as their physical bodies permit. They feel they can do this because they have a positive "can do" attitude to life, which itself is strengthened with the more races they complete over time.

24

"Each marathon challenges me a little, enhances me."
Elaine Doll-Dunn

"The confidence, determination and commitment in marathon
running complements my life in a very positive way,
and especially has helped with this breast cancer."
Carol Dellinger

"Every run is a gift."
Christian Hottas

Every marathoner brings their own unique context to the start-line.
Many individuals challenges have been overcome, or are about to
be. Running long distances strengthens that belief in oneself. It's
the stories we hear that inspire us and make us believe that, yes,
anything is possible if we have the resolve, determination, tenacity and belief in ourselves.

New Zealand messenger Tui Te Rupe had run more than 100 marathons when he retired several years ago, with a PB of 2:53. Tui's
story is remarkable and inspiring because he was a blind runner
who ran with a rope tied to a partner. In 1982 Tui won a silver medal in the marathon at the World Blind Championships, Vancouver,
Canada. In the following year he won the gold medal in Auckland,
New Zealand. Nine years later in 1992 he won another silver medal
at the World Blind Championships in Miyasaki, Japan.

In the United Kingdom messenger Paul Watts, or 'Blind Paul' as
he's sometimes referred to, has run more than 200 marathons. He
ran his first marathon in 1989, and has generally run an average
of about 10 a year (although in one year he ran 28 marathons).
He is currently doing a sports and recreation course at the Royal

National College for the Blind, with the view to becoming a sports instructor.

When asked why he ran marathons Paul said "Because I'm mad", but also because he has a "nice bunch of friends" in the United Kingdom 100 Marathon Club. Other marathoners run with him, and on occasions will run ahead at the end of the race so he can cross the line by himself. He runs with a Figure 8 pulley which is bound with yellow tape so he and the other runner can run close to one another.

Paul says he runs "for the fun of it", and usually assigns one event a year for charity. "I couldn't keep going around the same people always asking for money" he said, when interviewed over the radio.

In another interview, with the Hereford Times, Paul said "I do it just to prove that being blind means you don't have to sit down and do nothing."

He's hit the wall a few times and was injured one day doing a half marathon in Taunton, England. He and a friend were running close behind others who suddenly separated and left little time for Paul and his friend to avoid a median barrier between the lanes. He broke a few ribs, but within a few weeks he was running the London Marathon. He received a plaque to commemorate his 200th marathon milestone. Paul said "It is made out of wood with a Braille label and also has the figure 200 so you can feel it."

American Ron Bucy had open heart surgery to replace his aortic valve. After nine days in hospital, his right chest area developed a hematoma and was swollen several times the size of his left side. He also had fluid around his lungs and chest. Ron wrote in a North American 100 Marathon Club newsletter: "After 30 years on the road everyday it's become a real challenge for me to accept ... I guess we all have to deal with these issues along the line but at sixty-three I would have preferred it to be a little later in my life. Then you listen to the challenges that others face and you feel thankful."

Indeed, Paula Boone had one such "a-ha" moment last year at the Sunmart Marathon, Texas. Her uncle had just passed away and she was feeling tired. At this point in the run she was walking. A little boy came along the trail, saw her, and said "'you can run you know." All the excuses went through her mind for why she wasn't running but then she realized that the boy was right, she actually could, and she realized many people simply can't. She said to herself that "I can run and I'm very fortunate to run ...to be blessed to be able to do that at my age", and with that she resumed running the race.

When Don McNelly appears on panels to talk about his hundreds of marathons it's usually at running events and not with seniors groups. Don said in a recent Niagara Falls Marathon magazine article, "I think the reason is that around Rochester I am known as a crazy runner, and there are people probably saying to themselves you'll scare the hell out of them. I guess they're afraid I'm going to tell them to run a marathon a week or something."

Fellow American Chuck Commack started running in 1978 as a result of he and his wife making a complete change in lifestyle: "I was getting heavy and had quit smoking and tried to get in shape", he said. By 2004 he had run well over 100 marathons. But in September that year he was diagnosed with pancreatic cancer. He had the pancreas removed, and received six months of radiation therapy and chemotherapy. He was running right up until the day of the surgery and was running again two weeks after that. He kept running through his treatment, although not as much as previously. Chuck says his running and walking regimen helped keep his energy levels up through everything.

In April 2005 Chuck ran the Yakima River Canyon Marathon, but was in considerable discomfort. He later discovered he had fractured nine vertebrae during the race. The radiation he'd had from the cancer treatment had weakened his bones and the jarring from running had created the fractures. He then underwent an extensive period of recovery, including kyptoplasty, in which bone cement is injected into the vertebrae to fill in and stabilize it. In 2007 he ran a marathon in Eugene; his 200th – his first marathon in two years.

Boonsom Hartman started running in 1990 after she had surgery to correct a bladder problem. Her doctor told Boonsom she couldn't run or walk, so she tried to do exactly that. Now, because he told her she couldn't, every time she sees him he gives her a big hug. Boonsom was also having to cope with her daughter being diagnosed with a brain tumor. Running relieved the stress and made her feel relaxed. In addition, Boonsom has hypoglycemia (low blood glucose or low blood sugar), has suffered trauma in her life, has had a series of other illnesses, and a history of fainting spells.

Originally from Thailand, Boonsom is the mother of four children and is the youngest of twenty, yes, twenty, siblings. Her father died three days after she was born. Boonsom, which means 'wish for something good', now lives in Oak Forest near Chicago.

Before marathon running entered her world her passion was needlepoint. Every spare minute was consumed with needlepoint. She's now transferred that passion completely to distance running.

Boonsom ran her first marathon in Chicago in 1992. After a few years of running she set herself a goal of 50 marathons in 50 states by age 50. She did so with three years to spare. At the time when we talked, late 2009, Boonsom had completed 204 marathons, including 13 ultras. She typically completes a marathon in the time range of 4:11 – 4:45. She has now completed the 50 States twice and when we talked she had just two more states to run in for a third round completion.

Boonsom said "I'm really happy. You have control of your life. Marathon running made me happy and its fun, every marathon means something to me." If she could she'd travel and run every weekend. Her husband is very supportive, traveling with her wherever she goes, and often riding his bike or running alongside her when she's training. Boonsom said that marathoners are "happy, more mellow. They give you a big hug; they're so happy to see you – and it doesn't matter if you're a fast runner or a slow runner."

Boonsom is known as the Lipstick Lady because she always makes sure she is wearing bright lipstick during the marathon, especially at the finish (her favourite is Artistry Perfect Moisture Lip Color. Cherries Jubilee). "When you run a marathon, you want it bright", she says. "If you're a girl – wear lipstick, make sure you look good; it's important." To accessorize the lipstick she has 75 running outfits.

I talked to 47-year old American messenger Carol Dellinger two days after she had had a mastectomy. I had no idea that she'd just had this operation until the call itself, but Carol was insistent that we talk. "I'm glad you called, because I'm bored", she said. Carol had had a routine mammogram in October, and then radiation and chemotherapy treatment. It doesn't take long when talking to Carol to see that she has a wonderful positive outlook on life.

Carol completed her first 100 marathons by age 35. At the time she was the youngest woman to do so. But she is still the youngest woman to have completed 200 marathons (currently she has run more than 230 marathons).

A number of factors culminated in Carol's venture into marathon running. Her mother died at age 52 from bone cancer, her two sister's obesity (both weigh over 200 pounds) and their struggle with alcohol, and her connections with softball. Carol played at first base in semi-professional softball. Their short-stop was running a marathon and challenged Carol to run one. A year later she did: "I wasn't fast but I had great endurance. And then when I found that baseball was starting to compromise my running, I dropped the gloves."

Carol's first marathon was the 1989 Capital City marathon in Washington State. She has run that 20 times and has run the Portland marathon 20 times. It's a small world. Carol, it turned out, was at Bob Dolphin's birthday celebrations at Portland in 2009 the same day I was there.

Just like fellow messenger Rory Coleman explained with his own life, Carol surrounds herself with positive people and keeps the negative ones out of her life. "Marathoning has enabled me to maintain a positive outlook on life. I can accomplish anything in life and I owe it to marathon running." She see's marathoners as "outgoing, positive and very caring, a great group of healthy, positive people." "You can run a portion of a marathon with someone and be friends forever. You can have 2-3 hours of bonding, and yet there's still so much more to learn about one another too. There's a very strong trust element – we feed off one another with this trust."

Carol says that "a fit woman is a powerful woman. I'm built like a Toyota 4 Runner – muscular, powerful – like a steam engine. I'm out to prove you do not have to be thin to win." She told me she has "yet to shed a tear regarding cancer. You have to will yourself well, that 'can do' attitude." She has low blood pressure, low cholesterol, and a low heart rate. Little wonder then, that her doctors are amazed. Little wonder then that runners and non-runners alike are inspired by Carol. She does a lot of motivational speaking with youth groups and health care professionals.

When fully recovered from the operation Carol will continue to pursue her goal of running 500 marathons, although, she added, "each time I run a marathon that's my next goal. I never take a marathon for granted. My overall desire is to be a healthy, active individual."

In fact, just nine weeks after her mastectomy surgery Carol completed the Phoenix Rock 'n' Roll Marathon, and has since run several more. She told a reporter: "I ran that marathon on gut. There was no pity party for me; cancer picked the wrong woman to mess with. I never once shed a tear and looked at it as an inconvenience. That's how I approach life. I'm a very upbeat person."

American Elaine Doll-Dunn lives in Spearfish, South Dakota. She has worked as a guidance counselor at the local high school for 32 years, and is an adjunct professor at the local university. Now 72, Elaine only began running when she was 40. She is the proud mother of seven, and a grandmother of eighteen (three of her children have run marathons; all of her children are athletes in some way).

Running marathons was life changing for Elaine. She writes about her life, thoughts and experiences in three books; Running On... A Sole's Journey, FT HPNZ... A License to Run, and Gotta Run: Life is a marathon so double tie your shoes.

I talked to Elaine one morning before she headed off to the school. Elaine was born in Hebron, Nebraska in 1937. Her father had gone off and fought in World War II for two years and so, being on a ranch and with no brothers to work, Elaine quickly got into the rhythm of work-life on a ranch. Her mother took on many different jobs to overcome the hardships they faced. Elaine continued to work on the ranch when her father returned, but at least was able to enjoy riding her horse five miles to school every day.

Elaine has always had a passion for learning. At 17 she received her one-year teaching degree and started teaching at a country school. She married at a young age to her "childhood sweetheart" and they moved to France. In France she had three children and was pregnant with a fourth when her husband died from cancer. Elaine and her children returned to the United States, and moved back to her parent's ranch, whereupon she returned to college.

She remarried and had three more children. In addition to raising her children she obtained her bachelor's degree. At 65 she completed a Doctor of Philosophy in Psychology; her research focused on the self-efficacy of women who begin marathon running after the age of forty. Of her doctorate Elaine writes that "It doesn't get much better. It's like an emerald in my apron pocket; nobody sees it, but I like knowing it's there."

On her website she has an excerpt from one of her books "Only in retrospect do I realize that we run for, or we run from. I was running from and I didn't know it. The road has taken me places I never dreamed possible; mentally, physically, spiritually, and emotionally. Not bad for the price of a pair of Asics."

Elaine's second marriage did not work out and she was once again single. A third marriage changed her life yet again. Elaine met Jerry Dunn at the Black Hills marathon. In 1995 at the age of 57 she and Jerry got married during the Disney World Marathon.

They ran from the start-line to the Magic Kingdom where they had the ceremony. Elaine was wearing a traditional wedding gown and Jerry wore a tuxedo. Elaine slipped off her runners, put on her high heels, and the ceremony began. One of her daughters, an opera singer, sang 'Circle of Life' from The Lion King. "Seemed appropriate", Elaine said. When the ceremony was over the running shoes came back on and they ran the rest of the race. At the finish, Jerry picked up Elaine and carried her over the line. The Today Show was there too, as were several other media outlets.

Elaine told me she loves any kind of physical challenge. She is adamant that a positive 'can do' attitude will make a difference in people's lives. She believes it has enabled her to take on challenges and make the most of life. At age 55 Elaine ran the 113 miles Centennial Trail across South Dakota. A year later she "beat cancer." She has climbed Mt. Kilimanjaro when she was 58 years old. For her sixtieth birthday she ran 60 miles across Panama from the Atlantic to the Pacific. In 1998, at age 61, she won the Mrs. South Dakota Pageant. She writes on her website "I participated at the national level for Mrs. America. I was 30 years older than the other contestants, no, I did not place!"

Elaine's running had begun many years earlier when her second husband said "you can't run half a mile." He wasn't far off. But Elaine persisted, proving to others, but more importantly to herself, that she could. She started training with her friend Bill. They heard about the Black Hills Marathon being run nearby (Rapid City, 1978). Elaine said to Bill that he could run it and she would help him train. After a while Bill said to Elaine that since she's doing the same training she should run the marathon with him.

So she did. Even though she passed out at the finish line after completing the marathon, she wanted to continue running. "I swore I'd never do one again." Elaine is the only person to have run all 26 Black Hills marathons. She says that "running facilitated changes in my life – it was empowering."

Today Elaine has run 110 marathons and is the founder and race director of the Leading Ladies Marathon – an all woman event in the Black Hills, South Dakota. "It's my empowerment vehicle" she said. The Leading Ladies marathon event has grown exponentially. Elaine keeps it simple but invites inspiring guest speakers such as Kathrine Switzer, Helen Klein, Lorraine Moller, and Pamela Peak (a medical doctor from Nebraska). As for her own running, Elaine says "I used to race marathons. Then I ran marathons. Now I 'do' marathons."

Elaine said she "was born to healthy people, and I live healthy; physical and mental health ... I put myself to the edge, let's see what I can do... It also makes me feel good if I can make people happy and laugh." She also teaches children to read, encouraging them to bring a book from home that they are interested in: "it provides clues as to who they are, what they do." At some point, Elaine asks about what exercise they do. She has photos of her running on her office wall. These become conversation points and sources of inspiration.

In 2008 Elaine was the recipient of the Spirit of Dakota Award. The Award is made annually to one woman who posses qualities of leadership, courage, strength of character, and community commitment.

I first met Christian Hottas in Hamburg when I was there meeting several members of the German 100 Marathon Club. We had just finished the Elbe Tunnel marathon under the Elbe River in Hamburg. Christian invited me to his home on the outskirts of the city later that evening. He picked me up from the train station and drove a couple of miles to his apartment. We made some coffee and began talking about running. His English is better than mine. It was one of those evenings I'll never forget.

Christian started running marathons in 1987 at 30 years of age. He took on marathons because he was unfit and gaining weight. Seeing the writing on the wall he changed his diet and started to run. He increased his number of marathons each year until he started his family medicine practice (he's a Doctor; general & sports medicine, and a Chiropractor). Although his first wife didn't "accept it" at the time, his young daughter did. Christian used to push her along at various races. She was very proud of him.

As we read earlier, Christian has made his own marathon course in a park near his home in suburban Hamburg. "I don't do any training during the week; haven't for several years now" he said, "I just do my usual two marathons (or ultras) per weekend, but sometimes up to 10-17 in the same number of days in a row, between 80 and 171 marathons/ultras per year." His PB for a marathon is 2:59, while for ultras he has run 100 K in 8:14.

"During my runs I like to take lots of photos, I like to talk with many (old or new) friends, and I like to get many new ideas where I could run in the future. What I prefer running is an extraordinary or unusual course like on a beach, on the seabed, in a tunnel or a salt mine – or like the Grand Union Canal 145-Mile Trail Race from Birmingham to London which I did in 1998 and 2000, the West Highland Way Race, 95 miles, which I did in 2004. I love to meet my running friends and to run (and talk) some hours together with them."

Christian told me "every run is a gift. Every training run, every half-marathon, every marathon. We should enjoy every chance we have. A marathoner needs some respect for the long distance but it's not worth it to be anxious. We need to always be a little bit patient and most always look to our body. Run with it, not against it. Running hundreds of marathons needs to resist the temptation to pound the surface – you must be slow enough not to push yourself", he said.

"Marathons", he added, "help you experience nature, relieve stress, and give the body a workout. Running slow means there is less stress on the joints and less stress on your heart." He's been running them for years. He also introduced his future wife, Barbara (Basia) Szlachetka, from Poland, to distance running in 1997.

As Barbara was not a runner, Christian started her career by showing her running videos. In August, 1997, he made her a 4 K training route, which she ran with no trouble at all. They ran a half marathon together. At 14 K Barbara sped up, then with 2-3 K to go she wanted to walk. Christian said "no, let's run slow but not walk." Four weeks later she did her next half marathon. Then in November she ran her first marathon, in a time of 4:10. Christian had promised they'd go dancing afterwards, which they did. Soon after, she ran her first 50 K trail run. Barbara found running easy.

We had a break from talking while Christian went to another room and brought out several photo albums. We continued our conversation into the late hours as we flipped through the albums.

Barbara completed 52 marathons or ultras in her first year of marathon running. Over the next few years she transitioned into a world class distance runner. In June 1998, her 'rookie year', she became the German Champion in the 24-hour event in the 40-44 age group. In her second year she ran 251 K (156 miles) in a 48-hour road race in Cologne (a new Polish record). In March 2000, she ran 284 K (176 miles) in an indoor 48-hour race (an all age world championship bronze medal). In November 2000, in a 48-hour ultra in Dallas, she ran 304 K (189 miles), a course record. In March 2001 she ran 315.9 K (196 miles) in an indoor 48-hour race (a World cup bronze medal), and in May 2001 she broke the Polish record with 201 K (125 miles) in a 24-hour run, which earned her 5th place at the European Championships. In July 2003, she ran 348.9 K (217 miles) in another 48-hour road race; the second best ever in the world). In September 2003 she was the 3rd female finisher of the 246 K (153 miles) Spartathlon from Athens to Sparta in Greece.

Barbara set three Polish National Records in 24 Hours and six Polish National Records in 48 Hours. She set the 72-Hour National Record of 404.576 K (251 miles), and is "still the owner of all those records even today."

In July 2004, Barbara was diagnosed with advanced colon cancer.

She had her first operation which was successful, straight away. In August she had a smaller operation – on a Wednesday, and on the Sunday she ran the Longford marathon in Ireland. Despite the cancer, in 2004 she ran 27 marathons. These, Christian said, were more like "holidays from cancer", as she could enjoy the day, meet friends, experience nature and simply have fun. It was a very intensive period for Christian and Barbara, and they made the most of it.

Beginning in October 2000 and up to the time of her cancer she had been a member of the Polish National 24-Hour Ultramarathon Team. But things were never really the same. Barbara was diagnosed with more cancer at the beginning of 2005. She ran a few more marathons in 2005, but it was determined the cancer had metatastized and there was little chance for survival. Barbara told Christian she would "make murder" with her cancer. They both did.

She continued running up until July but then got fluid in her abdomen, which is very painful. Meanwhile, Christian, who had been running all through these years with Barbara, had amassed close to 1,000 marathons. Barbara told him to keep running – that she wanted to see him complete his 1,000th marathon. And so, in August 2005, Christian ran his 1,000th marathon, before the age of 50. Barbara ran the last few kilometers with him. It was the last run she was able to do.

She spent her remaining few weeks at home with Christian, who, as a doctor, provided her with around the clock palliative care. They set up a bed in their living room. Christian never left her side except for taking showers, running errands, making meals and keeping friends and family updated daily through the Internet. Barbara listened to her favourite running music in those last few weeks. She died on November 24th 2005. After the surgery and during chemotherapy, Christian said, "she enjoyed those last twenty-seven events (24 marathons and 3 ultras) as real moments of pure life."

As Christian was talking he paused and looked over to the couch. He said quietly "I suppose I should probably move the IV pole out." I looked over and saw Barbara's IV Pole still in the living room, wrapped-up in the branches, leaves and vines of the plants growing in the pot on the floor.

In less than eight years Barbara had completed 336 marathons and ultras. At the time of the interview Christian didn't have another goal in mind. But through some more recent correspondence with him it's clear he is in full swing again with the distance running. In 2009 Christian ran one 151 marathons, including 24 ultras. His grand total, as of early 2010, was 1,523 marathons, which includes 258 ultras. If people rank runners in terms of numbers of marathons run, this total of races places him at 'second' behind fellow German Horst Preisler.

Shortly after her death Christian wrote a memoriam letter for Barbara; the following text is excerpts from that letter.

Barbara Szlachetka has passed away. She died, in her home in Hamburg in the circle of her most beloved ones around 11:41 a.m. on November 24th, 2005, exactly the way she had prayed and wanted ... Running meant LIFE for Barbara. During her runs she was invigorated and forgot about her illness for hours... Basia completed her last running steps of about four kilometers at Kaltenkirchen Marathon on August 14th, 2005 while accompanying me to the finish line of my 1000th marathon. She did these final steps with the same motivation as the first - her love for me and desire to be together. Unfortunately, her wish to run with me the whole distance was not possible at that point any more.... Dear Basia, you now have finished your longest race with all your grace and charisma. Thank you for all the experiences and the endless love you have shared with your running friends and me.

I had arrived at Christian's home to talk about his running. As the evening went on the conversation moved to Barbara. Most of the photos we looked at in all the albums were of Barbara. I never met Barbara but she sounded like a remarkable woman. The photos showed a passion for life.

***

Nita Kay LeMay of Hawthorne Woods, Illinois told a reporter that when she finished her first marathon, Chicago, at age 40, she cried. "It was empowerment more than anything ... you are invincible. You can do anything. You can tackle anything", she said. That was October 1992. She was addicted. Twelve years later in October 2004 she ran her 100th marathon at the same race. Nita Kay has gone onto to run more than 130 marathons and ultras, including running a marathon on all seven continents in seven months in 2003.

Nita Kay is legally blind. When she looks directly at people she cannot see them as she has no straight vision. Nita Kay has macular degeneration, a hereditary disease and a major cause of visual impairment in older adults. She started to lose her sight in her twenties. She's now in her late fifties, and her eyesight has worsened over time. Her peripheral vision has also declined over the years.

Nita Kay told a reporter that she "doesn't consider it a handicap. It's just another one of those challenges that life gives you ... I don't want special treatment." She has learned to compensate, both during her races (and when she works at her job in a restaurant); she high steps on unfamiliar courses, for example. Typically though, with poor depth perception she needs to run slower than she would like, especially on rough trails. That said, her PB is still 3:54. She feels "very blessed" to be running the long distance races; her hope is that she can inspire others. "When my vision is completely gone, I won't look back with regrets, I'll look back with memories of those adventures ... I've been there, I've done that, got the t-shirt-type thought", she said in 2007.

Swedish messenger K-G Nystrom (Karl Gustav) used to hate sports as a child. But one day his Gym teacher made the class run around a circuit at school and then picked three of the students to run in a competition. K-G was one of them.

He was a natural runner. He became a school champion at age 14. While at university he was selected for Sweden's 1960 Olympic 4 x 400 metre track team. But he broke three bones in his foot while competing in a triple jump event prior to the Olympics and could not participate. He had a string of illnesses and injuries, including polio, meningitis and hepatitis. In 1970 at 32 years of age he was told he would never run again. In 1982 he was put in a wheelchair. After five months of not doing anything, he said, he "hated himself." He forced himself out of the wheelchair and got moving. His first one kilometre distance took 25 minutes. But he persevered and built up the distance training.

Six months later at 44 years of age he ran his first marathon. He didn't move for three days after that, spending most of the time in bed. But he got going again and a month later completed his second marathon. He discovered that the longer the distance and the slower he took, the better it was. He ran more and more. After 80 marathons he discovered that he could drink a beer without any side effects. After 150 marathons he discovered he could drink almost anything and it would not affect his running. Doctors, he said, claimed that "this was not in the books."

In 1997 he was diagnosed with lymph cancer. He told himself "I don't want that" and continued running four more marathons that year. The cancer went away. K-G told me that he hasn't slept through the night for 50 years. These days, because of hurting knees, he sleeps in total, maybe 5 hours. But he never feels tired. In 2001 he needed titanium rods in his knee. Five months later he ran a marathon on crutches, completing it in a time of 5:16. In fact he 'ran' a number of marathons on crutches in the first year after the titanium was put in his knee.

Through these experiences K-G has come to the conclusion that being active helps to significantly reduce the effects and likelihood of getting diseases. The body's cells, as some research is actually suggesting, continually rejuvenate as a result of the activity. "Marathons and ultra's", he said, "keep me alive."

At 71 years of age K-G has run 650 marathons and 120 ultras. In one year he ran 57 marathons and 5 ultras. He has also organized more than 200 races. "I get told I'm a nut", he said, "and I say 'Thank-you'". In 2009 he only ran ultras, but 16 of them. "Ultras are a very social thing … I'm going to do my last ultra when I'm 105!"

While on the one hand he may appear, as he puts it himself "crazy" with his running obsession, on the other hand he is making the most out of his life. "Your life is short" he told me, "and you're dead for a very long time. When they say you're crazy, I think what can I say … 'thank-you, you are the most perfect ordinary person I have ever met'?" In addition to speaking seven languages he has been a teacher, a scientist, the chief of development in a chemicals company, built houses, ran music stores and a travel agency, and been heavily involved in race organizing. In amongst all this his wife was killed in an accident. K-G has had a full life, and he shows no signs of stopping.

When I first talked to Australian 100 Marathon Club founder Bob Fickel he suggested that I get in contact with fellow Australian Stephen Mifsud. Steve is a financial planner in his early fifties. His story over the years is another testament to the words tenacity commitment, resilience, and perseverance.

Steve initially got into running because of injuries he received to his knee playing rugby league. And he almost died from a brain hemorrhage when he was spear-tackled in one game. Back then and still, he is in a "sit down job … I leave in the dark, I'm back in the dark ... the doctor told me to get out and run."

Steve ran 3-4 marathons a year for many years. In 1999 he almost died from meningitis on the eve of his ultra Six Foot 'buckle run'. In July 2003 he was to run what he said would be his last marathon, number 75 in Queensland on the Gold Coast. His knees held on and he finished, but on the 1,000 K drive home his knees got worse. He was forced to stop halfway and spend two days in a hotel room on pain tablets and rest his knees, in order to make the rest of the journey home. His doctor said "enough", and so he retired.

Steve told me that his life over the next five weeks was "miserable … I was depressed." A running friend suggested he not run but simply jog the marathon distance (his PB is a time of 2:58). So he set himself a new goal of running every state and territory in Australia in twelve months (eight marathons in total). His first race then, was just five days away in Adelaide – 1,500 K away. He needed to conquer his fear of flying to get there, which he did. It was a tough run with Steve hitting the wall, he says, after just one kilometre. But he persisted and made it to the end. His knees "gave up" in his second race in Sydney, but he'd been through this so many times before he knew the best solution was simply to run barefoot. In fact, in most of his races he has taken his running shoes off for 10-25 K of each one. Steve says this relieves the fluid draining from his knees into the bakers cysts at the back of his knees. His knee typically locks up around 20 K. If he takes off his shoes, and puts them around his waist, his legs straighten and the pain eases. "It's not painful running barefoot", he said.

In January 2004 he headed to Hobart, Tasmania for number 5 on the quest. He fell ill during the run and had to stop a few times, but still managed to complete it. The next marathon was Canberra. The day before the race he was bleeding internally. He said to his wife "if this was just any run I wouldn't start but its number 6 of 8 and we've already booked the next two." So he raced.

With marathons "you don't know if you're going to finish", Steve said, "until you get to that line." By 10 K he was very ill and "almost passing out from the weakness caused by the loss of blood." He made several toilet stops and managed to get through. Steve thinks this was due to the atmosphere and the other runners giving him support. Once home he had several tests and hospital visits. But as he comments "unfortunately the Friday before the Perth marathon I was still in hospital with my disease still undiagnosed, that was July 2004, so I discharged myself, flew to Perth, Western Australia [over 3,400 K away] and finished number seven."

With just one more race left on his internal quest – Alice Springs in the middle of Australia – he received word of the diagnosis; he had Crohn's Disease and Ulcerative Colitis, which meant he had trouble digesting solid food. He was put on a liquid diet, and prescribed steroids. He refused to take them. "I was an athlete", he said. "With Chron's disease you're not to run because you're bleeding internally", he said. Although it was hard, he completed the race successfully. Soon after, a New Zealand friend told Steve he couldn't stop there; that he had to run in New Zealand on both the North and South Islands – as part of the Australia-New Zealand 'spirit'. He took up the challenge, and in 2005 he successfully completed marathons in Christchurch and Auckland.

By November 2007 he had completed 91 marathons. People were encouraging him to complete the nine more required to reach his 100th. He said that in 2008 he "retired three-four times, but each time he started up again."

For his 100th marathon he planned to run the New York Marathon. During a race in Canberra 25 years earlier he said he "really suffered from the heat and almost passed out, but I found a New York Marathon Cap. I wet it and it cooled me down, kept the sun out of my eyes and kept me well enough to finish. I've run nearly all my marathons in that hat since, so now, after 25 years it is going home." And so in 2009 he and his wife and daughter, and Cap, travelled to New York to fulfill his dream.

After the race Steve wrote: "I got into 3:30 shape, but on the day I was overwhelmed by the crowd, over 3 million spectators on the course, this was a day to enjoy and take in the atmosphere - not to race. I decided to jog at an easy 4.30 pace and have fun; in fact as I entered Central Park New York, I slowed down, not wanting the marathon to finish. In the final few meters, I remember taking off my cap, looking at it and remembering my dream set 25 years ago of running New York and here I was only meters from finishing. Dreams do come true."

Steve's plan now is to officially retire. His long term goal has been reached. After New York, Steve didn't run for four weeks, but he kept fit by cycling, kayaking, and dragon boating. While on holiday one weekend in December he saw a half-marathon advertised. He ran it and surprised himself with a time of 1:41. But with marathons no longer his primary focus, he's putting more time into dragon boating. He has just been selected in his Australian's state's Squad. That said, he's also looking at running a marathon in Europe later in 2010 as well. It's hard to imagine Steve will ever stop running.

An "interesting fact" said Steve, is that "my date of birth is 25.02.58. My marathon PB occurred on my 25th marathon – a time of 2:58 even." He's also run more than 100 half marathons, and given his comment that "I run for that final 200 metres – you feel invincible – sometimes that feeling stays with you for weeks", it won't be a surprise to see his name regularly as a finisher in distance events.

When American Andrew Kotulski was visiting St. Petersburg a couple of days after the 2001 Moscow marathon he got up from a park bench to walk back to his hotel and felt the air had gone out of him. He had leaky valves and lung problems. It occurred, he said, at the same time as the 9-11 disaster in New York City.

Andrew became violently ill and couldn't leave his St. Petersburg hotel room for a week. He was driven to the airport, still very sick, and flew back to New York where he went to Emergency. They told him he had double pneumonia due to an unknown bacterial infection and that his organs were basically shutting down. He was told it would be unlikely he'd live to see the next day. He was given his last rites.

For reasons unknown he made it through that night. He remained in hospital for another two weeks, wasting away during that time. Andrew told me they could see his bones through his skin. "I was in very bad shape – fever, chills, diarrhea, vomiting, all that … It wasn't a total recovery but in retrospect, having the illness and recovering from it made me realize how blessed I was to be able to run; I was so happy to be alive and really to be able to live for the moment." Today he still runs low on oxygen. When we talked in 2009 he said that if he was in hospital 'right now' they would put him on oxygen immediately.

After complications, hernias and repair surgery from bladder surgery, 45-year old Oregonian messenger Fenny Roberts had to learn how to walk again. Her doctor recommended she start running to help with the healing process. Fenny wrote of this several years ago:

> [Her doctor] "encouraged walking as much as possible to strengthen my stomach muscles, with the aid of an abdomen brace. I was determined to get back to the fitness my body had one year earlier. After four weeks the brace came off, and I slowly, painfully, using walls, rails, I made my way out to the car and to the YMCA track once around. The next morning; (knowing I could walk around the track, hanging on to the rail), I went to the Y. Much to my amazement I was able to slowly shuffle my feet around the track not only once but four times. Friends watched in unbelief as I accomplished this task. The next morning at 6 am I went eight times around the track. I was on the road to recovery. Four weeks later, Dr. G. encouraged starting to jog with my brace one block first day, then added one block per day from then on. Friends from the Y encouraged me to run with them. Before long I was running West Salem hills: a task I thought I could never do even before my last two surgeries. I ran in March 1998 the Shamrock Run along with fellow Y runners. Due to a hip injury, I race walked the Steen Mt Run a few months later and took a third place. With Y runners encouragement I ran my first marathon in October 1998; The Portland Marathon.

"In 2006 Fenny completed her 100th marathon – the Pacific Crest 50K Trail Run at Mt. Hood, Oregon. One of her accomplishments in those eight intervening years was running 121 miles in a 24-

hour run in her home town of Salem, Oregon, in 2000.

Fenny is a fitness instructor at the local Y, teaching Yoga, Pilates and Tai Chi. She was previously a swimming instructor for 27 years. Fenny told me that she was diagnosed with type 2 diabetes five years ago – which, she said, is consistent looking back with how she felt growing up as a child, where she'd often feel sick if she didn't have her meals at a regular time. "But it would never show up in tests over the years", she said. She thinks this may be due, in part, because her diet actually mimics the very diet that a diabetic needs to have. Now, she feels, the longer distance running helps to keep her blood-sugar at the right level. Keeping fit and enjoying the outdoors through running makes a huge difference to her life.

In 2009 she injured her back again. Fenny's doctor told her to take some medication and not to run. But the medication proved ineffective and she was getting depressed. Fenny began pushing a grocery cart to get mobile again. She had lost a lot of leg muscle. Over the ensuing days people watched and wondered, including police officers, as she built up the distance in small increments and could walk up to 90 minutes at a time. Through this period Fenny had "found race-walking." She now belongs to the North-west Race Walkers Club.

Fenny said she "loves the outdoors and especially running the ultras and the trail races – its relaxation for me. It's a way to keep fit, enjoy the outdoors, sing, and listen." Now in her late fifties she suggests to beginners that you need to "discipline yourself to get out and do it." She quoted her chiropractor: "Movement is life and life is movement." Fenny's immediate goals now are to get herself up to 50 K race walking, and train herself back up to running 100 milers.

Fellow American messenger Cathy Troisi ran her first marathon in 1992 after participating in one of Jeff Galloway's running schools. She owned two pre-schools in the north-east of the United States, and selected marathons to run that coincided with school vacations. Now in her sixties, Cathy has run more than 265 marathons. Over the years she has raised more than $90,000 for charities, especially the Dana-Farber Cancer Institute in Boston, Massachusetts.

Tragedy struck Cathy's family in Christmas 2006 when her only child, her daughter Kimi, was diagnosed with cancer for a second time. Kimi died in August 2007. "I fell off the wagon", she told me. "I lost my motivation, interest, desire, everything. But I decided to do a marathon a month; I felt I needed to do it as a distraction more than anything. I looked for marathons that had no cut-offs. I needed to get to the marathon weekend each month, which felt good, but then when I was back at the apartment things hadn't changed."

In July 2009 her granddaughter asked her if she had allergies or anything, because Cathy's eyes were always red. The question transformed Cathy. A running friend said she'd help her get out of this "well of despair." They registered for Pikes Peak, the JFK 50 miler and the Lake Tahoe Triple.

"Pikes Peak got cancelled and I was pulled from the JFK, but the Triple 'worked, with times of 6:12, 5:57, and 5:47. Regardless, they got me out there", she said.

Cathy loves Lake Tahoe. "It's the one place I can go on the planet and find a sense of peace." After her last visit for the triple she came up with the idea of running around Lake Tahoe twice for a total of 144 miles. It's a goal she knows is attainable if she sets her mind to it. Cathy believes the training required will be just the thing she needs to move her out of current thinking. "Running has been a salvation for me" she said, "it's given me normalcy after my daughter's death." Based on her own experience she says it's important for everyone to "never judge how someone is doing a marathon as you never know what they're dealing with as they come to the start-line."

Cathy also has an Achilles companion who has a heart transplant, so sometimes she will walk a marathon with him. Achilles is an international organization that began in 1976 when Dick Traum, an above knee amputee, decided he needed to do something about his own fitness. He joined a YMCA and started running – short distances at first which later grew into longer distances, culminating in him running the New York marathon. Seeing the difference running made to his life, he founded the Achilles athletics club in 1983 to help other disabled runners, many of whom train with volunteers such as Cathy. Her Achilles partner had his heart transplant twelve years ago. He has run marathons in more than 30 states.

Siri Terjesen is a university professor with specific research interests in international entrepreneurship, strategy and business. She has authored several book chapters and her papers have been published in numerous academic journals. She has studies and held academic positions around the world, including England, Australia, China, Norway, Canada and the United States.

Siri was born in 1975 in Akron, Ohio. She had always wanted to run marathons as she was growing up. She completed her first marathon in Copenhagen, in 1997, one week after graduating from the University of Richmond in Virginia. She said "I found a sub-culture and I was hooked – an eclectic fun group of people … happy, outgoing, fun, slightly crazy group of people." Siri told a reporter that she admires "something in every person I meet at ultras." With an obvious natural talent she has gone on to win 40 marathon and ultra events in 15 countries, and has represented the United States in major international competitions. She was the British Ultrarunner of the Year in 2003, and also represented England in 2003 and 2004. In 2003 she was the United Kingdom Champion in the 100 K. She was the Australian Champion for the 50 K in 2006. Her PB for the marathon distance is 2:58:35, and for the 50 K is 3:35:19 (the fastest time for an American woman in 2006). Siri's PB for 100 K is 8:22:09, which was the fastest time for an American Woman in 2003.

Siri said that running "has been a blessing." She was diagnosed with scoliosis at the age of seven. This is a genetic curvature of the spine; if you look at the spine from behind instead of looking straight it looks more like an 'S' or a 'C'. Siri wore a full brace for nine years, during which time she could only remove it for one hour each day. Regardless, she still ran while she wore the brace.

By age 16, doctors concluded the brace was not working; in fact her condition was getting worse. Siri had surgery. Two steel rods were inserted from the top of her neck to down to her tailbone. "Running" she told a reporter, "has always been a wonderful escape time." After a long period of inactivity following her operation, she got back into running and rediscovered her love for the sport. "I really love the camaraderie and find that ultrarunners the world over are a fairly eccentric but friendly bunch, full of energy and laughs." When she trained for her first marathon in 1997, she said "this time it wasn't to escape the brace!"

You get a sense that Siri embraces life to the full. She is open to new experiences; "adventure is the best souvenir" she says, and meeting new people. To Siri "runners all have similar karma regardless of age, gender, nationality." Siri's positive attitude enables her to race the long distances. She thinks about her accomplishments, friends and family. "When you're going that far you really have to manage your head. If you start to think about negative things, it's easy to stop."

Siri said she is "so lucky … I travel so much with my work and can coordinate this with my running. With academics we can plan our days around the running. If I don't have running the other stuff doesn't work well either. I throw myself into work the day before so the run seems like a reward and down time after."

Her running and research are taking a bit of a back seat in 2010 as she has just had her first baby, a boy. It shouldn't be a surprise to anyone that knows Siri that she has now "gotten into long distance walking in the interim, since that's super safe."

25

"Although we are in the same races Bill is always ahead,
but only because he has a good woman behind him!"

Pauline Howes

"Through running you realize there's a connection with people
no matter what country you go to.
In marathons, everyone starts on equal footing.
You realize that we're really all the same people."

Yen Nguyen

A number of messengers are married couples – that is, both spouses have each run more than 100 marathons. Steven Holehan and Parvaneh Moayedi from Texas, for example, ran their 100th marathons within a few months of one another in 2007. They became 50 States finishers in October 2006 at the Cape Cod Marathon in Falmouth, Massachusetts, and plan to run all of the continents together.

Also based in Texas is another married couple - Steve Boone and Paula Boone. In December 2009 Steve, at age 60, completed his fourth cycle of the 50 States. He hopes to have his fifth cycle completed in 2010. Steve has run more than 430 marathons while Paula has run close to 300 races.

Based in Houston, they are perfectly situated to travel around the continent because Houston is a hub for air travel. They are able to get some good deals as well as direct flights to destinations. As a result of their extensive traveling they have, as Steve explains, "learned a lot about the country, the history, learned lots about the people, and lots about the places; we've gone to places you'd never find on a map even!" When I asked Steve how they manage to do so much running he said "we don't put ourselves in a box ... we always keep our eyes wide open for opportunities, new travel deals ... we don't get caught in a rut of the typical weekend, like going to Walmart and buying things all the time ... we have friends all over - we have friends who finish in 2:07 and those who finish in 6:07. Slow, fast ... it doesn't make a difference." The usual comment about Paula and Steve's running from family and friends is 'Why??!!??' "Most of our friends are runners", Steve says, "and they still think we're over the edge. Our non-running family members don't even understand what marathons are."

Paula said she "loves to eat and my next favorite thing is travel. Marathons get me to do these things." Even though she says she's not fast, she trains on weights every day, swims four times a week, and then runs marathons on the weekends. "I would always choose to run with Steve because he is my best friend and favorite traveling companion, but he runs too fast for me to keep up with him." Steve tries to run 6-8 miles 4-5 days a week and also walks every evening. If they are not at a marathon, they will do a 12-14 mile run on the weekends.

Pauline and Bill Howes from England have both run more than 100 marathons. 'It' started quite innocently when Pauline was at home with three children and wanted to get fit. She saw an advertisement for raising money for 'Save the Children' by running the Woman's Own 10 K race. She said "I really didn't know how far 10 K was, but I entered, got accepted and began to run. Bill would come home from work and I would leave the children with him and go for a run. Bill was running [training] the football teams and thought this was another of my phases and would diminish. At that time, he had no idea that he would run one day."

Pauline completed the 10 K run in 50 minutes and then started to train for half marathons. After running a number of half marathons and seeing the London marathon on television, Pauline decided to do a marathon. She completed her first marathon in 4:27. She knew immediately that she wanted to do better. Bill on the other hand thought it would be her first and last. She joined a running club and around the same time Bill finished his commitments with football. He and Pauline then ran the Great North half marathon. Bill then took up running, got faster and faster, and, at one point, won every cup in the local running club. Pauline broke the 4:00 hour mark in the marathon while Bill went on to a PB of 2:51.

Their friend John Dawson meanwhile was accumulating more and more marathons. As Pauline commented, "we were (and still are) amazed and inspired by him." Through John they became friendly with other 100 Marathon Club members. Gradually they ran more and more marathons, until they decided they too wanted to become members of the club. They completed their 50th marathon in Madrid together, and completed their 100th together a few years later in Benidorm, also in Spain. Pauline makes the point that stresses that "although we are in the same races Bill is always ahead but only because he has a good woman behind him!"

Susan and Paul Adams from England have been running together for many years. At age 31, Paul ran his first marathon in Scarborough, his home town. Paul said he "started running initially to lose weight and become more healthy, as I smoked cigarettes and suffered migraine headaches badly." He was heavily influenced by friends and mentors who were runners. They helped him gain both fitness and confidence, especially the confidence in his ability to complete the distance.

Paul says that these days, marathons provide relaxation from the stresses of his work (he's a partner in a large architectural firm). Running marathons "has become a lifestyle providing lots of events to attend and enjoy." His best friends are fellow runners. Importantly, with Susan taking up running as well, the marathon experience has become a "family affair." Several years ago Susan and Paul 'found' the Swiss Alpine Marathon in Davos. They ran that race for their 25th Wedding Anniversary and have done it each year ever since.

Susan started running marathons to prove she "was capable", after completing a nutritional research project on endurance runners that looked at preventing them hitting the wall by keeping energy levels stable. Running marathons has increased her personal capability, particularly as the act of running a marathon signifies the achievement of "what I set out to do through my own effort and no one else's." She says it's great to meet up with "some fantastic people and hopefully inspire others to have a go."

Both Susan and Paul have completed the Brathay 10 Marathons in 10 Days Challenge, which is run over the Brathay Windermere Marathon course in the Lake District of England. They both started the 2008 challenge but Susan had to withdraw part way through due to a foot injury she had sustained at an earlier marathon. She remained there on crutches supporting Paul's success in the 10 in 10 challenge. For Paul it was an emotional moment when he crossed the finish line in the tenth race. As he said "completing the 10 in 10 is probably the best feeling I have had in running." Susan returned in 2009 and successfully completed the challenge. Obviously delighted, she says that the Brathay Windermere Marathon "is close to my heart after completing the 10 in 10."

A couple of years ago, I drove down to London from the Lake District in England having just met members of the UK 100 Marathon Club at the Windermere Marathon. I was off to spend a few days interviewing club members about their running experiences. My first interview was with Michaela Sanders, who I'd been emailing before leaving Canada. Michaela's instructions for meeting at a bookstore just of the M5 motorway were straightforward but for the uninitiated was as complicated as the script for The Matrix.

I successfully, well miraculously, went around about twenty roundabouts, some several times, and went repeatedly up and down ramps to the motorways, by the motorways, for the motorways, and to the motorways again. It was with great delight that we sat in comfy chairs in the bookstore drinking coffee and talking about marathon running.

Michaela is in her mid-forties, and works in the health foods sector just north of London. She runs marathons for the friendships and the ability to see different places. The fitness element also appeals. "Running is a great way to be outdoors and doing something good for yourself." Despite having run more than 100 marathons she still considers herself a "totally non-sporting person."

Michaela started running in 1993, almost flying off the treadmill she bought the first time she got on it. When she got a membership at the gym, she gave the treadmill to her brother. She got hooked logging the distances she was running and the weights she was lifting at the gym. She then joined the Fairlands Spartans Running Club, and started running "anytime" to encourage her friends to run as well. "At the time running was my escape – I could completely clear my mind and deal with things." As well as experiencing the runners "high", she was continually meeting new people and friends, some of whom were members of the 100 Marathon Club who were encouraging, supportive, and simply good fun to be with. After running an 18-miler, she realized she wanted to run, and could run, the marathon distance.

About a dozen friends joined Michaela for her 50th marathon in Amsterdam; they'd come to run and celebrate. She had severe flu, felt sick and couldn't eat, but with so many friends having spent money to come and share the weekend with her, she felt compelled to run. Her husband Mark, who has since also become a member of the 100 Marathon Club, ran in front of Michaela, passing her jelly-babies along the way. She was running for everyone else. As she said, "resilience, tenacity and stupidity."

But essentially she is a goal setter; from identifying short running distances during a race, like lamppost to lamppost, to broader running goals and life in general. Her overall outlook is best captured by her comment: "Don't spend the rest of your life making more regrets."

Once she started running marathons Michaela went on to become the runner to finish 100 in the shortest amount of time, averaging a marathon every 11 days. She eased back considerably after she reached her 100th. Her goals since then have been to get her body back in better condition, to run fewer marathons and to get her times down again. Her times had increased as her number of marathons accumulated. More recently, she was also the fastest person to complete 100 *different* marathons or ultras, (at an average of just under 18 days each marathon), in her 123rd event.

In the longer term, she'd like to "break the 4-hour time, run 200 and 300 marathons, or run a marathon in every county, every letter of the alphabet ... there will be something" she says. But the social side of the lifestyle is at the heart of the experience: "Without the marathon running I wouldn't have been social, met up with friends, seen the places I've seen... never would have done it otherwise." Meanwhile, her husband Mark accelerated his tally of marathons and went on to complete one hundred as Michaela slowed the rate of hers.

Michaela and Mark have travelled with many different runners to races in Europe and across the United Kingdom. Another couple, also in their mid-forties from the UK 100 Marathon Club, they have run and socialised with are Linda and Dave Major. It was Dave whom I met on the train platform in Athens. Linda and Dave openly acknowledge that their lives revolve around marathons, or to be more precise, around the total marathon experience. Almost *every weekend* they are off to run a marathon or an ultra event somewhere, and sometimes two in one weekend.

Dave says they do this for three main reasons; fun, friendship and fitness, which, he says, used to be the other way around. Dave says he is driven by goals, whereas Linda is driven by happiness. Dave's happiness also relates to Linda's. When I asked Linda about juggling marathons with life in general she replied simply "you earn enough money Monday to Friday so that you can enjoy the weekends and the holidays."

With running a marathon or more every weekend, there is less need to train in between. Their bodies have become conditioned to the distance, perhaps even addicted to the weekly long run. Dave has not gone more than three weeks in the last four years without a marathon, so long runs are not a concern. One or two 5-mile runs during the week is the most they will do when they are running marathons every weekend.

In 2009 they ran outside of the United Kingdom on more than twenty occasions. A typical weekend in Europe may consist of meeting friends at the airport, flying to the destination and having a night out when they arrive. On Saturday they will pick up their race numbers and look around the location. In the evening they'll go out or take it easy, preparing either way for the race in the morning. A Mexican restaurant will be in the plans if Dave can arrange it. Sunday morning is race morning, followed by the retelling of stories about the race and other marathon-related experiences with friends and then traveling back home ready to start another week at work and gearing up for another marathon, somewhere, the following week. Dave wrote to Lenore Dolphin once "I am known for having a drink, alcoholic, before (during, sometimes) and after a marathon and certainly believe in celebrating each marathon achievement before it happens as well as afterwards."

Linda said to me "I thought that by doing marathons every weekend you can eat what you want. How wrong I was – I still need to watch what I eat compared to how much training I do in a week. I have learned, over 100 marathons, that I can't eat spicy food the night before, can only have water on the course, and need to have a very bland breakfast, like banana and toast. I can't have fizzy drinks directly after either."

In 2009, Dave ran 59 marathons and ultras and Linda ran 52. For those achievements they were awarded second and third place respectively in the Marathon Maniacs Club 2009 Male and Female Maniacs of the Year awards. Dave has run just over 400 marathons and Linda just over 300. As important as the numbers may be for achieving goals, Dave and Linda do what they do for the shear enjoyment of it all.

Back in the United States, in Houston, Texas, and not far from Paula and Steve Boone, Yen Nguyen and her husband Peter Bennett integrate their passion with running marathons with their passion for travelling. As Yen explained, "One of the reasons I run is that I can travel, and see the world at the same time."

Yen and Peter met at an Enron corporate track meet in 1999. In

2002, just moments after being proclaimed the 100 millionth visitor to the Eiffel Tower, Peter proposed to Yen. They got married the following year in Hawaii, which Yen says is one of their favorite destination marathons.

The couple have run past tanks in Chile during protests against a new government, and run with poverty stricken children in Tanzania. Peter gave out candies to the children as they ran for long distances alongside he and Yen. On a trip to Belgium for the Maastricht Marathon they arrived but their luggage, including running gear, did not. As everywhere closes on a Saturday in Belgium they contacted their hotel and explained their situation. The manager was a runner. Within a short period of time she had contacted friends in the running community and Peter and Yen were quickly decked out in full running gear borrowed from Belgian runners. "I looked like a European runner", Yen said, "you know, bi-shorts, spandex stuff …." Yen now travels wearing her running gear, just in case.

Peter is a lawyer and Yen is an accountant. With so much travel, at one point they had accumulated one million air miles. "It's more a question of getting the time off work than the financial side of things" Yen says. Having run in more than 40 countries, "the challenge" says Yen, "is not so much the actual distance, but getting there." In fact, Yen keeps a journal of the "bad travelling experiences." In 2008 they estimated they spent about US $40,000 on travelling and running marathons. "People spend money going to the movies, drinking at bars or on expensive cars … we spend it on running", Peter says.

They are quick to point out that getting to know different cultures and people is important. "Although we don't always speak the same language it's still a people's sport, and there is a common bond; it's kind of neat, people are nice everywhere", Peter said in a newspaper article. "Through running you realize there's a connection with people no matter what country you go to." Yen added that "In marathons, everyone starts on equal footing. You realize that we're really all the same people."

In New Zealand, Chris Leahy is scheduled to run her 100th marathon in June 2010. Her husband Mike, meanwhile, is close behind with 84 marathons. Chris got addicted to marathon running several years after having her two children in 1983. At the time, it was a way to keep fit. Chris was quoted in a New Zealand newspaper as saying, "There have been times I've thought, 'what the hell am I doing out here', but you just get out there and you do it."

Her best time is 3:20, although, due to a back injury a few years ago she now completes marathons at a brisk walking pace. "Plenty of friends think I'm absolutely crazy", she told a reporter, "but we all have our funny ways I suppose. While you're fit and healthy why not do it?"

Swedish messenger K-G Nystrom.

Some of Germany's many messengers: Sigrid Eichner, Joachim Meyer (1200+ marathons) and Juergen Kuhlmey.

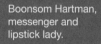

Boonsom Hartman, messenger and lipstick lady.

Wedding day at the Disney Marathon for messengers Elaine Doll-Dunn and Jerry Dunn, pictured here with 1972 Olympic marathon gold medalist Frank Shorter.

Pam Penfield at the top of Pikes Peak (14,115 feet).

Messengers Elaine Doll-Dunn and Jerry Dunn, with Baron.

Paul Selby, South Africa.

British messenger Mark Sanders, running his 100th marathon in Germany

Siri Terjesen, representing Team USA, World 100 K championship.

American messenger Todd Byers, 80 marathons run barefoot...and counting.

British messenger Jim 'Manic' Mundy,
finishing his second 10 marathons in 10 days challenge

Danish messenger
Tor Rønnow

Paul Adams, finishing
his 10 marathons in
10 days challenge,
Lake District, England

American messenger Cathy Troisi at the Lake Tahoe Triple.

British messenger Michaela Sanders after completing her 100th marathon.

Sean Meissner winning at Yakima. Photo courtesy of Adrenaline Event Photography.

Messengers at the 2010 Yakima River Canyon Marathon:
Jose Nebrida, Lenore Dolphin and Bob Dolphin.
Photo courtesy of Adrenaline Event Photography.

British messengers Pauline and Bill Howes.

26

"People ask me why I run, and to me the question really is:
Why don't you run? Running is living a good life
and running a marathon is a wonderful way to travel"
Andrew Kotulski

"I'm seeing and meeting the real people in the real countries
– bringing down the barriers."
John Maddog Wallace

The world becomes a smaller place when you travel. The beauty of destination marathon travel is that runners have an ideal opportunity to see so much as they run the events, and meet runners from the destinations themselves and from around the world.

John Zeleznikow is a professor of information systems based in Melbourne, Australia. He's run more than 150 marathons since he first started in 1971. He runs marathons as a way to see the world, especially when he's on sabbatical outside of Australia. "Marathon running is just another part of life," he said, "the key is to have a balance – a quality of life – for myself and my family. My achievements come from other things. I run marathons because I enjoy them. It's a great way to go sightseeing. You see different cultures plus you have a commonality. I don't run hard, but I don't get injured as a result."

Don Kern is a 50 States finisher who has the distinction of also having completed the seven continents three times. His second completion, in March 2007, took only 35 days. In December that same year, he completed his third round in just 33 days, and became the only person to run all seven continents twice in one year.

Like many messengers, Osy Waye's passion with running coincides with his passion with travel. I met Osy in London's Hyde Park. We sat on a bench one afternoon on a perfect summer's day. Osy is a church caretaker and also runs a dog kennel. He took me through his photo albums while we talked about marathon running. Some great photos. He has traveled around the world running marathons. For his 100th he ran the North Pole marathon. In a Polar Bear suit.

He first tried running in the suit at the London marathon. At the North Pole all the runners wore snow shoes although it was felt they would only have to do that for the first lap. But with the snow so soft they had to run in the snowshoes for the entire distance. Fortunately, although it was minus 10-13 degrees Celsius (8.6 to 14 Fahrenheit), there was no wind to make it worse.

Osy also ran the Antarctic marathon at the other end of the world. It was the year the ship could not land due to the sea conditions. With a large number of runners specifically on the tour to run the marathon, it was decided to run the marathon *on* the ship instead.

> When someone suggested running on board, we were overjoyed. Doing over 200 laps was, well, quite funny, as I used to hate doing a 2 or 3 lap marathon. As well as the 240 laps on what was quite a small ship, we had to hop over 400 bulkheads and at the front of the ship we had to go through the doors inside. Quite near the start, I managed to trip over a bulkhead and bash my head on some other part of the ship. I remember it made quite a noise and gave me a gash to the forehead, and quite a bit of blood, but I have a thick skull, and no way was I stopping. I remember hiding my blood and wound under my hat to make sure no one was going to stop me. It did stop bleeding after a few laps. Running over 200 laps? Very interesting, relaxing, it was no race, just that desire to do it, there were always runners passing or you passing others, so lots of camaraderie. ... All we could hear beside

the patter of running shoes and encouragement was a sort of distant thunder, which we were told was the glaciers moving. If we had time to look over the side of the ship we would have spotted some whales, dolphins, and seals, and over on land, thousands of penguins. Magic."

Osy said, "You see so much in such a short amount of time when running marathons; you get to places you wouldn't get to otherwise." A few years ago he ran the Beirut marathon: "You go there with trepidation. Hide in your hotel. Should be safe with 2,000 runners you think. I've never found a place that has been more friendly than Beirut. Then this year, a week before the Beirut marathon, they had to cancel it due to the Lebanon conflict. I saw on TV the craters on the road that I'd run on."

Over the years Osy has collected more than 90 Hard Rock Café pins on his travels to marathons around the world. In Japan, for example, he ran a marathon and was able to visit seven Hard Rock Cafes. He's now a Pin Master for Beijing, and was Pin Master for Nottingham, England before it closed.

Like Osy, 68-year old American Andrew Kotulski has travelled the world, running marathons in over 76 countries. Like Osy, he too found Beirut to be "so friendly, so helpful." Andrew has accumulated more than 600 marathon finishes, including 30 Boston marathons. He is a member of the Quarter-century Club – runners who have active streaks of running the Boston marathon at least 25 years in a row. He's also run the 50 States almost six times, and the Canadian provinces almost four times.

In his younger days, Andrew had a five mile trip to get to school each day, one way. He could go by foot or take the bus. He loved the five mile runs. As he grew up, his sporting life revolved around tennis in New York City in the 1960s. He started running to improve his tennis, to get fitter, get in better shape. It changed his life. "While it was hard to find tennis courts available in New York, with running you simply went out the door." The more he ran the more he thought about marathons: "I didn't know if I could do it", he said, "Plus there were not many marathons around back then."

Andrew, a former smoker who smoked two packs of cigarettes a day, has had some significant hurdles to overcome in his life. But running marathons has been an integral part of his life. At one point he had a running streak of 26 years – running at least 4 miles every day. "Things are not that bad after you finish a run, no matter what the problem is", he said, "It's tough to cry and run at the same time."

"When you think about it, your health is the best gift that you can give to your family, your parents, your children, and to yourself." He says he will be running "as long as I can; till death do us part."

Messenger Ashis Roy of New Delhi, India, ran his 100th marathon in January 2010. His first marathon was the Rath Marathon in Delhi in November, 1985. Dr Roy has also traveled widely, with over 60 of his marathons being run outside of India. He's known as the "Marathon Man of India." He ran his first marathon at the age of 52, and has plans, at the age of 78, to run the Yakima River Canyon Marathon in Washington State in April, 2011.

But you don't have to travel a lot to run 100 marathons or more. The most prolific New Zealand messenger, Michael Stewart, has now run close to 500 marathons, most of which have been run in New Zealand. In fact in a Runners World article in 2006, written by Australian messenger Julia Thorn, he noted that he had not run any marathons overseas. It's quite remarkable when you consider that even now New Zealand only has a population of 4.3 million people, and there are simply not a lot of marathons to run each year. Michael ran his first marathon, as an 18 year old in 1970, and clocked a time of 3:29. His father had started him running."It's addictive", he said about running in Julia's article, "but it's good for you. Running has led me into learning about nutrition and how to look after my body."

Helmut Linzbischler alternates life between Austria and Michigan. To say he has had a full life would be an understatement. He ran his first marathon in 1985 at Graz, Austria and completed his 100th marathon there in October 1998. He has now run more than 250 marathons. His other passion is mountaineering; he's climbed all over the world including in Turkey, Iran, Pakistan, Alaska, Russia, Mexico and South America. As well as completing a marathon in all 50 States in 2005 he also reached the 'highpoint' in all 50 States and photographed all 50 state capital buildings, plus DC. As well, he climbed to the summit of all 57 peaks in Colorado that are higher than 14,000 feet and explored the Cascade Range volcanoes. The most challenging part of this quest, he said, was the logistics involved in coordinating the marathons, high points and state capitals.

His other running feats have included the 1992 Transamerica Footrace from Huntington Beach, California to New York in 64 days; a 350 K solo race in 1994 along the River Mur in Austria, a 1,300 mile solo double crossing of the Austrian Alps in 2000 in 40 days; a number of American 100 mile races, the 1998 Badwater 135 mile race that starts in Death Valley and finishes at Mt. Witney, and the Climbathon in Borneo which, with more than 15,000 feet total elevation, is considered to be the "world's most gruelling half-marathon." He is also a licensed pilot, certified ski instructor and a referee, and a licensed instructor for rescue swimming.

Fellow European, German Juergen Kuhmley, has travelled the world with his business and his passion of long distance running. He owns a pharmaceutical company specializing in cancer therapy. It has done well, and as a result Juergen has the financial means to run wherever and whenever he wants. Juergen ran his first marathon in 1985 at Karlsruhe, Germany. Sixteen years later he ran his 100th marathon at the Dead Sea. He ran his 300th marathon in 2007. He has run the seven continents in one year, as well as the North Pole Marathon (in snowshoes), and has run the Mongolia 100 K, the Mt. Everest Marathon, the Sondershausen Marathon (minus 2,300 feet), the Antarctic Marathon; and the Desert-Atacama Marathon (Chile) and Titicaca Lake Marathon (Peru).

As a child he said, he always wanted to run when he was walking. Although he was quite a good runner at 5-10 K at High School he didn't start running marathons until he was 48. Now at 70 years of age, he is running as much as he can. "I'm a runner" he confessed, "I have a feeling when I walk that I have to run." At university he studied chemistry for 11 years, which, he says, is a "real test of endurance." He makes the connection between chemistry and marathon running. "In each marathon the body is exhausted but you have to keep going, exhausted – a challenge for the body; that's where the mind kicks-in."

His wife is not into activities like Juergen but is still into fitness walks. When they visit New York each year as Juergen runs the marathon, his wife will focus on the musicals.

Like Juergen, John 'Maddog' Wallace has also run the Dead Sea marathon. That was en route to John becoming the first person to ever run a marathon in 100 different countries. He travels to most races with his wife, Nicole, of 35 years, who doubles as his 'sports manager'. Now, retired at 65, and with more than 330 marathons to his name, Maddog continues to train daily, and still pushes himself in the marathons.

John originally hails from Carleton Place, just outside of Ottawa, Canada. He completed a degree in engineering at Queen's University in Ontario, and started running marathons at 33: "I stopped smoking and was putting on weight" he said, "so I decided to start running." He ran a mile and threw up. It became an obsession, he said: "I'm gonna get my ass in shape."

John found that the longer he ran, the better he liked it. A couple of years later he moved from Canada to the United States. His career saw him move from engineering to sales and marketing in the high technology sector. "Running", he said, "became the stress reliever."

He ran his first marathon, the Silver State Marathon in Reno, Nevada in 1982, in a time of 3:28. He ran it hard but hit the wall and had to walk the last few miles. John's clearly goal oriented. His first goal after this first marathon was to break three hours. Then it was to "do the 50 states." "When I make a goal it becomes an obsessive goal", he said.

His nickname Maddog came in his early working days in Dallas, Texas. He was one of a group of runners who were all around 40 years old. There was always a run of some sort each weekend. They would typically run a race on Saturday and then go for a 10-13 mile run on Sunday. "We were all fanatics," he said. They decided not to do their Sunday run at a 10 K pace, but a bit slower. What started out at a 6:30 mile pace whittled down to a 6:00 pace later in the run. With a couple of miles to go, John would take off – like a mad dog. The Maddog label stuck. So as he runs, even today, mentally he often changes over the last portion of his runs to 'Maddog' as he pushes himself to the finish line.

Almost on the day he retired from his executive position in 1999 his wife had an opportunity to work in England. Off they went. John kept busy through this time running in as many countries as possible – 31 different countries, in fact.

While in England, people asked him which countries he had run. He discovered that no-one had run a marathon in all the European countries. This was his new goal. He went back to run in the countries he'd missed while his wife was working in England. By 2004 he had run marathons in 54 European countries and called it "Europe." By now his grander country total was getting close to 80 different countries.

But it wasn't until 2008 that he made 100 countries his goal – and to complete them by age 65. Maddog ran in 10 different countries in the last eight months to reach his goal, two months earlier than his 65th birthday. He completed his 100th different country in Tahiti, at the Moorea marathon in 2009. Fittingly, he met up with Horst Preisler who happened to be running the Tahiti marathon at the same time. Singapore in December 2009 was his 101st country, at which point, John said (before he went there), "this obsession with countries will be over." As of September 2010 he was up to 105 different countries.

Maddog formed the 'Country Club' a few years ago, membership to which is conferred if a runner has completed a marathon in at least 30 countries. There are 18 club members. It would be an amazing evening to have these runners share their experiences of traveling and running around the world. The experiences of Mad-dog alone would keep me listening. He has run past famous icons such as the Eiffel Tower, Mount Rushmore, and the Kremlin. He's run the Mount Everest marathon. He's run past tanks and camels in Egypt, and had soldiers carrying machine guns following him in a Jeep. In Israel, rockets were firing overhead and to the north of him. He avoided elephants in India and huge snakes in Cambodia. As there was no official marathon in Cambodia, he had to mark off a course and run it, at night, which he did with the assistance of a taxi driver driving alongside with headlights on. John recalled to a journalist the time he ran past refugee camps in the Sahara Desert. He said children were following him and asking for his shoes. "Despite all of our problems, we've got it good", he said.

One of Maddog's most memorable experiences is a small event in Ukraine a few years ago. As he 'was doing' Eastern Europe, he needed to run a marathon in each of Belarus, Ukraine and Moldova in one trip. He had met a Moldovian Olympic marathoner in another race, who helped him with the language and finding races. One of these races was in the middle of nowhere in Ukraine. He got off the train, he said, and was met by the race directors who had enlisted the help of an English professor, Tanya, to be his interpreter. He stayed for three days. After the marathon, in which there were just 13 runners, the race director took Maddog back to his small apartment for a special dinner to commemorate his visit. He also invited an Opera singer who sang a song she had written and dedicated to Maddog. "They were the nicest people and yet the poorest – they were very sincere and friendly. I'll always remember that."

In all his travels, however, he says he's "never had a problem with people by being American." And that's part of his enjoyment. Regardless of systematically achieving his running goals: "I'm seeing and meeting the real people in the real countries – bringing down the barriers." He writes about his running and travel experiences on a web blog and posts photographs of his travels. It's a lesson in geography, and makes you feel like packing your bags and immediately taking off somewhere. He told a reporter one time that "A quarter of the places I've run, I wouldn't have even considered going to if there hadn't been a marathon. And then when I get there, I really enjoy the country. Because every country's got interesting things to see and typically the people are wonderful."

While Osy has collected Hard Rock café pins from around the world, Maddog has focused on teaspoons. He has collected a spoon from almost every country. It was quite a challenge in some third world countries, he said, even Russia, as they don't have a good tourist infrastructure. Only in two countries – Cuba and Albania – was he unsuccessful. In Cuba, he had to make do with a small ceramic dinner bell and in Albania, a carved wooden cigarette holder. Maddog also collects another souvenir from each country, which he says often proves to be more challenging than the souvenir spoons. In each country he collects a silver charm for his wife's charm bracelet. Often he would have to have one made by a local jeweler or go to a flea market and buy one. Regardless, it has to be representative of the country (for example, the Eiffel Tower for France). He's managed to get one in every country. His wife, he says, has two unique charm bracelets that are still growing!

He knows he's continually pushing his body – and is now getting too many injuries. His good friend and mentor, Canadian Wally Herman, has been telling John to slow down to avoid the injuries. It seems he's starting to take notice because he wants to be running the long distances for as long as he can. He needs, he says, to cut down now to a marathon just once a month. For a five-month period he was injured, and depressed. "It was extremely boring", he said. If he couldn't run he'd likely bike, then swim. "If I couldn't exercise I'd probably just say good-bye."

His friends don't believe him when he says he doesn't have any more goals. Good call, because he does have one; to run one more sub 3:30 – he thinks he "still has one left in the tank." But he acknowledges lately that he's "walking the fine edge between staying healthy and being injured." He has never run an ultra because, as he puts it, "when I cross the finish line that's it, there's nothing left. I'd probably kill myself as I'd run it [the ultra] the same way as I run a marathon."

When Maddog's not running somewhere in the world, he lives in the Rocky Mountains in Silverthorne, Colorado in the summers at an elevation of 9,000 feet. Great for training, he says. In the winter he and his wife live on Longboat Key, Florida, where he trains on flat bike paths at sea level.

27

"I haven't found any other activity
that makes my body go into a higher level of function.
It really makes me feel alive."

Van Phan

We've already met several runners who have been able to run over fifty marathons in one year. Some, like Dave Major and Horst Preisler, have run more than 50 marathons every year for several years. Increasingly more and more messengers are running 50 or more marathons in a year. But it wasn't always like that.

Texan Bob Fletcher is the author of *'Spaghetti Every Friday'*, a book which recounts his experiences as he ran 50 marathons in 50 weeks at the age of 50. It's a great read; his experience made even more significant by the fact that he completed the feat in 1983. Logistically alone, not having the Internet to locate and guide you to which races to run, where and when, and not being able to register online, makes Bob's achievement even more remarkable. Bob and his wife Lou Ann travelled all over the United States, driving more than 36,000 miles in that one year.

Bob has since gone on to complete more than 200 marathons. He'd still be running marathons now, but he fell off the roof of his house six years ago and pinched a nerve in his neck. "I'm effectively running on one leg now", he said, although he's still running about 5-6 miles at a time when he runs. "I'm running so slow now", he said, "I have a problem where you run so well for so many years, it's mentally discouraging to think, to imagine, running a 5-hour marathon ... that's a big deterrent for me."

Bob's PB is 2:45. He ran his 100th marathon in Houston back in 1986 at 54 years of age (in a time of 2:58). Not many people had run 100 marathons in 1986, so there was a big party. Bob was written up in the newspapers and appeared on television. He completed his 200th at the age of 70 in a time of 3:34. He's run the Houston marathon 20 times, but considers the Munich marathon "the best" because he was able to run on the same 1972 Olympic course where Frank Shorter won the marathon gold for the United States.

When he reflects on his 50 in 50 at 50, he sees it as "doing something you're not sure you could do"; in essence testing yourself – pushing your physical, mental, emotional and spiritual capacity to places they may not have gone before. And once you "get there", whatever "there" looks like, you've climbed to a different plateau that will elevate the soul and make other challenges, less challenging.

In 2008 Dane Rauschenberg wrote a book titled *'See Dane Run'*. The book chronicles Dane's 52 marathons in 52 weeks, which he did to raise money for L'Arche Mobile, the charity organization he was running for, which provides care and support to individuals with intellectual disabilities. All this was done while he was working full-time as a lawyer in Washington, DC. Like Bob Fletcher before him, the challenges it seems, were not so much the marathons, but the logistics in getting to them and back home, all the while raising money and working.

Dane's very first marathon was in Harrisburg, Pennsylvania in 2001. A "horrible time" he said, made worse by the fact that when he finished he found out his grandmother had died during the night. During his 52 in 52 Dane said he was inspired to run by L'Arche Mobile but also by his father, who "has been crippled for 30 years and never complains about not being able to walk. It makes me get up and run every day."

Dane had run just a handful of marathons before he embarked on his quest for 52 in 52. He took to running marathons while at law school so he could lose excess weight he'd put on playing rugby, and to get back in shape. He sees himself as "an average runner who happens to be extremely stubborn." Essentially though, he wrote on his web blog he's a "swimmer who realized that it is easier to find the road open than the pool."

I met Dane at a marathon near the end of his 52 in 52. Encouraging, supportive and more than happy to talk with anyone, he's been an inspiration to many runners. He's since left his job in Washington, DC and now lives and runs based out of Salt Lake City, Utah. He has a web blog that he regularly updates and links to other sites. It was no surprise that he hit the 100 marathon milestone in 2009.

Dane (and others) admit that he's "gifted biomechanically." In fact he says he has not stretched for the past ten years. But he's not had any injuries from running and his times have been consistently between 2:50 and 3:30 for the marathon distance (his PB is 2:49). He also runs ultras and in 2010 he successfully ran the 204-mile relay Odyssey race from Gettysburg to Washington DC, by himself, to raise money for a local wellness center.

On the other side of the Atlantic is Steve Edwards, who lives in Moreton-in-Marsh, England. I've met and run with Steve a few times. His running feats are somewhat legendary even though he's only in his mid forties. In a 12-month period between 1991-1992 he ran 87 marathons, which was a world record at the time (later surpassed by Jerry Dunn, Horst Preisler and more recently Larry Macon). Typically, marathons are run on Sundays in the United Kingdom, but in Europe they also have marathons on Saturdays.

In the Netherlands Steve wrote his car off after a Saturday marathon, and is lucky to be alive. He missed the Sunday race but fortunately he had his life! At another marathon he fractured a bone in his foot and limped for 15 miles. Although he was told not to run, he had to keep running, he said, as the record for most marathons completed in a year was in sight. He completed 87 to become the world record holder. His average time for a marathon that year was 3:14.

Most recently, Steve has set another goal for himself – to run 500 marathons under 3:30 before he turns 50. He has already run 500 marathons or ultras, which is significant in itself, but his 500 marathons in under 3:30 puts him in a class that arguably very few could be a part of.

When Steve is not running marathons he'll typically run 30-40 miles a week, but seldom runs more than 5-6 miles at a time, which he feels will "keep the speed in his legs."

Steve says he runs for relief from the various "pains in life." It's also a chance to clear the mind and de-stress, and "it's great for your heart and lungs." He had always dreamed of being an elite runner but realized that although he can't run "that fast", he has plenty of stamina. Other reasons for running marathons, he said, are the camaraderie: "you can line up in the field with the elites and the back runners, plus you're always competing against yourself."

His marathon running started with a bet with mates in a pub; Steve would win a pint of beer if he was able to run a marathon. He ran his first marathon, in Coventry, at 19 years of age, in a time of 3:38. From there he started running approximately one marathon every month. When he was 26 years old he met up with the UK 100 Marathon club members, including Richard Byrd who was attempting 52 marathons in one year. Inspired by this, Steve set his sights on becoming the youngest person ever to complete 100 marathons. He did this at age 28.

Steve's name is almost synonymous with the Brathay 10 Marathons in 10 Days Challenge in the Lake District of England, which he has now completed four times (2007-2010). In 2008 he set a Guinness World record for the fastest 10 in 10 (35:20). He is an inspiration to other 10 in 10 runners with his wealth of knowledge, his support and enthusiasm, and for his care and concern over the safety and interests of others. In addition to raising thousands of pounds for the Brathay Trust he has raised money for many other charities including the Spinal Injuries Association – a UK charity that supports 40,000 people in the UK who are paralyzed through spinal cord injury.

We met Jerry Dunn from the United States in an earlier chapter, but he too has accomplished significant goals in his running career. Those accomplishments have been reported on CNN, ESPN, the NBC TODAY SHOW and in numerous television and newspaper articles. Jerry says "Don't limit your challenges, challenge your limits." He's known as the 'Lean Horse' and sees it as a metaphor for his life. It comes from when he ran across the United States while raising money for Habitat for Humanity. A farmer offered Jerry a night's sleep in a real bed. The farmer told Jerry that a lean horse runs a long race.

"I've gotten a lot of media attention" Jerry said, "and it's given me the opportunity to suggest to people that even though what I do is pretty wacky and is addictive behavior, it's much better than the addictions I used to have. It's about motivation, discipline, goal-setting and tenacity."

In 2000, Jerry ran 200 marathons. Most of these were not official races and thus he was not eligible for any world record status. Nonetheless, at 54, he still completed 200 marathon distances in one year. He completed 21 official marathons but also ran their 26.2-mile official length courses another 179 times on his own. Jerry would travel to a marathon city two weeks prior to its race and run the course as many times as possible before running in the official event. His average finishing time was around five hours, although he finished his 200th in 4:05, which was his fastest time of the year. His PB is 3:23 (1985).

An article on Jerry explained that: "Many years of living a self-described renegade lifestyle and an ongoing 20-year recovery from past alcohol and drug use have instilled a cavernous determination within Dunn. What else but deep ambition could motivate a middle-age man to awake at 4:30 a.m. and complete a 26.2 mile

263

run by 11 a.m. for nearly three weeks out of every month?"

I asked Jerry if he could reflect on the 200 in 2000 with the hindsight of several years gone by. This is what he wrote:

This first paragraph is taken from my log (pre-blog days)

"The human body, mind and Spirit are inextricably intertwined, and today I am so very thankful, to God, that I have made it to the eve of completion of this self imposed test of MY body, mind and spirit. To say it's been an incredible year is inadequate. To say it's been a successful year is an understatement. So when I figure out how to describe how I feel, I will. But for now, suffice it to say......Hallelujah....and AMEN! *(Jerry Dunn, Dec. 9, 2000, on the eve of completing his 200th marathon distance run in a single calendar year).*

PHYSICALLY: Surprising as it may seem, I felt great. I was probably in the best shape of my entire life. Nothing hurt, nothing broken.....just a lean, mean running machine. A fact that was proven when number 200 turned out to be my fastest of the year. (A blazing 4:05:30) I figured....what the heck, what's the worst that can happen.....I bonk, and have to walk most of it? Who cares....I made it.

MENTALLY: **Relieved**...knowing that I didn't have to get up the next day and do it again. **Sad**....that it was over. Having spent most of 1999 putting this project together and all of 2000, executing it, I thought.......what next? This not being my first event/project/endeavor of this kind, I thought I was prepared for the inevitable "crash and burn" syndrome that occurs after any kind of project of this magnitude. So, from that 200th finish line on Dec. 10, until December 20th I was on an emotional high. I had done it..........200 in 2000. But on the night of the Dec. 20th, less than a block from home, at the start of local, holiday ***Run for the Lights*** run around our little town of Spearfish, I slipped on some ice and turned my ankle. Rather than "run through it" as I would have done anytime earlier in the year, I walked back to my house – headquarters of the event and post run party, and began to eat the delicious holiday fare spread out on my dining room table. No, I didn't turn immediately into a 200 pound recluse, but this night was the beginning of a downhill emotional slide that led me to the lowest point I've ever allowed myself to tumble.....mentally.

I termed my condition "mild" depression. Others in my life suggested that it may have been a bit more than that. Physically I still felt great, but mentally, not so good. I couldn't shake it until mid summer. By then I was out of "the groove" as far as any regularity of running. And now, almost 9 years later, I'm finally finding the discipline to train/run consistently again. In the interim, my love for running, which is also my salvation, did not wither and disappear completely. I now direct a couple of success-ful running events and have plans for a couple more. (Oh yeah, I did throw in a 60-miler on my 60th birthday in 2006. I did 480 laps around the field house track at Black Hills State University......just to prove I still had it (14 hrs: 48: and a few odd seconds).

It's been said that running is a lifetime sport. I find it to be more of a life *style*, and for me, that has proven to be a good thing.

SPIRITUALLY: I had close to 1000 hours of "road time" to contemplate the meaning of life. Okay, so I only used 10 or 12 for that purpose....

The spiritual journey of 200 in 2000 was incredible. Each morning I ran was another opportunity to be thankful. Thankful that I was able to do it one more time. Thankful for the changes running had wrought in my life. Thankful for the opportunity to smile at, and say hello to, total strangers and watch them respond in kind...often pleasantly surprised.

Running is a simple activity, and to spend nearly two-thirds of the days of an entire year running 26.2 miles, lent itself to me coming to the realization that most all of life is simple. We complicate our lives unnecessarily.... think about it.

The over-arching lesson of the whole experience would have to be humility. Even though I thrived on the attention of the media; the accolades of strangers; the excitement of the travel; and the "oh-my-god-I-can't-believe-you-are-doing-that" comments.....at the end of the day/year, it was still just Jerry Dunn, a skinny little kid from the Southside of Indianapolis, runnin' a bunch of miles in a lot of different places. And that was fine with me. I proved to myself that it could be Dunn."

Jerry has only completed about seven marathons in the last nine years since his 200 in 2000, but at 64 he's now getting back into running. "We need goals in order to accomplish things", Jerry says. "Running marathons gives you a lot of self-confidence in life. Half-marathons are great but there's something different about the next 13.1 miles."

The Marathon Maniacs Male Runner of the Year Award in 2009 went to Larry Macon, who ran 94 races in the year. Larry, a 64-year-old San Antonio, Texas, lawyer, could perhaps feel he had a quiet year given that the year before, he ran 105 races, a world record.

That's right, 105 official races in one year. Worth repeating. An average of two marathons a weekend. "I've always been driven", he told a *Runners World* reporter in 2009. "I used to work most weekends. My co-workers say that my running is the best thing that happened to them. Now they don't have 400 e-mails waiting for them on a Monday morning." In a way, 105 should not have been a surprise to anyone. In 2006 he ran 79 marathons, and in 2007 he ran 93. If it shows anything, it's that he improved his logistical skills in 2008.

The *Runner's World* article outlined how some weekends unfold for Larry. "In August, he finished the Frank Maier Marathon in Juneau, Alaska, at 12:30 p.m.; drove to the airport for a 2 p.m. flight; landed in San Francisco at midnight; then started that city's marathon at 5:30 a.m. Or there's the time he drove from the finish of the Cow Town Marathon in Fort Worth, Texas, to New Orleans (which took him 12 hours), arriving five minutes before the start of the Mardi Gras Marathon. And thanks to holidays like Memorial Day and races with Saturday night starts, he squeezed three marathons into one weekend five times in 2008."

Larry started running in 1992 at the age of 49. He ran his first marathon in 1994 as part of a dare.

On weekdays Larry is up at 4am and is either working out with a personal trainer or running with others. Come the weekend he rushes through one finish chute only to head off to another marathon (In the course of researching this book, I heard other marathoners talk of 'Larry Macon sightings' as he raced away in rental cars to his next event). As Larry himself said to a reporter, "if I have time, I'll shower at the hotel … but usually life isn't that good. So I'll change at a stoplight. I've gotten good at it. I haven't been arrested for indecent exposure yet." In 2009 he tallied 200,000 airline miles flying to and from races.

His running partner, Justice Rebecca Simmons, commented in a newspaper article that "Larry is a gifted trial lawyer … to be as successful as he is, you need to be aggressive and competitive. I think running has made him a better lawyer. It gives him time to think through cases."

Larry told a reporter that he runs so many marathons "because I love it. It's such a joy to be outside. If you're a lawyer, you meet a lot of jerks. There aren't many jerks out here. People are all nice and friendly."

Larry's tally of marathons and ultras is now well over 600. There appears to be no stopping his relentless pursuit of marathons, and yet he says he has no particular aspiration to become the world record holder for the most marathons completed. Simply, he enjoys it. And as long as he continues to enjoy it he'll keep running.

***

Some messengers may take two-three decades to complete 100 marathons, while others may reach that target within two-three years. The commitment to detail that the passion of long distance running requires is there regardless of the time it takes to reach 100. It takes time to arrange the logistics for each race. This includes how and when you travel, where to stay and for how long, registration, coordination with work schedules, race day packet pick-up, food and drink requirements, and the coordination with friends and family who may be coming to the event. And if the runners bring friends or family along, the logistical demands increase again. Regardless of the location there is almost always a cost incurred.

The messengers are dedicated to their passion of long distance running. The total experience of the long distance run provides both the solitude and social connections all in one. If you enjoy the total experience why would you not come back for more?

28

Several years ago the Basher - Dasher Chronicles emerged in the United Kingdom to document the ongoing running challenge between messengers Jack (Dasher) Brooks and Roger (Basher) Biggs, two members of the UK 100 Marathon Club. Jack and Roger are the only two non-Americans who have run a marathon in each of the fifty states. What follows here are excerpts of commentary that 'roll back the years' of that ongoing competition, which still continues into 2010, as written by Jack Brooks.

The Basher - Dasher Chronicles

'After all this excitement at home Dasher was free to prepare himself for Abingdon Marathon on Sunday, 18th October 2009. His plan was to set off like lightning and keep going for as long as possible. Actually, this is his usual plan, but he usually runs out of steam after the first hundred yards or so. However, for once his scheme worked and he finished in 3 hours 35 minutes, some way ahead of Basher. Basher advised at the finish that he'd been "caught short" four times during the race thus prompting Dasher to point out that he'd actually been caught short for over 60 years'.

'If your rental car ever breaks down pray that it doesn't do so in Lee Vining, California. It is a one payphone town and as that payphone appears never to be emptied it is impossible to put money in and make outgoing phone calls. There is only so much food that one can eat and coffee that one can drink and even those options ran out at 9pm as the last eating place in town closed its doors. It is not much fun playing "spot the lorry [truck]" when only one passes every 30 minutes or so'.

'Over the years Dasher has discovered that it is possible to defeat

Basher on trail marathons by using the terrain. Thus, at the start of the Dovedale Dipper on 2nd August 2009 he felt fairly safe in the knowledge that whenever he was knee deep in mud this would mean that Basher would be waist deep in it. Indeed, as conditions got progressively worse he charitably hoped that Basher had remembered to take his snorkel with him. With his usual dastardly cunning Basher had deployed Carol Ann and Patsy in a particularly glutinous part of the course at about the half way point and briefed them to request a piggy-back from Dasher. Being the gentleman he is Dasher chivalrously declined and promptly toppled over into the quagmire'.

'Sunday morning arrived far too soon and at 5am it was time to join the queue for school buses to get to the race start in Folsom. It is a little known fact that American school buses were designed to give those of Basher's stature an unfair advantage over those of normal height. Basher whistled nonchalantly as Dasher endeavoured to move his legs from where they were wedged in behind a seat. Some people will do anything to gain an edge. Once at the start area it quickly became apparent that the warmest place was a bus and as Dasher was once again shunted into the window seat Basher impressed some girls with a few pre-race vaseline tricks (unless, of course, it was his psychedelic race shorts that they were giggling at). As Basher trotted out his "Do I look like a runner?" speech, Dasher looked around expectantly in the hope that someone might know the answer. Dasher followed on by recounting his experience in Genk a few years ago when a Belgian runner advised him that if he could learn to run as fast as he could talk he might turn out to be a half decent runner. Nevertheless, it soon became obvious that Basher had made the deepest impression on the audience as a star-struck 6 year old approached him and requested his autograph'.

Phoenixes and Ashes (October, 2008)

'Dasher has now attempted more comebacks than he has had hot dinners. However, on their latest US foray it was Basher who was suffering with an injury. Selflessly, Dasher reasoned that the next best thing to running was responsibility, so he immediately appointed Basher to the jobs of chauffeur and head bagman. Basher suffered this indignity with such good humour that Dasher had to playfully resort to programming the wrong addresses into the Satnav in order to provoke a reaction. In spite of all this Basher was loyally waiting at the finish of the Indianapolis Marathon as Dasher finished in 3.46.28 ready to commence the 250 mile dash to Grand Rapids, Michigan and beat the 7pm registration deadline. Dasher had merely pulled on trousers and a shirt and then dived into the car. As the journey progressed he became increasingly aware of the thin covering of gatorade adhering to both his skin and his clothing. By the time their destination was reached he felt as though he had been coated in plaster of paris and almost required a hoist to manoeuvre him out of the car. This, of course, was Dasher's excuse for picking up someone else's number at race registration'.

"Sister" Warren proves that running is habit forming at Fargo Marathon 2008. Warren and Dasher arrived in Fargo the Thursday before the race. Dasher promptly proceeded to damage his knee on the hotel treadmill. However, it always pays to go on holiday with a nun and once Warren had donned his habit on the Saturday morning for his 200th marathon it was time for Dasher to demand divine intervention. 50 Hail Marys and several strong pain killers saw Dasher lining up beside an inconspicuous looking "Sister" Warren speculating on how many nuns can actually boast a Chelsea tattoo. The 2 kept together for much of the first half of the marathon with Dasher hampered by his knee and Warren tripping over his habit, but Dasher just edged ahead in the second half as it became considerably hotter and finished in 4:00:34 with Warren just behind in 4:04:36'.

'The Neolithic Marathon starts very close to the stone circle in Avebury and finishes right next to the Stonehenge Monument. The undulating off-road route runs through the beautiful Vale of Pewsey and then across Salisbury Plain. Dasher did speculate at one stage at the sound of gunfire quite how the ancients had got hold of guns, but it was later explained to him that part of the course is alongside an army target range. Apparently, as a quid pro quo for allowing the race to run through army owned land a few snipers are permitted to pick off the front runners. It was somewhat hurtfully pointed out to Dasher that this meant that he was in no danger'.

'Dasher had slipped United Airlines a tenner to ensure that Basher would have a turbulent outward flight. However, he hadn't anticipated that the over-zealous pilot would also delay Basher's flight for almost 3 hours. Basher joined in the spirit of things by losing his wallet en route and eventually arrived frustrated and pleading poverty. Had this been enough to tip the scales in Dasher's favour for the next 2 races'?

'Early on the morning of 21st October at Breakers Marathon (Rhode Island), Dasher found himself running in front of 3 girls, which was nice. He subsequently realised that they were not there simply to admire his lean physique, but were using him as a wind break as the course followed a particularly exposed area of shoreline. Behind the girls lurked Basher and as soon as more sheltered terrain was reached he took off like a scorched whippet'.

'8th October 2006: A Major Achievement!

Sunday arrived and Fast Fu'd disappeared into the distance with the front runners as Linda Major and entourage forged their way across the start Line of Munich Marathon on 8th October 2006. Gentleman John Dawson (the metronome) set a steady pace for Linda's 100th marathon as Basher, Dasher, Slasher, Manic, The Kid, Blueboy Steve, Norry Longworth, Warren D, Uncle Tom Cobley and all enjoyed demonstrating to a receptive audience that UK runners know how to have a good time on tour. Was it Linda's Spice Girls dress, Basher's hat and pigtails or Warren D's Rastafarian wig that excited spectators most? We'll never know, but the applause rose to fever pitch as the 17 UK runners entered the Olympic Stadium and Conga'd across the finish line'.

'24th September 2006: A Revelation for Dasher

Dasher has often heard Basher waxing lyrical about negative splits. He has nodded his head meaningfully (a good tactic to adopt with

Basher) assuming that negative splits were distant relatives of Basher's favourite dessert, the banana split. However, Dasher's world has now been turned upside down as it appears that at Berlin Marathon on 24th September 2006 he actually ran a negative split. Hitherto Dasher has always remained ignorant of his times during races and has strictly adhered to the "don't press any buttons until you've finished" rule. In fact he has chuckled quietly to himself as Basher has loaded himself down on race days with GPS's and other assorted paraphernalia. Dasher considers that it is a prerequisite for any race to load Basher down with as much as he can carry. Indeed, he had speculated about buying Basher a grandfather clock to take round with him until it dawned on him that there would be problems getting it through airports'.

'16th July 2006: Torrid Times in Torshavn

Torshavn is a place where a storm pulls no punches. A gale is a gale in the Faroes and there is one around the corner most days of the week, but particularly on Sundays. Where there's a maelstrom there's a marathon and Dasher can well remember shivering on the start line on of the Torshavn Marathon on 16th July 2006 with 6 of his comrades in torrential rain and a howling gale. This was his first race since he'd injured his knee and he'd come prepared to limp, but not to swim. Actually, he had suggested forming a huddle for warmth, but a couple of the girls gave him distinctly funny looks. As the race progressed and Dave "tri-man" Farthing took a commanding lead, the only Faroese with smiles on their faces were those manning the drinks stations as the rain had saved them the trouble of filling up the cups (or, at least, those cups that hadn't been swept away by the wind)'.

'29th April 2006: Dasher runs marathon and Basher tries his first duathlon. Triple Crown Trail Marathon

After a long Friday flight Basher and Dasher arrived early on Saturday morning at White Clay Creek State Park, Newark, Deleware, USA for a "friendly and non-competitive" trail marathon. After 2.5 miles Dasher went ahead and after wading across the first of 4 river crossings his confidence grew in the certainty that Basher would shortly be out of his depth. Sure enough Basher started his duathlon when he reached the river and was swiftly swept off his feet. The route was not short of obstacles such as tree stumps, rocks, steep ascents and sharp descents and Basher found them all. However, Dasher claims that his one tumble equals Basher's three as he has much further to fall than the little fellow'.

To misquote A. A. Milne:
The wonderful thing about Bashers
Is Bashers like winning and things
So crushing defeats over Dashers
Means everyone's telephone rings

'Paddock Wood Half Marathon on 2nd April 2006

All was going to plan until they encountered some serious head-wind between miles 9 and 11. Basher claims that this affected him although Dasher maintains that as all the hedges were 5 feet high the wind could only have hindered him and that Basher would just have used them for cover'.

29

'Wisdom: experience and knowledge
together with the power of
applying them critically or practically'
Oxford Dictionary

'Knowing yourself is the beginning of all wisdom'
Aristotle

Each Messenger has accumulated more than one hundred marathons and ultras since they ran their first 26.2 mile event. There is wisdom gained from running a single marathon. The commitment and passion associated with running more than one hundred – that journey to Apathia – creates and reinforces that sense of unperturbedness – that unworried state of mind.

It is a *state of being*; not unlike, perhaps, the various gradations of 'master' at the black belt level in martial arts such as karate. The more experienced masters, the Sensei's, exude a sense of calm and self-confidence in the dojo and in their everyday lives. They have mastered what it is to be karate-ka – the wisdom, skills, techniques and accumulated experience – of a karate practitioner. While the distance running messengers may not be Sensei's they have the wisdom of accumulated distances, of people, of places, of self, that knowingly and unknowingly they share with others. The experience never stops at the finish line; it flows onward into the next race, the next week, the next season, the next year, and most importantly between those moments of running.

The messengers live their lives by example. They have a positive outlook on life and a deep appreciation for what they have. They are happy not because of money or material objects, but because of the experiences accumulated and shared, the social bonding with other runners and the realization that they have the physical ability and the mental and emotional fortitude to continually challenge themselves and reap the rewards for doing so, and to face life's challenges as they emerge.

The messengers are adaptive – redefining their happiness as the context changes. When I talked to Norm Franks in the nursing home he was not bemoaning his situation – he was talking about when he would be running next. I talked to Carol Dellinger a couple of days after her mastectomy but you would not know it; I didn't know it in fact, until Carol told me. But I was clearly talking to a very positive upbeat person.

And the research evidence tells us that our own health improves by having more positive people in our lives. Social connectedness is one part of happiness, but who you connect with, the type of person, is also important. Happiness begins inside, and is maintained by the connections with others and the desire and ability to be involved in experiences that you are passionate about, with the people who feel like you do.

None of the messengers talks about a time in the future when they won't be running long distances, or being physically active. They know that time will come of course but the plan, if there is one, is to delay that for as long as possible. When they can't run, they'll walk. When they can't walk, they'll crawl. If an adverse event occurs in their lives they will overcome it. Being adaptive as they are, they will redefine their happiness according to their new context. Holly Koester has wheel-chaired well over one hundred marathons now. As with the other messengers, her life is not unfolding as she would've predicted growing up.

And as we've seen in this book, the rewards of distance running are many. Triumph over adversity, transformations into new, healthier lives, raising awareness and support for others less fortunate, living a good life to the full. And simply being healthy in the most holistic sense of the word.

The messengers have plenty of advice for others. Above all else, the key message for anyone running a marathon is to enjoy themselves. Worry less about your times, for example. Jeff Galloway said that he's "never heard anyone say because they got their personal best time their lives changed for the better."

Australian Harold Copeland, who at eighty-one years of age was running six to eight miles a day, once said "Enjoy the run. That's the answer. Enjoy whatever you're doing. Biking, running, or life." Fu in England said he runs marathons "enjoying the race and sense of achievement, enjoying the company of friends, getting new PBs ... plus the benefits of having a healthy mind and body." Fellow Brit Peter Graham said "Go out and enjoy yourself on the day; it doesn't matter what time or what place you finish it should be the challenge of completing the course in one piece." Bill Inskip said "smile all the way and run as you feel."

Several messengers advised new marathoners to simply "throw away the watch." Australian Jim Barnes said "be prepared to work hard; if you really want to do it you'll put the time in." Todd Byers said it was important to learn to run marathons well so that they can run safely and enjoy the actual event. "Enjoy the whole experience' and don't think solely about the run itself; combine it with a holiday." Jeffrey Horowitz said it's important to "gather as much information as possible, but decide for yourself what works and what doesn't. Never stop learning." Susan Daley said "enjoy the people you're running with."

I asked Jerry Dunn what advice he would give beginners. After a long contemplative pause he rattled off a series of questions he felt beginners need to ask of themselves: First, he said don't take the race too fast. Then he added, "ask the questions:

Why have you decided to run marathons?
Do you have any friends who are runners?
Look for people to run with.
Do you have opportunities to run/train with experienced runners?
Have you picked an event to run in?
Have you looked online for coaches?
Have you thought about the time it will take
away from other parts of your life?

And he also emphasized that "there's fun to be had, but you need to know there will be some pain … don't over-train, don't get discouraged; and don't beat yourself up if you don't make the mileage."

Similarly, Englishman Dave Major offered this advice:

- "Have a reason to run it first
  (for example, health, sponsorship, friendship, challenge)
- Buy a good pair of running shoes and some decent kit. Warm or Cold!
- Set yourself 3 months of specific training if you already run and 1 year if you have done nothing.
- Complete long runs up to about 20 miles at least 3-5 times prior to the big day.
- Don't do too much training too soon. If you started doing 1 mile a week and increase it by 1 each week, that's 52 miles after 1 year. That is more than enough to complete a marathon.
- Enjoy your training. Run a few 10 K's or half marathons to get use to race day nerves / arrangements.
- Pick a big race where there is crowd support if possible.
- Learn from or enjoy the past runs but on the big day run as to how you feel, not what you should achieve.
- Irrespective of your time when you finish your 1st marathon look back at where you have come from and take pride in that.
- Don't assume your 2nd marathon will be faster or any easier!! Your body will now know what 26.2 miles is like. More importantly, your mind will as well!!"

Some reflection on those points is all the more reason perhaps for why there is a strong sense of achievement when completing a marathon. Susan Daley said "there's always a feeling of satisfaction finishing a marathon. Like you see people finishing, they're all got that look of achieving something – that's what it's all about."

Tor Rønnow felt that in the process of training you become happier with running. "It shouldn't be just vanity running a marathon – it should be a more deeper experience than that", he said. Over the long term, Tor added that as his children get older, he plans to take them with him to races and he will reduce the number of marathons and ultras he runs, but at the same time he will show them the world through the running.

What about during the race itself? Several messengers stressed the need to enjoy the event but the fact remains that you are still covering 26.2 miles. That takes time; a lot can happen. With 400 marathons under his feet Dave Major broadly summarized the distance as follows: The first 1-10 miles is social and sightseeing. You take in the rush of the event as the new experience unfolds. Already there's a sense of accomplishment as you've made it to the start-line and actually 'doing it'. The next 10-13 miles, he said, is the time when you'll "probably feel the best you are going to for the whole race." He says the next 13-20 miles are work-like; "get these out of the way. They are nothing miles where you start to feel all the little injuries you may have. It also starts to hurt a little bit and tiredness can set in." At the 20-25 mark "it's all mental now. Keep going forward as the line will get closer if you do this. Think of all the good reasons why you run. Try to hook up with another runner or start a conversation." And finally with 25 miles to the finish line, "don't do anything stupid now. Celebrate your last 25 miles and take in all the euphoria in finishing this great distance."

Similarly, Fu commented, "try to run to 16 miles in 'autopilot' with your legs, heart and lungs all working in a steady state. This is the best part of the marathon when you feel invincible and you can run forever. Things start getting harder at 16 miles when fatigue sets in and where the real work begins." "Run within yourself and save something for the end", said Wally Herman.

Christian Hottas felt that "a marathoner needs some respect for the long distance but it's not worth it to be anxious. Always be a little bit patient and most always look to your body. Run with it, not against it. Run slow and steady." The first marathon is a challenge, Christian said, "it's an adventure, it's your test – the second is to become better." But "take in what you see around you", said Gina Little, "embrace the experience."

"And if you do get injured", said Bob Dolphin, "listen to your body. Don't mask injuries with analgesics; try alternatives while mending injuries – do anything to keep the heart rate up." Yen Nguyen agreed; "Listen to your own body, not your friend's, and be comfortable with yourself – do your own thing – have fun at it. We all have our own personal goals, but we're all doing the same thing – it's a distance you've got to respect." The point is equally applicable to the experienced runners.

Sean Meissner emphasized that it's important to "listen to the veterans for advice, but try things for yourself to see what works best for you. Everybody is different." Indeed, New Zealander Dave Penfold commented that first timers should "go and have a yarn with someone experienced to learn how to schedule a marathon. Hold back, hold back. Keep the petrol in the tank. Use it for the whole journey."

Takatoshi Yoshino, the secretary general of the Japanese 100 Marathon club, says that we should run with three spirits *Challenge*, *Codawari* and *Humor* (enjoy the run). Codwari is Japanese for each person having a personal goal that they work towards, while at the same time respecting the fact that other runners may have different goals.

At his home in New York Andrew Kotluski explained to me that you need to "have the mindset for the training that you're your

own best investment. So spend an hour every day on that investment. People's biggest problem is that they will squeeze health
and fitness into everything else, yet it should be the most important part of the day. You've got to believe it's possible – and get to
that level of fitness, build up, forget yo-yoing – keep training. You
are you're best investment."

No far up the road in Boston lives Dave McGillivray the Boston
Marathon Race Director. Dave has dedicated his life to running
and *giving back* – helping family, friends and those in need. There
is an inextricable link between his running and his giving. At the
end of his book he writes "I will keep going until some higher
power decides it's time for me to stop. Just as with running a
marathon, you don't want to say at the end that you had a lot left
to give. If you run a race correctly, then you planned wisely and
gave it everything, so that by the time you finish, you've given
your all. At the end of my life, I'd like to think I gave everything I
had and then some, right up until I simply ran out of time."

Juergen Kuhlmey, Germnay, at the North Pole Marathon.

Dane Rauschenberg, 52 marathons in 52 weeks.

American messenger, Dave McGillivray.

Yen Nguyen of Houston, Texas, in a rare moment when she's not running.

Steve Edwards, 500 marathons later, after it started with a bet.

Dasher Brooks and Basher Biggs, friends of Ben and Jerry.

Christian Hottas and Barbara Szlachetka at the start of the
Eurasia Marathon 2004.

Osy Waye's 100th marathon. Assembling at start, North Pole Marathon.

Osy Waye finishing his 100th marathon.

American messenger, Dave McGillivray en route, across America.

30

"Whoever is happy will make others happy too."

Mark Twain

The idea for this book began two days before the Athens marathon after a chance encounter with one of the messengers. He told me about his marathon running experiences and described his 100 Marathon Club. A couple of days later I was filled with the experience of completing the Athens marathon. And aching all over as I passed through the finish-line and chute, and began my so-called post-race recovery.

One of my biggest thrills from that day was hearing a booming "Malcolm" coming from the stands as I walked out of the finish chute. It was Dave Major again, his wife Linda, John Dawson and Jim Mundy. We'd only met once, but here they were, genuinely pleased to see me, and happy that I'd finished. So was I.

Although I'd finished and was, I think, smiling, my body was dreading the thought of moving anywhere. My legs were Giant Redwood tree trunks. I was hungry and hoping to be horizontal as soon as possible. Stairs became my enemy for the next few days. The messengers meanwhile looked as if they had just been for a stroll in the garden. We chatted for a bit. It was like meeting up with old friends, yet I hardly knew them. That chance meeting at the end of the race embodied the spirit and passion of the messengers. In any case, they were soon heading back to their hotel and getting ready to celebrate the completion of Dave's 200th marathon.

***

To many people, happiness is a function of living a good life. I would be surprised if there was anything that ranked higher in our lives than happiness. Psychologist Martin Seligman says that happiness involves positive activities and positive emotions. It's well known that distance running is a positive activity; hundreds of research articles also show that physical activity is good for your health. It also increases self perceived short term well-being. The messengers certainly exhibit the traits of positive emotions. These positive emotions, Seligman says, consist of past, present and future emotions.

Past emotions are reflective – satisfaction, contentment, pride and serenity. The sense of accomplishment and goal attainment reached by the messengers exemplify these attributes. *Present* emotions include pleasure and gratification. Completing marathon after marathon and enjoying the total experiences of doing so, being given a medal to show achievement, sharing stories, and connecting socially on a regular basis with friends easily instill pleasure and gratification. *Future* emotions refer to optimism, hope and trust. The continuation of long distance running training and events builds self-confidence and self-esteem, leading to optimism and a sense of hope for future experiences such as new runs, longer runs, better times and new places to visit, as well as a sense of self-trust in trying to attain new goals and trust in others as the bonds of friendship grow stronger over time.

It's all relative to our own context. Most runners *and* non-runners don't have it in us to run more than 90-100 marathons *in one year* like Steve Edwards, Jerry Dunn, Horst Preisler, Larry Macon or

Christian Hottas. Others, like Dave Major, have run more than 50 marathons and ultras, *every year*, for several years. They do it, in part, because they can, and they do it because it feels right – it's meaningful on a variety of different levels, the contours of which vary according to each messenger's own context.

The messengers have layer upon layer of total distance running experiences, each building upon one another, the accumulation of which creates the apathian landscape on which they live.

There is spiritual growth from physical actions, especially when those actions are directed towards a messenger's own defined goals. Some messengers may understand it as such. Others may never explicitly recognize what they do as being connected to any spiritual path. For Jerry Dunn, the spiritual connection may be felt strongly when he runs across the United States because it seems to be the right thing to do at the time. Thousands of others may also benefit from his physical (and spiritual) expression in ways not even known by Jerry. Marshall Ulrich had an epiphany while running Badwater in 2001. He discovered that he was not running for himself anymore but running for others. Marshall talked about the immense satisfaction he felt when he realized that he could help others; he stepped out of himself – "doing for others is the essence of life," he said.

Sean Meissner and Jeff Hagen may reach their heightened spiritual moment heading into miles 70 and 80 of their many 100 mile events, or perhaps when they are hallucinating from the stress they have placed upon their bodies as they challenge the long distances and landscapes on which they run. The rewards are huge, but they have nothing to do with personal financial gain. That's partly why they go back for more. Monetary reward is never the goal. It is much deeper than that. It's about conveying and re-conveying messages to themselves, and to others, who can also benefit from this in many ways.

Apathia, like George Sheehan's monastery, is a place – a place in the messengers' minds that they arrive at – the conduit for which are the physical encounters of running long distances and all the experiences embedded in those physical challenges. Each of the messengers have their own apathia, and it varies according to the different context of each messenger – where they are and where they have come from spiritually, emotionally, mentally, socially and physically. Their passion for long distances leads to that place in their minds that is defined by themselves and no-one else. But the common bond is an inner peace, that sense of mental unperturbedness and tranquility, that unworried state of mind that the accumulation of long distance running experiences provides.

To run 100 long distance events or more, you must be comfortable with yourself; with who you are, and where you fit in the world. Otherwise, it's a long time to spend with your own thoughts. Why would you put yourself in long distance events if you were not comfortable with yourself? You must be willing to face and endure the challenges in front of you even if you are not fully sure of what they will be. There is a comfort zone within uncertainty. It speaks to confidence.

Confidence is gained through experience. Confidence in knowing you can overcome adversity. Confidence in pursuing challenges. Confidence in putting yourself to the test. Confidence in knowing that you can set and achieve goals. Running long distances builds confidence. What looks like a very physical experience – the simple act of running – is a much broader and deeper experience that gets at the very heart of what it means to be human. It carries over into our everyday lives.

While Dennis Bramble, Daniel Lieberman and Bernd Heinrich show us *why* we run in the evolutionary physical sense, we have also carried with this a psycho-social need and desire to feel the benefits of such activity. We make connections with ourselves and, equally important, with others. After all, we are social animals.

The messengers continually reiterate the enjoyment and the happiness of the social connectedness that completing hundreds of distance running events provides. For them, the more events they complete, the less importance is the physical challenge. Over time more importance is transferred to the social side of the total experience.

Ultimately, it is all about the connections that long distance running provides to the messengers. The ongoing connection with others is vital to their happiness and to the happiness of those with whom they are in contact with. "Happiness", said Aristotle, "is the meaning and the purpose of life, the whole aim and end of human existence ... happiness depends upon ourselves."

Social networks, say Nicholas Christakis and James Fowler, shape our lives. For the messengers, these are built around their club affiliations. When you've run more than 100 distance events, you get to know many people. The social networks increase geographically and numerically with the more races completed.

The marathon clubs and the *connectors* inside these clubs are the ties that bind the messengers with one another. Reporters who want to know more about the messengers, for example, simply contact the respective clubs and talk to the official representatives. Lenore Dolphin, Tom Adair, Steve Boone, Takatoshi Yoshino, Bob Fickel and Roger Biggs among many others, will happily provide information and direct you to the appropriate individuals anywhere in the world. The growth of the Marathon Maniacs club and the Fifty States Marathon club is further proof of the desire to socially connect with other long distance runners and share in the total long distance running experience. It is a social movement, one that will lead to more and more runners completing 100 marathons and ultras.

**

In many ways this book has only touched the surface of the total experience of the messengers. It's easy to forget the fact that each event these athletes have completed has been 26.2 miles or more; each athlete finishing more than 100 of these events. It is still a long way no matter how many times you've travelled it.

Completing a single marathon is a significant achievement. Many people have completed the distance to prove something to themselves and possibly to others. The single act of achieving something, putting oneself to the test, reaching for something they are not sure is possible, can be transformational.

But there is a certain magic that brings some people back again and again. Kelvin Marshall, Gina Little and Big Dave, for example, watched a marathon unfold in front of them, and said to themselves "I could do that." Chris Warren was so caught up with the experience watching his girlfriend complete her marathon that he decided to do one too. And that one turned into two, which has turned into a lifestyle.

Running more than 100 long distance races is not for everyone. But for those for whom it is, they have definitely found something. It is something we all would like to have. Tellingly, it is consistent with the latest scientific research evidence.

The messengers are happy. They are especially happy when they are out experiencing their passion. Happy, despite, for a number of them, the adversities faced and the challenges they have had to overcome.

They are also healthy in the broadest sense of the word. They are resilient, tenacious and positive in outlook. I will always remember Norm Franks saying to me as he was recovering from a stroke, after 965 marathons, that he will complete 1,000 marathons even if he has to use a walker. He then starts laughing loud and hard. Truly a golden moment. I'm privileged to be sharing the spirit of the long distance runner. And I think, physically, if he can, he will.

Norm embodies so much of what it's all about, not just for the messengers in this book, but for all of us. People like Norm are inspirational. If I was a ten-year-old listening to Norm and being given one of his medals he would 'have me', and my life would be changed just like that.

The messengers inspire. They give back.

**

All marathoners inspire in some way. They lead by example. They achieve what they set out to do. They endure. They transform.

They may transform themselves. They may help to transform others. One single act of pushing their limits can be enough to compel others into action; inspire children to run; inspire adults to get up and get moving, inspire others to attempt a long distance run. In this age of inactivity, overweight populations and rising rates of obesity, the modern day long distance runner is a perfect role model for effecting positive change in society. The messengers' passion for distance running exerts a positive influence that rubs off on others, and likely in many ways that they will never really know.

Given the messengers' positive outlook on life, it is no wonder that the continuation of their social relations only further reinforces their personal resolve to seek new knowledge about themselves and others. They reduce the social distances with other runners and non-runners alike, thereby expanding their knowledge about the world even further.

And they seek new knowledge about the places they visit. They are *travelers* and not tourists, in the same way American social historian Daniel Boorstin describes: "The traveler was active; he [sic] went strenuously in search of people, of adventure, of experience."

The pursuit of new experiences, and the knowledge implicitly woven within them, is addictive – it is a passion after all – and builds confidence. It contributes to that unworried state of mind; that deeper understanding of the universe and our place in the universe.

The messengers are role models. And proudly so. We can all be role models; our smallest actions and our quietest comments can have profound effects on those with whom we are in contact. Like the messengers, we may never know the full extent to which what we have done or said has inspired the positive actions of others.

What then, are the key messages that the messengers provide?

- The rewards to the passionate long distance runner include greater self-respect, greater respect for others, greater self-esteem, and greater levels of confidence.

- It is possible to draw happiness from one of the most fundamental activities we know of.

- Through running long distances the messengers form and build strong social networks which contribute to their happiness and the happiness of others around the world. There is a desire to connect and reconnect socially.

- Physical activity contributes to building happiness and our emotional, spiritual, and mental well-being. Being happy is addictive.

- The emotional, spiritual, mental and physical well-being derived from running long distances creates a sense of the unperturbed, a level of contentment; a sense of the unworried. The more races run, the further along one is on the road to Apathia.

- It is possible to overcome adversity; never give up.

- It is possible to transform your life.

- The achievement of goals set positively contributes to building a 'can-do' attitude that embraces life and its infinite possibilities. Failure is only failure if one never tries.

- Believe in yourself; have courage; anything is possible.

- Inspire.

- Be inspired.

- Enjoy what you do.

Movement is life. We are not made to live sedentary lives. Being active reaches back in evolutionary time and better attunes our physiological bodies to be in harmony with the world in which we live. To the messengers, that harmony is made possible when they journey along the road to apathia; with their mind, spirit and body as one. And it is made possible by the social connections that are enriched by the ongoing participation in running events around the world. The messengers may run alone, but they are by no means lonely.

The messengers have found a place that perhaps we all need to reach. Through their passionate pursuit, unknowingly on the road to apathia, their world makes perfect sense, and they are the better for it.

31

It's a late Thursday afternoon in November, Kingston, Canada. I'm on the road, actually *on the road*, filming a television show on marathon running. One of the runners we are following for the show is Lori, who is running around and around a residential area while we film her. Lori is training for the Goofy Challenge at Disney World in Orlando, Florida in a few weeks. It will be her second marathon.

Lori has Type 1 diabetes and uses an insulin pump. She must take insulin regularly each day, every day for the rest of her life. The pump regulates the flow of insulin into her body. Lori also has an immune system disorder, asthma, allergies, some hearing problems, and other health issues. She is also a single mum with a seven-year old daughter, Isabel. Right now Lori is training with a damaged ligament.

She's running and she's smiling.

Lori is one of the happiest people I've ever met. Lori simply gets on with things. She doesn't complain about anything. If there is a barrier or adversity, she looks at ways to overcome it. I later tell Lori that I'm inspired by what she does, but she doesn't see why I feel that way.

Lori has not run 100 marathons, but like the messengers she too has a positive, happy, 'can-do' approach to life. It's contagious. We all 'can' if we try. Even if whatever we try doesn't work out we are still better off for the simple act of trying.

We all have an opportunity, and a responsibility, to inspire others. We can be inspired by the great achievements of others – the fastest marathoners, for example – but we can find inspiration in the people around us in their acts of courage, commitment, passion and kindness.

And we may never know the extent of our own influence. We can all be messengers. We need to recognize that even the smallest connections we have with others may ripple and evolve in ways that improve their lives and make them happier. The research evidence shows it.

The messengers around the world have found something. They are out there running for health and happiness, passionate about what they do, and leading lives that inspire others in ways they may never know. We can all learn from the messengers.

Anything is possible.

Her finely touched spirit had still its fine issues, though they were not widely visible. Her full nature, like that river of which Cyrus broke the strength, spent itself in channels which had no great name on the earth. But the effect of her being on those around her was incalculably diffusive: for the growing good of the world is partly dependent on unhistoric acts; and that things are not so ill with you and me as they might have been, is half owing to the number who lived faithfully a hidden life, and rest in unvisited tombs.

George Eliot, last paragraph of Middlemarch (1871)

Acknowledgements

I am extremely grateful for the support, patience, and encouragement shown by the messengers while writing this book. I am indebted to them because they trusted me to accurately and ethically express 'who they are', 'what they do' and 'why they do it'. The massive challenge has been to compress engaging and amazing stories of more than one hundred individuals into one compact book. Whether I've succeeded or not is over to you, the reader, to decide.

But I do need to sincerely apologize, in general, to everyone I interviewed, because each messenger's story is significant in itself. The magnitude of the achievement – completing 100 marathons and ultras – still seems amazing to me. I feel quite guilty for reducing many peoples' achievements and lives down to just a few paragraphs, if that. But had I not done so, this book would, in fact, be volumes.

I should also say that I did everything I could to provide up-to-date information. But the runners keep running, times change and there are new places always being visited. It was also a challenge to make sure every piece of data was correct, as sometimes the data – such as race times were reported differently, stated to me differently, or I may have inadvertently changed a number recording what was told to me. Ultimately I take responsibility for any errors you may find. That said, I'd like to think the numbers – the details – are less important than the bigger things we learn from the experiences of the messengers.

I have travelled to many places to meet the messengers, and I've run and laughed a lot with them as well. Sue, Paul, Dave, Linda, Robbie, Juergen, John, Jim, Selina, Bob, Steve, and Jeff are just a few that come to mind. I've talked to messengers around the world, at all times of the day and night. I continue to keep in touch with many of the runners you have read about in this book.

My fear in thanking specific individuals is that I'll miss someone. But here goes. I ask for forgiveness in advance if I do not mention your name. First I'd like to thank, in no particular order, Lenore and Bob Dolphin, Linda and Dave Major, Christian Hottas, Juergen Kuhmley, Bob Fickel, John Dawson, Tom Adair, Jeff Galloway, Dave McGillivray, Shinichi Nose and Dave Penfold, all of whom were instrumental in assisting with contacting people, providing material, or giving input on my many questions. Runners such Jeff Hagen, Lester Smith, Horst Preisler, Jack Brooks and Steve Edwards in particular, also provided insights that made a lot of the pieces 'fit' in my mind.

I could not, of course, talk to all those who have completed 100 or more marathons and ultras. The book would never be finished if I tried to do so. My apologies, all the same, to those who I did not get an opportunity to talk to.

Writing books is not my full-time job, unfortunately, so it has been a challenge, to say the least, to find the time to do so. Simply, life (and work) get in the way. I did not receive any advances to write the book either. That would be nice to receive – fantastic in fact – but unfortunately, for my bank account anyways, I also funded every part of the book myself. I have no regrets, because what I've learned has made a significant difference to my own life, and I hope it can make some kind of difference in other people's lives as well. Which, really, is the purpose of the book.

The book has also taken a long time coming, and the patience of runners (and many others) interested in it has been remarkable. I thank you! I could easily write another book explaining the course of events that have transpired through the book's development. Incredibly, some of the runners in the book have completed more than 100 marathons in the time I've taken to write it.

I'd like to say a big thank-you to Jacqueline Venditti for the graphic design work and to Lyn (Baker) Mikesell, Gary Wright, and Susan Donaldson for their editorial comments on the book.

Finally, a very special thanks to my boys, Callum and Jack, who have made the best and biggest difference in my life and who, quite unknowingly, were the reasons I started running marathons a few years ago. I'm hoping that they will read the book one day. And I hope they like what they read.

Malcolm Anderson, 2010

About the Author

Malcolm Anderson is a New Zealander now living in Canada. He took up running in 2006 in a bid to get back in shape. He discovered that running was much more than just simply putting one foot in front of the other. That certainly helps, but he realized he was undergoing a transformation – one that started with a desire to get fit – but one that continues because of all the other things being active does for you. He's now run 35 + marathons, including two ultras, one of which was the 90 K Comrades Ultramarathon in South Africa, and the Brathay 10 marathons in 10 days Challenge in the Lake District in England. His most important event was a 5 K Wolfe Island race which he ran with his sons Callum and Jack in 2008. A 100-miler is in his sights sometime soon. Malcolm writes about marathon running as well as humour pieces. Often the two go hand in hand. He is the host of a television program on marathon running and is the founder of Run for Tomorrow – a global charity event that will be held in 2011 and 2012, in which a team of 10 core marathon runners will be running a continuous relay around the world. There's more on Run for Tomorrow on his website www.runplaces.com. When he is at his day job he finds himself conducting health services research and evaluation as an Assistant Professor at Queen's University, Kingston, Canada. If he's not conducting research, or writing, or running, he's typically found on a small farm outside of Yarker, which is not quite in the middle of nowhere, although you can see it from there.

The Messengers | Comments by Runners

"It's awesome!!! Very inspiring." (Canada) • "This is by far the best running book I have ever read!" (United States) • "I am reading it at the moment and I have not put it down. It has interesting & inspirational stories and when reading it you want to get out into the fresh air." (United Kingdom) **"The Messengers is the perfect title."** (United States) • "I consider this one of the best books I have ever read. The writing is incredible." (Canada) • **"So many interesting stories, and cleverly woven into each other."** (United Kingdom) ***"A great read … very inspirational."*** (New Zealand) • "It's very entertaining!" (United States) • **"A great read."** (United Kingdom) • *"I've barely been able to put it down."* (United Kingdom) • "I love, love the book … It is really inspiring." (United States) • "Fantastic. A great book!" (United States) • "The Messengers is the BEST running book that I have ever read in my 16 years of running." (United States) • "I read it almost all in one sitting, it is a page turner for me. I thought that you put what we (repeat marathoners) do into words beautifully… To sum it up, I love, love it!" (United States) • *"Awesome read."* (United States) • *"If you can inspire someone (us) who as you have so eloquently written is "inspired" already, I would accept this as the ultimate compliment."* (United Kingdom) • **"You are a talented writer, very inspiring and you have made the next 4 Marathons within reach."** (Australia)

"The Messengers comes with *our highest recommendation*… This *wonderful book is inspiring in and of itself.* It is *a breathtaking accomplishment.* If you want a book that will not only inspire you to run a marathon, but may inspire you to run 100, then *this book is for you".*

i-Run magazine, Canada

"Malcolm Anderson has truly put together a *well-written* ample book that will make *a lasting contribution to distance running*, from the non-elite side, and *we urge everyone to get a copy".*

NORTHWEST RUNNER, United States

"This book is full of inspiring stories about how people *change their lives* for the better through running."

Jeff Galloway, US Olympian, www.RunInjuryFree.com

"Throughout our lives, we are constantly inspired and motivated by what others have achieved. We witness ordinary people doing extraordinary things. When we hear about their accomplishments, a phenomenon occurs where *we begin to believe that we, too, can achieve what one once thought was impossible.* Malcolm Anderson's book, The Messengers, is a collection of so many of these inspirational stories that will leave the reader **believing they can accomplish anything want to** if they are willing to make the sacrifices involved and if they have the courage and guts to make the commitment."

Dave McGillivray, B.A.A. Boston Marathon Race Director

"'The Messengers' features runners and their inspirational stories from all over the world. Meticulously written, The Messengers contains a collection of stories about runners that is unheralded within the running book genre. **The Messengers is not only about running but reveals the heart and soul of each runner."**

Marshall Ulrich, Author of 'Running on Empty', Adventure racer and 4-time Winner of the Badwater 146-mile race across Death Valley

"The pulse of life finds its rhythm in running. The joy of life is found in human relationship. **Heaven is where running and personal relationships intersect.** The MESSENGERS in this book have something to say about life and how they have chosen to live it. They are not talking about the number of miles they have run, but about the people they have met along their journey. Each MESSENGER seems to bear the same message…to live is to run, and to run is to live. **It's not about the miles…it's about the smiles.** I'm honored to be one of the MESSENGERS in this book, and I feel privileged to be a member of this unique tribe."

Jerry Dunn, America's Marathon Man

Also by Malcolm Anderson

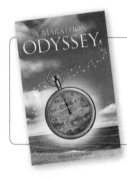

A Marathon Odyssey

A new marathoner's journey through history, travel, training, three marathons, and the social movement of marathon running.